Urban Housing and Poverty Alleviation in Tanzania

by

Milton Makongoro Mahanga

DAR ES SALAAM UNIVERSITY PRESS LTD.

Published in Tanzania by:
Dar es Salaam University Press LTD.,
University of Dar es Salaam,
Uvumbuzi Road,
P. O. Box 35182,
DAR ES SALAAM.

ISBN 9976 - 60 - 343 - 6

Copy editing and book design: *Bernhard J. Sanyagi*

Contents

FOREWORD

This book is an outcome of a thorough research work undertaken by author in all phases. I am particularly impressed by the completeness of the data gathering and rigour of the author's analysis.

While it may be true that the scholarly community has to statistically prove a linkage between poor housing conditions and poverty, there has been some work done that suggest the two conditions exist simultaneously. Logically, this seems to be true; but the question for policy makers is to determine which problem to solve initially. The real long term solution to both problems is to provide an opportunity for all citizens to work their way out of poverty and into better living conditions. Most recent studies seem to suggest that government programmes which are aimed at solving current problems without long term employment solutions are doomed to fail. A general rule of a democratic society is to enact policy which is in best interest of the majority while at the same time considering the basic needs of all members. While the poor may not be the majority, their basic needs must be addressed.

I am extremely impressed by this work, and I believe that it should easily withstand any peer review. The work should also be brought to the attention of government officials, policy makers and researchers. The author should also consider writing opinion pieces for editorial pages in major newspapers. This work can have a significant impact on policy.

Michael Busler, *Ph.D.*

Washington International University, July 2000

ACKNOWLEDGMENTS

I wish to express my earnest gratitude to my former employer, the National Housing Corporation (NHC) for sponsoring me to undertake the executive *Ph.D.* degree programme at the Washington International University. I am also indebted to the whole management of NHC for their unwavering support during the whole period of my research work. All staff and management of the students affairs and academic departments of the Washington International University were also very helpful during my study.

My very special thanks go to Dr. Michael Busler of the Washington International University, who was my chief research supervisor, instructor and advisor. Without his guidance and support, the completion of this work would no doubt have been much harder and more painful. Professor Lusugga Kironde, of the University College of Lands and Architectural Studies (UCLAS), was immensely helpful during the initial research plan and writing of the proposal. Indeed, his careful analysis of issues helped me to properly orient my work as well as locate the relevant literature.

My special thanks also go to Prof. Matthew Luhanga of the University of Dar es Salaam, Dr. B.B.K. Majani and Mr. Alphonce Kyessi both of UCLAS, for their continued support, encouragement and guidance during the research for this book. Dr. Chris Kabwogi of the NHC assisted me with factual and literal editing of the work as well as availing me some relevant reference materials. Many more people helped me in one way or another; these include Mr. Hermes Mutagwaba of the NHC, Mr. G.G. Bhuko of Dar es Salaam Water and Sanitation Authority (DAWASA) and Mr. Felix Kaiza a renown journalist.

I am also indebted to Mr. C. Rweyemamu and his assistants for the wonderful interviewing job they did; not forgetting of course the Yombo Vituka respondents to the questionnaire administered by the above mentioned research assistants. To my colleagues at NHC, UDSM, UCLAS and the Institute of Finance Management, relatives and friends I can only say thank you so very much for your support and friendship. Finally I have to recognize Mrs. Pulcheria Lukanga for typing the original manuscript of this work.

ABBREVIATIONS

AHF	- African Housing Fund
ANOVA	- Analysis of Variance
BAHSO	- Bureau for Aid to Social Housing Collectives (Senegal)
BNH	- National Housing Bank (Brazil)
BoT	- Bank of Tanania
BRU	- Building Research Unit
CBOs	- Community Based Organizations
DCC	- Dar es Salaam City Commission
DDCs	- District Development Councils
ECA	- Economic Commission for Africa
EIUS	- Environmental Improvement of Urban Slums (India)
ERP	- Economic Recovery Programme
EWS	- Econmically Weaker Sections
FRG	- Federal Republic of Germany
GDP	- Gross Domestic Product
GRP	- Gross Regional Product
HABITAT	- United Nations Centre for Human Settlements
HDFC	- Home Development Finance Company (India)
HDI	- Human Development Index
ICP	- International Comparison Project
IDWSSD	- International Drinking Water Supply and Sanitation Decade
IMF	- International Monetary Fund
IMP	- Integral Measure of Poverty
IMR	- Infant Mortality Rate
IUCN	- International Union for the Conservation of Nature
JICA	- Japanese International Cooperation Agency
KAIRP	- Katchi Abadi Improvement & Regularization Programme (Pakistan)
KfW	- *Kreditanstalt fur Wideraufbau* (German Development Bank)
LBT	- Labour Based Technology
LOGIT	- Regression model in which the dependent variable is dichotomous and the cumulative distribution of error term, *u*, is logistic
MBS	- Mortgage Based Securities
MMM Master Plan	- Marshall Macklin Monaghan Master Plan
NASACO	- National Shipping Agency Company (TZ)

NHC	- National Housing Corporation (TZ or Kenya)
NHDP	- National Housing Development Policy (TZ)
NIC	- National Insurance Corporation (TZ)
NIGP	- National Income Generation Programme
NPF	- National Provident Fund
NSSF	- National Social Security Fund
PPF	- Parastatal Pension Fund
PPP	- Purchasing Power Parity
PROBIT	- Regression model in which the dependent variable is dichotomous and distribution of is logistic
PROMEBAD	- Project for the Improvement of Disfavoured Districts (Cape Verde)
PTA	- Preferential Trade Area
REPOA	- Research Programme on Poverty Alleviation
RoB	- Registrar of Buildings
SCP-T	- Sustainable Cities Programme - TZ
SDP	- Sustainable Dar es Salaam Project
SHASU	- Scheme of Housing and Shelter Upgrading (India)
SHHA	- Self Help Housing Agency (Botwsana)
SIP	- Slum Improvement Programme (Bangladesh)
SOPROG	- Real Estate Promotion and Management Company (Congo)
THB	- Tanzania Housing Bank
TPHF	- Tanganyika Permanent Housing Finance
UCLAS	- University College of Lands and Architectural Studies
UDA	- *Usafiri Dar es Salaam* (commuter transport company)
UNCDF	- United Nations Capital Development Fund
UNCED	- United Nations Conference on Environment & Development
UNCHS	- United Nations Centre for Human Settlements (*see*, Habitat)
UNDP	- United Nations Development Programme
UNEP	- United Nations Environment Programme
UPE	- Universal Primary Education
URT	- United Republic of Tanzania
WASH	- Water and Sanitation for Health
WES	- Water and Environmental Sanitation
WHO	- World Health Organization
WTP	- Willingness to Pay
WWF	- World Wildlife Fund

LIST OF TABLES

FIGURES

PREFACE

In developing countries, poverty has usually been associated with rural areas. Indeed empirical evidence suggests that poverty is more rampant in rural areas. However, the unprecedented urbanization, particularly in developing countries like Tanzania, coupled with the effects of world recession, has resulted in a significant increase in the scale of urban poverty. It is in view of such rapid urban growth which manifests in high levels of urban poverty, shortage of adequate shelter and other essential services and poor environmental conditions, that it was found necessary to carry out this research which was also a condition for the award of the Executive *Ph.D* degree in Business Administration offered by the Washington International University in the USA.

Specifically the research for this book was conducted on the premise that there is a serious problem in the structural frameworks and conceptualization on the part of the government of Tanzania, like most governments in developing countries, and other stake holders concerning the whole question of provision and improvement of housing and living conditions of the urban poor. It seems that no proper and empirically derived linkage had been made between poor housing conditions and poverty. The role of improved housing and its environment in alleviating poverty had also not been well perceived. Worse still, the true players and their roles in this task seem to have not been properly identified by most researchers and policy makers. In other words, there are gaps between conceptual, contextual and empirical understanding of housing poverty in our country. This research seeks to fill in these gaps.

The approach adopted is first to review the available literature on urban housing development and improvement policies in developing countries generally and Tanzania in particular, and highlighting their impact, if any, on alleviating housing poverty. Empirical analyses are then undertaken to show the causal relationship between housing and other poverty manifestations with the aim of showing that improving housing conditions is, in fact, improving the living condition, and thus, reducing poverty, among poor urban people. The willingness and ability of poor urban people to pay for improved housing and related services is also positively tested. More importantly, it is empirically evidenced that any attempt by the "overclass" (politicians, bureaucrats, professionals, researchers and donors) to exclude the poor people in planning and implementation of poverty alleviation programmes affecting their (poor people's) communities would only be a futile undertaking.

OVERVIEW OF THE BOOK

As an introduction, chapter one of this book deals with the conceptual background by propounding the importance of housing, defining housing, poverty, and analyzing the severity and manifestations of housing poverty in developing countries generally, and Tanzania in particular. The chapter then states the significance of the urban housing poverty problem before underlining objectives and hypotheses of the project. The methodology for carrying out the work is lastly elucidated.

Chapter 2 sets out the conventional definition and determination of poverty before linking poverty with poor housing conditions and environmental degeneration. The contribution of housing to poverty alleviation is amply demonstrated in this chapter. The chapter also presents evidence suggesting that the urban poor are poorer than the rural poor basically because of housing poverty. The rapid urbanization and severe housing problems in Africa and other developing countries are then traced.

Chapter 3 reviews the global experiences on policies and practices for providing and improving housing and related services and infrastructure to the urban poor. This analysis is aimed at enabling conceptualization of the severity and magnitude of the housing problem and poor urban services. The concept of partnership as the only viable option in redressing housing problems for the urban poor in developing countries like Tanzania is brought into perspective. The role of various stakeholders in the provision, improvement and financing of housing for the poor urban is also reviewed.

Chapter 4 highlights the poverty situation in Tanzania, after reviewing the political and economic background of the country. Several attempts by the country to eradicate poverty and its manifestations are briefly highlighted including research works undertaken to guide policy decisions in this regard. It is, however, argued that despite such attempts, policy makers and researchers have not yet properly and adequately addressed the question of urban housing poverty and the proper measures for its eradication or alleviation.

Chapter 5 reviews several attempts by the public to redress the problems of housing and associated social services since independence. The chapter starts by bringing into perspective, the urbanization crisis in the country and the poor land delivery system and urban infrastructural services. Sources of housing supply in Tanzania are then highlighted before tracing the history of housing development and financing in the country before and after independence.

Chapter 6 narrows down the literature review of housing and related services in the city of Dar es Salaam, within which the study area of Yombo Vituka is situated. Using secondary data, the chapter suggests that despite Dar es Salaam being the largest urban centre in Tanzania, the housing situation and other related services like land delivery system, transportation system, health delivery system, water supply system, solid waste management and sanitation system are in deplorable state.

Having reviewed the literature on housing and other related social services, chapter 7 expounds on the conceptual and methodological framework introduced at the beginning, highlighting on the research design, sampling design and methods of data collection. Fieldwork planning, limitations and other problems are also presented. Presentation and initial analysis of data collected from the research survey are presented in chapter 8, while chapter 9, 10 and 11 seek to empirically test the four hypotheses mentioned at the beginning, mainly using statistical models such as sampling distribution, regression analysis and contingent valuation models.

Applying regression analysis, Chapter 9 tests the hypothesis that poor housing conditions are consequential and combined effects of not only the low income households, but also other manifestations of poverty like overcrowding, lack of safe and adequate water supply, poor sanitation and sewerage system and other housing characteristics and attributes. Chapter 10 tests the hypothesis of income generating capacity of poor households and uses Contigent Valuation models to test poor people's willingness and ability to pay for both housing and non-housing goods and services. Chapter 11 uses sampling distribution to test whether low income and/or insecure land tenure hinder or demotivate poor people from improving their housing stuctures and housing conditions.

Chapter 12 summarizes findings and draws recommendations and conclusions arising from the issues raised throughout this book.

It is my great conviction that this work has not only enabled me acquire a *Ph.D* degree, but also that it will go a long way towards supplementing current literature and research efforts on urban poverty alleviation as well as guiding policy decisions and practice on urban housing and urban regeneration in general.

Milton Makongoro Mahanga, *Ph.D*
Dar es Salaam, July 2000

1
INTRODUCTION

CONTEXT

Housing is a major component of the world stock of physical capital, and save for food, it is the largest single category of consumer expenditure (Diamond and Lea, 1995). In fact housing is a human basic necessity. As aptly put by Premadasa (1981), housing and shelter are people's birthright. It means that housing is a right that every citizen must enjoy. Every country, every government, realizes this fact. The need for adequate housing also features in various human rights instruments including the Universal Declaration of Human Rights (Article 25), the International Covenant on Economic, Social and Cultural Rights (Article 11), the International Convention on Elimination of all Forms of Racial Discrimination against Women (Article 14) and the Convention on the Rights of the Child (Article 27). The World Bank (1995) considers housing for low-income households as a formal safety net.

Housing is a major factor determining the life and welfare of the urban poor. As alluded to by Wikan (1990), although housing is not an isolated issue, it is one of the key existential concerns i.e. one of human basic needs, others being food, clothing and health care. Housing has been a basic human requirement since humans sought caves for protection against wild animals and external elements some 20,000 years ago (Ranson, 1991). A person who lacks such basic human need is poor. Although poverty is mostly understood from lack of income or assets because these can easily be measured, generally poverty implies deprivation or human needs that are not met (HABITAT, 1996d). Moreover, even data on income and assets are usually unreliable, and therefore poverty measurement based on income has been a contentious issue. In the absence of reliable statistics on poverty based on people's incomes and assets, one possible way of estimating the extent of poverty would be to determine how many people live in poor quality homes or neighborhoods that lack basic infrastructure and services that are essential for good health (HABITAT 1996d). This is what is referred to as housing poverty.

According to the 1992 Human Development Report, UNDP estimates that the rate of urban poverty is increasing at about 7% per annum, particularly in urban slum and squatter settlements facing social and economic exclusion, limited access to basic social infrastructure and services, with no credit for improved housing, thus even reducing their capacity for productive activities (Salewi, 1999). This implies that urban poverty is accentuated by housing poverty. In fact, housing poverty is even directly associated with the general income poverty. Perhaps it has not been sufficiently appreciated that housing is a productive asset, and that decent and adequate housing can supplement households' income, thereby significantly contributing towards poverty alleviation.

Although investment in housing and related services does not directly add to household income, it is an important contributor to the income (Arrossi, *et al*, 1994). For instance, improvements in water systems often provide better quality and greater quantities of water at costs well below what people previously paid to private water vendors. Paved roads significantly improve transport services. Many small informal enterprises operated within the improved households and in the neighbourhoods and improvements in the facilities there, may increase the amount that can be earned through such activities. Improvements in housing conditions also reduce the incidences of diseases and injury, which in turn, can ensure that income is not lost through time off work or spent on medical expenses. Additional rooms may be rented out, providing a further source of income. In some cases, particularly when households have legal tenure, the increase in the value of the house may provide an asset to secure a loan from conventional sources for investing in either further improvement of the house or for other business ventures.

It is estimated that between one fifth and one quarter of world's population (about one billion people) live in absolute poverty, without adequate food, clothing and shelter, with more than 90% of these living in the South (HABITAT, 1996d). As regards urban areas of developing countries, it was estimated that in 1985, some 330 million urban dwellers in these countries had incomes so low they were characterized as living in absolute poverty. In 1995, the estimate had risen to 430 million people (HABITAT, 1996e).

It should be stressed from the outset that housing covers not only the physical structure or shelter, but means the whole concept of human settlements. As defined by HABITAT (1986), human settlements are

> ...not simply housing or for that matter, merely the physical structure of a city, town, or village, but an integrated combination of all human activity process - residence, work, education, health, culture, leisure etc - and the physical structure that support them.

The United Nations (see Massawe, 1996a) also defines housing as:

> ... the residential environment, neighbourhood, micro-district or the physical structure that mankind uses for shelter and the environs of that structure, including all necessary services, facilities, equipment and devices needed for the physical health and social well-being of the family and the individual.

In other words, our basic concern is with healthy housing. As defined by World Health Organization (Ranson, 1991: 1), healthy housing is:

> A human habitation that is structurally sound and relatively free from accidental injury hazards, provides sufficient space for all normal household activities for members of the family, has readily and easy available and adequate supply of potable and palatable water, has a sanitary means of collection, storage and disposal of all liquid and solid wastes, is provided with appropriate installed facilities for personal and household hygiene and cleanliness, is sufficiently weatherproof and watertight, provides proper protection from the elements, especially for those persons who may be particularly susceptible, for physical and/or physiological reasons to these potentially adverse environmental conditions, provides a hydrothermal indoor environment which is healthful and comfortable, is free from excessive noise from both interior and exterior sources of the structure, has natural and artificial means of illumination that are safe and adequate in quality and quantity for the fulfillment of all normal household activities and functions, is free from toxic and/or noxious odors, chemicals and other air contaminants or pollutants, has adequate but not excessive microbial and thermal characteristics, provides sufficient but not excessive solar radiation, provides adequate protection from insects and rodents which may be reservoirs and/or vectors of disease agents, and is served by the necessary and/or desirable health, welfare, social, educational, cultural and protective community services and facilities.

It is estimated that by 1990, 600 million people in urban areas of Africa, Asia and Latin America lived in poor and unhealthy homes and neighborhoods because of the very poor housing and living conditions and lack of adequate provision for safe, sufficient sanitation, drainage, removal of garbage and health care (HABITAT 1996d). These 600 million people are obviously regarded as poor (they lack income and assets to enable them afford better quality housing and basic services) even without calculating and measuring their income and assets. If such "housing poverty" is included in measuring general poverty, this greatly increases the extent of urban poverty when compared to conventional income-based poverty lines. Most of these 600 million people live in cramped, overcrowded dwellings with four or more persons sleeping in one room or living in tenements, cheap boarding, subdivided land or in disaster-prone places such as areas with frequent floods. In fact, millions of them are completely homeless and sleep in public or semi-public spaces. These include pavement dwellers and those sleeping in bus shelters, streets, graveyards, train stations, parks or other such public places. For instance, in 1994, there were 1,075,000 people in South Africa who were living in shacks, hostels or outbuildings in urban areas alone. This was 23.8% of all urban households in South Africa (Gilbert, et al, 1997).

Poverty is therefore much more than just lack of income - it includes all other aspects of deprivation that go with inadequate income. If this fact is appreciated, then any initiative to improve housing, health, environment, transport and other basic services such as water, sanitation, sewage and disposal of garbage becomes part of poverty alleviation. Evidence suggests that in the Pacific countries, apart from low cash income levels, poverty has been exacerbated through declining health and nutrition levels, overcrowded housing, increased school dropout rates and increased stress upon physical and social environments of low-income urban dwellers (Bryant-Tokalau, 1995). Therefore current poverty alleviation efforts by developing countries will yield minimal results unless immediate measures are taken to address the issue of urban housing that is seeing millions of people flocking into urban areas every year demanding proper housing.

It is in consideration of such pathetic situation facing millions of urban poor, that low cost housing schemes have been part of many government development policies. Although many studies had previously indicated that low-cost housing construction and its attendant problems were so unique, and that housing improvement is an end in itself rather than a means to the broader end of eradicating poverty, it has been established (Drakakis-Smith, 1981) that low-cost housing provision problems do not form a unique and separate segment of the development process. They are the product of complex linkages that extend throughout the entire social-spatial field from cultural traits to political psychology. Shelter cannot therefore be isolated from other aspects of urban life and its production and consumption are closely linked to other difficulties and poverty aspects experienced by low-income groups. According to the HABITAT Agenda (HABITAT, 1996c), adequate shelter for all and sustainable human settlements development are not isolated from the broader social and economic development of countries and that they cannot be set apart from the need for favourable national and international frameworks for economic development, social development and environmental protection, which are indispensable and mutually reinforcing components of sustainable development.

Unfortunately, the argument that housing policy is part of social policy has always been contentious. Social scientists usually accord very negligible attention to housing issues; while housing experts on the other hand, also often neglect the social aspects of housing, and do not therefore consider housing policy or housing provision as being a social policy matter (Clapham, et al, 1990). It would appear that this lack of correlation between housing policy and general social policies is attributable to the fact that most housing policy issues seem to be geared towards economic and environmental objectives rather than social policy objectives as such. But it is evident that unlike housing policies, social policies including health services, education system, sanitary and water services, personal social services and the social security system usually dominate political and public debate.

But what is social policy? Social policy can be defined as a policy on all those areas of consumption in which the state plays a central role, either by regulating the provision of services, underwriting the cost of their provision, or providing goods and services in kind (Clapham, *et al*, 1990). This definition clearly includes housing, since housing policy can be regarded as any form of intervention (by the state or state organs and state collaborators) in housing provision, distribution or consumption that affects the location, character and availability of homes or rights associated with housing occupancy. Therefore, housing policy cannot be understood in isolation from the wider political and economic context (Malpass and Means, 1993).

Housing policy is thus inextricably linked to social and economic policy of any country. To improve housing conditions is to improve social and economic well-being of the inhabitants. Adequate housing promotes security, health, wealth and welfare of the people. Adequate housing is a pre-requisite for national socio-economic development. Unfortunately, in many developing countries, the housing problem is perceived entirely as a welfare problem whose only solution is the transfer of physical or financial resources to people who cannot accommodate themselves. This is a wrong perception. The HABITAT Agenda also urges that to improve the quality of life within human settlements, the world must combat the deterioration of housing conditions that in most cases, particularly in developing countries, have reached crisis proportions. The housing problem facing urban people in developing countries, including Tanzania, should therefore be considered as one aspect of the general problem of poverty (Massawe, 1996a). In other words, measures to alleviate urban poverty must, of necessity, include measures to ameliorate the condition of housing and related services and infrastructure.

POOR HOUSING AND URBAN SERVICES IN TANZANIA

Like many African countries, Tanzania resolved to combat poverty immediately after attaining independence through "free" provision of health, education, water, housing and other social services. As regards to housing, Tanzania realized that there was a significant mismatch between demand for decent shelter and housing supply. The government's immediate response to the rising demand for shelter was to involve itself directly in both construction of dwellings and financing of the same.

Initially there were some successful housing schemes including provision of basic services and amenities around the environs of urban settlements. The schemes included slum clearance, sites and services upgrading, construction of low-cost houses by the National Housing Corporation (NHC) and other government agencies, and other self-help schemes. In Zanzibar, there were also several low cost housing schemes (Mchenga and Hassan, 1998). However, as years went by, most of these schemes were either stopped or carried out at a very slow pace. This situation was attributed by government financial constraints. However, the slum clearance scheme was stopped in 1969 largely because more slums were being demolished but fewer houses were built in their place.

Consequently, after decades of efforts to eradicate poverty through, among other things, the provision of decent shelter to Tanzanians, particularly urban dwellers, the situation has not improved (Kironde, 1985; Kabwogi, 1997; Kyessi, 1996; and Mahanga, 1998). Many people still live in squatters and slums in unplanned areas, with horrifying environmental conditions with their consequential health hazards.

Apart from differences in terms of income and expenditure between the poor and the better off households in Tanzania, the World Bank (1993) also found stark differences in their access to water, housing conditions, durable goods and education. In general, 40% of all Tanzanians spend more than 15 minutes to reach the nearest water source (with 26.1% of rural people using 30 minutes). Only 33% of all households in Tanzania live in houses without mud walls, while 53% of houses have no metal roof. For the poor, these values are 21% and 68% respectively. The World Bank also found that the literacy rate in Tanzania was 68% (61% for women and 76% for men). 80% of the illiterate people live in rural areas, while 70% of illiterate Tanzanians are women.

The poor have less education. In fact 34.9%, 32.2% and 19% of the very (hard-core) poor, poor and better-off people respectively have no education at all, while only 1.3%, 2.2% and 11.3% of the hard-core poor, poor and better-off respectively have attended secondary education. These manifestations of poverty, though rampant in rural Tanzania, affect the poor urban people in a different, and probably worse dimension. This book attempts to correlate poor urban housing conditions with these and other facets of poverty, namely, illiteracy, inadequate clean and safe water supply, poor health services, lack of secure land tenure, high mortality rates, malnutrition, environmental degradation, and unemployment.

THE PROBLEM

As already pointed out, the government of Tanzania has, since independence, been trying to involve itself in the provision of housing to the urban population. However, such efforts have been disappointingly insignificant in bridging the gap between demand and supply of housing, let alone improvement of existing housing stock and other urban services. In fact, experience worldwide shows that nowhere has it been possible for governments to make direct provision of shelter for everyone. In order to realize the goal of adequate shelter for all, there must be concerted efforts of central and local governments, community-based organizations (CBOs), building industry, financial institutions, donor community, non-governmental organizations (NGOs) and, not least, the people who need shelter. There must therefore be a shift in the role of governments from being direct providers of housing to "enablers", facilitating a regulatory and financial environment in which the private sectors, community groups and individuals can play an increasing role in meeting their shelter needs (Vanderschueren et al, 1996; IUCN/UNEP/WWP, 1991, and Arrossi et al, 1994).

As in many other developing countries, there seems to be a serious problem in the structural frameworks and conceptualizations on the part of the government of Tanzania and other stakeholders in the whole question of provision and improvement of housing and living conditions of the urban poor. In the first place, no proper and empirically derived linkage has been made between poor housing conditions and poverty. It seems that the role of improved housing and its environment in alleviating poverty has not been well perceived. Furthermore, the potential and desire of poor people in improving their housing and environments have not been well exploited. The important questions to be asked are thus: How have the poor and unhealthy housing and environmental conditions compounded poverty situation in poor urban settlements? What are the potentials and pre-requisites of the households and the private sector (CBOs, NGOs etc.) in housing provision, improvement and environmental regeneration in urban Tanzania?

THE BOOK'S SIGNIFICANCE

Much of government policies and research work on poverty eradication in

Tanzania can be viewed from two general perspectives: rural poverty and income poverty. In Tanzania, poverty is usually associated with rural areas since, as evidenced by empirical data, poverty is more rampant in rural areas (World Bank, 1993). However, the unprecedented urbanization taking place in developing countries, including Tanzania, coupled with the effects of world recession, has resulted in a significant increase in the scale of urban poverty. According to HABITAT (1992), between 1970 and 1985, the absolute number of the world's poor increased by 22%, but the percentage increase among the rural poor was only 11% as compared to 73% for the urban poor.

Urbanization projections indicate that total urban population in developing countries which was about 1.8 billion in 1996, is likely to double before 2020 and reach 4 billion by year 2025 (HABITAT, 1996e). This implies that urban centres in these countries are likely to absorb approximately twice the population over the next 30 years than they have over the last 30 years. In Tanzania, one in every two people is expected to be living in urban area in twenty years hence. It is in view of such horrifying urban growth that manifests in high levels of urban poverty, shortage of adequate shelter and other essential services coupled with poor environmental conditions, that research on urban poverty, and by extension housing poverty, is significant.

This book is also significant due to the hitherto little understanding and appreciation of urban housing poverty. Poverty eradication measures in developing countries are viewed as those strategies and actions that reduce income poverty of the people. It is unfortunate that even when considering the plight of poor urban dwellers, attention is focused on their income poverty rather than housing poverty. In the first instance, the number of the poor in a country is usually measured with respect to single income level (poverty line) for both urban and rural areas, when in fact, there are enormous variations in the cost of basic necessities. According to Hardoy (1995) and as also evidenced by Nyerere (1968) and World Bank (1990), it is more expensive to live in cities than in rural areas.

In Tanzania, like in many other developing countries, apart from the unrealism of income poverty line for urban poverty *vis-a-vis* rural poverty, there is also an apparent lack of recognition of housing poverty in urban areas. Much attention is normally generalized in income poverty. Although related, income poverty and housing poverty are in fact, not synonymous. While income poverty is primarily about necessities for subsistence and the adequacy of resources for dignified living conditions, housing poverty is about the price-access to sanitary housing, to affordable rent-income ratios, and to satisfactory health and environmental conditions in low-income living areas (HABITAT, 1996e). Housing is also related to the generation and distribution of "urban welfare" which is not only associated with primary income from earnings and other monetized sources, but also the value of social benefits (and costs), housing-related externalities in locational (dis)amenity and environmental conditions (HABITAT, 1996e). Undoubtedly low income is frequently a major cause of housing poverty, but such housing-related conditions as low housing supplies, ineffective land policies, inappropriate building codes and standards and imbalances in tenure and housing finance can also be significant in assessing housing poverty and affordability.

OBJECTIVES

The objectives of this book are as follows:

a) To explore how poor housing and environmental conditions exacerbate poverty among the poor urban households. Although low level of income seems to be the main manifestation or indicator of poverty, there are several other similarly grave indicators such as poor health, illiteracy, inadequate clean and safe water supply, high mortality rate, malnutrition, unemployment, environmental degradation and homelessness or poor housing. Again, although poor housing and environmental conditions are generally regarded simply as some of the indicators of poverty, it is hereby argued that these, in fact, directly compound the other poverty facets like illiteracy, insanitation, poor or inadequate water supply, poor health conditions and unemployment. Improved housing conditions could therefore be a means of fighting almost all other symptoms of poverty;
b) To assess the role of decent and adequate housing in alleviating income poverty of low-income households. As earlier mentioned, housing is a productive asset. To low-income households, housing is a shelter, commodity and investment. An adequate and decent home is a workshop, a store and a source of inputs such as water and electricity.
c) To assess the potential contribution of the poor people in the provision and improvement of their housing and the environment, given the inability of the government to directly and solely do this. Given the massive investment in terms of financial and technical resources required, provision and improvement of housing and related services such as water, sewage system, collection of garbage, access roads, electricity and maintenance of the housing and its surroundings, need the participation of not only the central government, but also other stakeholders and donors (Jakande, 1994), with the active material and physical contribution from the affected households. Unfortunately, it seems that the government, in formulating schemes for housing and social

services affecting housing and living conditions of the poor, has assumed that most of these poor people can not afford or are unwilling to pay or contribute for such services, and therefore the services must be provided at full cost by the government or must be heavily subsidized. Apparently it has not been fully realized, even by the poor households themselves, that the affected households can meet the cost of providing such services, with the assistance of CBOs, NGOs and local governments. According to HABITAT (1996a), as a result of poor services and/or poorly maintained services, there has been lack of citizens' willingness, rather than ability, to pay for social and infrastructural services;

d) To pinpoint and assess factors that discourage or constrain the efforts of poor people and other stakeholders to improve housing conditions despite their ability and willingness as pointed out above. Main factors to be evaluated are access to secure land/tenure and access to credit;

e) The last objective of the research shall focus on policy recommendations, direction and actions for improving housing and the environments of poor urban dwellers in Tanzania for poverty alleviation and sustainable development.

PARAMETERS AND LIMITATIONS

As already presented, this book deals with housing and living conditions and the environments of the urban poor. All these collectively derive housing poverty facing many urban poor. It is important to state that the book's emphasis is on housing and environmental problems facing the poor urban dwellers but not environmental hazards which are particular to developed urban cities. As alluded to by Leitmann, *et al* (1992), the nature, range and mix of environmental problems found in any urban area is influenced by the general level of development of the country concerned. Generally environmental problems affect different economies as follows (Leitmann et al, 1992):

a) Low-income urban economies

Lack of basic environmental services such as water supply, sanitation, drainage, and solid-waste collection; a few temperate cities with severe air pollution from use of low-quality coal; uncontrolled land development and use; severe damage and loss of life from natural hazards.

b) Lower middle-income urban economies

Low levels of sanitation and sewerage treatment; poor drainage; severe water pollution from municipal and industrial wastes; severe urban air pollution in some cities from vehicle emissions, use of low- quality fuels, and/or inefficient use of energy, inadequate solid-waste collection and disposal; lack of hazardous waste management; ineffective land-use controls; frequent disasters from natural and man-made hazards.

c) Upper - middle- income urban economies

Severe water pollution from municipal and industrial discharges; severe urban air pollution in some cities from vehicle emissions, use of low-quality fuels and/ or inefficient use of energy; inadequate solid-waste disposal, cumulative man-made hazards ("time bombs") - for example, hazardous waste dumps or nuclear power plants; frequent disasters resulting from natural and man-made hazards.

e) High-income urban economies

Health concerns from urban air pollution; loss of recreational amenities from water pollution; management of hazardous and toxic wastes; less subject to risks from natural and man-made hazards.

Tanzania is basically in the first category, but some problems in category (b) affect also the country. However, these are beyond the scope of this research. For our purpose, and given research limitations and relevance, this research is concerned with only problems of category (a), i.e. housing for the poor and environmental problems facing them as regards water supply, sanitation, drainage and waste disposal. The focus is on the most affected areas that are mainly found in the informal and some low-income formal settlements.
For lack of adequate resources and time, the research has been conducted in planned (formal) and unplanned (informal) settlements in only one area of Yombo Vituka in the city of Dar es Salaam.

METHODOLOGY AND SAMPLING

Apart from analytical and applied methods in which available literature on housing sector development and urban services improvements in the world are analyzed and evaluated, the research upon which this book is based used empirical analysis, mainly through the application of computer statistical packages such as Minitab, to measure economic welfare of the poor urban people in Dar es Salaam city in Yombo Vituka area which has both formal (planned) settlements and informal (unplanned) settlements. Obviously Dar es Salaam best exemplifies the magnitude of urban shelter problems in Tanzania.

Although welfare or utility of a household may not be measurable, it is assumed to derive from consumption of housing and non-housing goods and services. We therefore empirically take a theoretical framework of the consumption of a bundle of housing and non-housing goods and services that contributes to welfare or utility, and "measure" the welfare of households and their ability to pay for these housing and non-housing goods and services, given quantity and budgetary constraints.

Adequacy and conditions of housing, and multiple usage of housing space is also analyzed to determine the contribution of housing to income generating activities. Furthermore, various housing variables related to demographic (overcrowding), economic and tenure aspects; age and type of housing as well as income and occupancy rates of poor households are empirically analyzed to understand how such housing characteristics and attributes together with other housing poverty manifestations such as poor water supply, poor waste disposal systems, and insanitation are directly related to poor housing conditions. The willingness of households to pay for housing and related social and infrastructural services affecting their homes and environments are also analyzed.

Factors such as access to secure tenure and access to credit which hinder or discourage both the households and other stakeholders to adequately improve housing structures and other housing-related services are analyzed, empirically showing their causal relationship with poor housing conditions.

Some specified and structured quantitative models, such as regression analysis and contingent valuation models are used in this analysis, explicitly documenting the assumptions and logical relationships in the models. It is believed that the use of techniques and methods of analysis to housing policies and decisions is crucial. As observed by Willis and Tipple, (1991b), the application of such techniques and methods of analysis to housing research and policy decisions will improve judgements on housing issues.

In this book, probability or random sampling is used as a sample design. The methodology involves the use of both secondary and primary data, employing appropriate questionnaires to a randomly selected sample of infinite universe to collect information and data which form the basis for empirical analysis and hypotheses testing.

THE BOOK'S STRUCTURE

This book is divided into four parts. Chapters 1 through 3 provide the introduction and literature review; while chapters 4 through 6 provide the background to economic, poverty and housing situation in Tanzania. Field work findings and data analysis are presented in chapters 7 through 11; while chapter 12 draws the conclusions and presents some recommendations.

2

URBAN HOUSING AND POVERTY ALLEVIATION

POVERTY: MEANING AND MANIFESTATIONS

Poverty reduction is priority one on the agenda of Tanzania's Development Strategy. But what is poverty? How is it measured? Who is poor? What are the manifestations and incidences of poverty? What are the linkages of poverty, housing and the environment? These are some of the questions addressed in this chapter. The chapter further seeks to propound the extent of poverty in urban areas of developing countries, which has manifested itself in the form of rapid urbanization and the consequent acute housing shortage, poor housing and environmental conditions. This analysis is considered vital since any attempt at measures to alleviate urban poverty, and particularly housing poverty, must take cognisance of the unprecedented urbanization in developing countries.

Most English dictionaries define poverty as a condition of being without adequate food, money etc. However, in economic terms, poverty is a multi-dimensional concept whose definition is not that straight forward since its measurement and assessment follow different approaches. The most commonly used dimension of poverty is income. Using income, poverty can be defined as the inability to attain a minimum standard of living. In this sense, poverty is measured by income or expenditure level that can sustain a specified minimum standard of living. There are two main approaches in defining and measuring poverty: absolute poverty and relative poverty.

Absolute poverty

Absolute poverty, from which the income approach definition explained above stems, focuses on the absolute economic well being of individuals or households in isolation from the welfare distribution of the entire society (Semboja, 1994). It is therefore a lack of subsistence level of food (Shubert, 1996). This definition implies knowledge of the minimum standard of living, i.e. poverty line. The absolute poverty line is the income required to meet a minimum calorific consumption level (Cooksey, 1994).

However, poverty is not just an economic condition. As probably best defined by the former President of the World Bank, Robert McNamara (UNEP, 1992), a definition which has been adopted by this study: "absolute poverty is a condition of life so limited by malnutrition, illiteracy, diseases, squalid surroundings, high infant mortality and low life expectancy as to be beneath any reasonable definition of human decency."

Relative Poverty

Relative Poverty is an arbitrary concept (Likwelile, 1998) which refers to the position of an individual or household as compared with the average income in the country, which again is based on some predetermined poverty line, a line which is set, for example, at one-half of the mean of income or quartile/quintile of income distribution. Relative poverty is some unsatisfied basic needs or income below a relative poverty line based on some minimum basket of food, goods and services (Shubert, 1996)

A recent definition of poverty, the Integral Measure of Poverty (IMP), covers not only the two criteria of absolute poverty and relative poverty, but also the qualitative evaluation of unmet needs that incorporates, for instance, freedom, women's liberation and stresses aspects such as education, community organizations and management (Shubert, 1996). This definition is in line with McNamara's definition of poverty (UNEP, 1992).

Determination of the Poverty Line

Although there are several methods for determining the poverty line, the most used method is to ascertain the income needed to purchase a nutritionally adequate diet consistent with the food preference of the poor, and then multiplying this figure by a certain factor which is dependent on the food consumption budget. For example, such a factor may be 1.4 for Tanzania where the poor spend about 71% of their income on food (Semboja, 1994). The model for determining the poverty line in this case is as follows:

$$P = [1 + (h - 1)] px$$

Where,

P = the poverty line

x = the vector of food requirements
p = the corresponding price vector
h = the reciprocal of the share of expenditure on food.

Poverty Measurement

After determining the poverty line by which to distinguish poor from better-off households, measurement of poverty on each individual or household depends on the poverty index. Poverty indexes are chosen depending on what aspect of the households below the poverty line one wishes to look at. Is it the number of households below the line (incidence), in which case the method to use would be headcount index; or how far below the poverty line their consumption lies (depth) or how many of them are extremely far below the poverty line (severity), both cases in which the poverty gap method would be used?

The Headcount Index

This is defined as the proportion (percent) of the population below the poverty line. This is the easiest and most understood poverty index.

The Poverty Gap

The poverty gap provides information on the amount needed to raise the incomes of the poor to above the poverty line thereby eliminating poverty. The computed aggregate income shortfall as a percentage of aggregate income provides a poverty gap measure, showing the extent of poverty in the country. The superiority of the poverty gap measure over the headcount index is that, unlike headcount index, the poverty gap gauges the extent of poverty, i.e. it provides the extent to which the poor fall below the poverty line. In figure 2.1, EF is the poverty line.

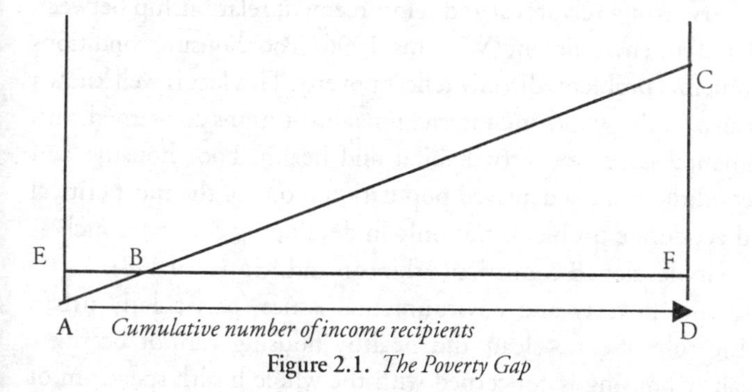

Figure 2.1. *The Poverty Gap*

There are at least four poverty alleviation policy measures that can be derived from the poverty gap as can be observed from figure 2.1. These policies are as follows:

1) The redistribution potential, which is obtained by dividing the area BCF by ABE
2) The marginal taxation to alleviate poverty, which is obtained by dividing the area ABE by BCF.
3) The reallocation of government expenditure potential, which is obtained by dividing government expenditure by the area ABE.
4) The percentage of government expenditures necessary to alleviate poverty, obtained by dividing the area ABE by government expenditure.

In a national context, poverty is usually measured based on Gross Domestic Product (GDP) to estimate the per capita income of a country. Despite the shortcomings of this measure it is still the most widely accepted measure of poverty of nations. Using this measure, the World Bank's national poverty lines are US $ 370 and US $ 275 for poor countries and extremely poor countries respectively (UNEP, 1992). In other words, a country whose per capita income per year is below US $ 370 is considered a poor country; while that with a per capital income below US $ 275 per annum is considered extremely poor. Tanzania, whose per capita income was US $ 130 in 1995, according to the World Bank, is therefore extremely poor.

POVERTY AND THE ENVIRONMENT: THE ROLE OF A HEALTHY HOUSING ENVIRONMENT

Most people living in African cities are poor, and their urban conditions and amenities reflect their own and their country's poverty (Peil, 1994). In fact, there is a very strong reciprocal and reinforcement relationship between housing, poverty and the environment (Williams, 1994). Poor housing conditions and their environmental problems directly reflect poverty. This fact is well known by governments all over the world and international institutions concerned with general developmental issues, poverty, habitat and health. Poor housing and environmental conditions and a deprived population is one of the most critical sets of social and economic problems not only in developing countries such as Tanzania, but also in developed countries (Atkinson and Kintrea, 1998).

When considering poverty and environmental issues (particularly urban environment), the role of safe, clean and healthy housing cannot be overemphasized. Healthy housing is concerned with the whole health spectrum of physical and mental health as well as the hygienic design of the shelter and social well-being, both within the dwelling and in the residential environment (Ranson, 1991). Poorly designed and constructed housing with unhealthy and unfriendly environmental facilities, lack of maintenance to housing and other essential household infrastructural services, all work towards environmental degeneration and contribute significantly to poor healthy conditions affecting the poor, and other not-so-poor people who live in poor urban squatters and slums. Available evidence suggests that environmental problems that might affect only the poor in other parts of the world are part of the daily lives of most African urban dwellers because quite a few people living in low-income areas (squatter settlements and slums) are not poor by local standards (Peil, 1994). Stephens (1994) also indicates that mortality rates for infants are between 2 and 10 times higher for people living in squatter settlements of cities than for those in non-squatter areas. However, many health problems affecting urban areas of developing countries are the same or similar to those affecting developed nations. These are (Ranson, 1994: 4):

- Lack of effective land management
- An insufficient supply of low-cost housing
- Unauthorized residential expansion outpacing and impending the provision of an adequate infrastructure and public services
- Unemployment, poverty and all that follows in their wake

According to the World Health Organization (1995), within the next 15 years, between 20 and 30 cities in the world will have over 20 million people each, and human-made environments will account for the living space of most of the world's population. WHO states that health problems in cities are aggravated by growth and development that is largely unplanned, uncontrolled and under-financed. In a recent policy paper The World Bank, has clearly stated the salient association between housing conditions, poverty and environmental problems as follows (Williams, 1994):

- The increased incidence of sickness and death is closely associated with housing that is too crowded, poorly built, located in unsafe areas or inadequately serviced with water and sanitation.
- Higher than expected prices combined with low incomes can result in high levels of overcrowding, low vacancy rates and homelessness.
- Poor quality housing is characterized by impermanence, fire-proneness, dilapidation and poor maintenance.
- Lack of residential infrastructure - intermittent or unsafe water supply, non-existent sewage, drainage and garbage disposal.

- Land tenure is insecure which can result in eviction and demolition.
- Housing is poorly located - either for economic opportunities or in unsafe locations, subject to natural and man-made hazards.
- A close association exists between quality of the urban environment and the performance of the housing sector.
- Slums and squatter settlements are places of lower environmental quality.
- Polluted water, inadequate sanitation, indoor pollution caused by wood burning etc. are major causes of disease.
- Illegality reduces motivation to invest in improving quality of the local environment.

Experience indicates that many developing countries suffer from having more or less the same horrible housing and environmental conditions, particularly in urban centres. For example, Hong Kong, which has almost six million people living on such a small piece of land, has the world's highest population density. Apart from such high density, Hong Kong faces serious environmental hazards through production of tonnes of solid and liquid waste. It produces 23,300 tonnes of solid waste, 21 tonnes of floating refuse and refuse from ocean-going vessels and dwelling boats, 2 million tonnes of sewage and industrial waste water every day, as well as 100,000 tonnes of chemical waste per year (Chan, 1994). Furthermore, although Hong Kong boasts of a very high GDP (US$ 12,069 per capita in 1990), there are large scores of low-income housing with poor community facilities and environmental conditions. There are also significant nutrition and hygiene problems in the living environment (Chan, 1994). As regards environmental hazards, the poor households in Hong Kong who live mainly in the midst of industrial areas or by the side of highways suffer from dual impact of pollution problems from the adjacent industries and environmental deterioration in the residential neighbourhood itself.

Tanzania has given prominence to environmental protection in its national development programme. This is in keeping with the resolution adopted by governments represented at the 1992 UNCED Earth Summit in Rio de Janeiro, where it was recommended that cities should develop their own environmental strategies and action plans in the context of their local circumstances. The world realizes that a sustainable development approach is urgently needed in the management of the urban environment, since with the current high rate of urbanization in developing countries, if effective and appropriate interventions are not made, sooner than later, we shall witness a situation whereby the environmental problems currently afflicting developing country urban areas will simultaneously intensify and become more extensive (Williams, 1994). In fact, development without concern for the environment can only be short-term development (Khan, 1995).

Growth and poverty alleviation are the keys to the preservation of environmental sustainability, although sometimes growth-induced environmental damage in some developing countries may be a temporary casualty to poverty alleviation (Khan, 1995). Ligthelm and Wilsenach (1995) also share this view arguing that environmental degradation is often a result of economic development and large-scale poverty. Simultaneously, environmental degradation in its many forms constitutes a threat to economic development and growth. This means that the only way to ensure that any form of economic development is not in direct conflict with the environment is to have sustainability conditions built into any economic development strategy - i.e. the optimal use and sound management of the natural resources and not their degradation or exhaustion.

HOUSING AND POVERTY ALLEVIATION

Housing for the poor is one of the most effective ways of improving their overall living conditions, thereby eradicating poverty amongst them. Housing is a central aspect of urban poverty and wellbeing. Housing policy cannot therefore be regarded merely as a social policy having little impact on, or connection with, economic growth. It is an investment which can be used as a positive influence in development planning to affect both the pace and direction of growth (Drakakis-Smith, 1981: 34). Milanzi (1996) also reiterates that the housing problem in developing countries is part of the general developmental problems and should be viewed as such. Yet to-date housing has not been included in the human development index despite the work undertaken by United Nations and World Bank on developing housing and urban indicators (HABITAT, 1996e). The importance of housing in the overall life of the urban poor, and hence in poverty eradication amongst them include the following:

a) Economic Development

Housing investment in developing countries like Tanzania, accounts for 3-8 percent of GDP, and 15-30 percent of gross capital formation (Sa Aadu, 1997). According to Arrossi, et al (1994), developing countries invest between US $ 150 and 200 billion annually in the construction of their urban centres. This includes also the value of the efforts of individual households, and of the public and private sectors in building new houses, enterprises, public buildings and commercial centres, new schools, health centres, and in the construction undertaken by the people themselves to improve the urban environment in which they live. Irrespective of the level of economic development of a country, construction accounts for more than 50% of the gross domestic fixed capital formation, of which housing represents 20-50% (Sweet and George, 1976). Furthermore, housing investment's share of GDP rises as economies develop (Malpezzi, 1991). However, in Tanzania, housing investment has not developed significantly. As a percentage of annual fixed capital formation, investment in buildings (both residential and non-residential) has hardly reached 10%. In 1993, for example, total investment in buildings was 8.6% of total fixed capital formation, with residential housing accounting for only 2.9% (see Table 2.1).

Table 2.1: *Expenditure on Gross Fixed Capital Formation, 1993 (Tanzania Mainland)*

ITEM	AMOUNT (T.Shs, ml.)	PERCENTAGE
1. BUILDINGS		
(a) Residential	12,646	2.9
(b) Rural (own account)	3,590	0.8
(c) Non-residential	21,585	4.9
Sub-Total	37,821	8.6
2. OTHER WORKS		
(a) Land Improvement	17,805	4.1
(b) Roads and Bridges	23,224	5.3
(c) Water Supply	3,983	0.9
(d) Others	38,140	8.7
Sub-Total	83,152	19.0
3. EQUIPMENT	316,122	72.3
GRAND TOTAL	437,095	100.0

Source: Bureau of Statistics: National Accounts of Tanzania, 1976-1993

Housing investment can be used as a positive influence in development planning to affect both the pace and direction of growth. As earlier alluded to, housing is a major component of the world's stock of physical capital, and save for food, it is the largest single category of consumer expenditure. For example, housing investment in Tunisia represents 50% of households' savings and 22% of family consumption (Driss, 1999). Housing is also a productive asset. For many households (particularly low income families), housing is a shelter, commodity and investment all in one. A home is a workshop, storehouse and a source of inputs such as water and electricity. Improved housing therefore increases productivity within the household economy. It is thus a major form of asset creation and savings (Wegelin and Borgman, 1995). Poor landlords, for example, also use housing to earn some income in the form of rental charges.

b) Job Creation

Housing is a key source of employment. The relatively higher labour-intensity of residential construction results in increased job opportunities. In Tunisia, for example, the housing sector employs between 7% and 8% of the working population (Driss, 1999). Many new rural immigrants to towns who can not get urban employment immediately are usually absorbed in the construction industry which provides them with erratic but an important source of income (Drakakis-Smith, 1981). They can later find other income generating activities in the town. In fact, income and employment opportunities affect household formations. According to Ermisch (1990), income and employment opportunities can affect household formation in a particular geographical area in three main ways:

- They can alter the number and composition of family units in an area's population by influencing marriage, divorce and childbearing patterns;
- They can change an area's population by affecting migration into and from the area;
- They can influence the probability that unmarried adults and family units form a separate household.

c) Multiplier Effect

Housing investment has a multiplier effect on the economy as a whole. For example, it is estimated that the building industry purchases three times as much material from the non-industrial sector of the economy as does manufacturing (Drakakis-Smith, 1981). The housing sector contributes to the development of the building materials industry, which in Tunisia, for example, attracts over 40% of investments earmarked for the sector (Driss (1999). A housing programme can be instrumental in developing savings and releasing unproductive capital into the economy (Materu, 1994). Housing construction activates construction related industries such as cement factories, timber felling and furniture making.

d) Disease and Delinquency Alleviation

Improving housing and basic services greatly reduces the tremendous health burden facing most low-income groups due to poor quality housing and lack of basic services. Indeed there is a close relationship between health and housing.

Improvements in death rates from infectious diseases such as cholera, typhoid and tuberculosis owe as much to improved standards of housing as to microbiology and antibiotics (Ranson, 1991). Poor and unhealthy housing also causes stress-related diseases such as hypertension, migraine headaches, depression, neurosis, alcoholism and social diseases manifested by pathologically derived antisocial behavior like crime, violence, street mugging, vandalism, child abuse and mental or sexual disorders (Ranson, 1991).

e) Other Related Social Benefits

Shelter is an important element in the other social aspirations of households. It affects material and psychological well-being, privacy and children's school performance. All these combine to increase the individual's mental and physical capacity to work. Another theory of housing which has a special significance for gender issues and the way we perceive subsidies in housing is that it is an asset with capital value and it is contributory to the production of goods and services (HABITAT, 1996e). The goods and services include "domestic sector" i.e. home-based production of meals, laundering, nurturing of children, and other things. A decent home is therefore essential to the wellbeing of every household, and can have a real effect on people's health, their education and their employment prospects. Improvements in housing can give people increased pride, not just in their homes, but also their communities as a whole (Scottish Homes, 1994).

THE POPULATION-POVERTY-ENVIRONMENT CIRCLE

Quoting UNICEF (1994), Chambers (1997) suggests that there is a negative link between population and the environment. More people cause environmental degradation which in turn causes more poverty and so a larger population (see figure 2.2). But he also cautions that beliefs on these negative relationships may be unfounded. More people may not always and necessarily mean more environmental degradation.

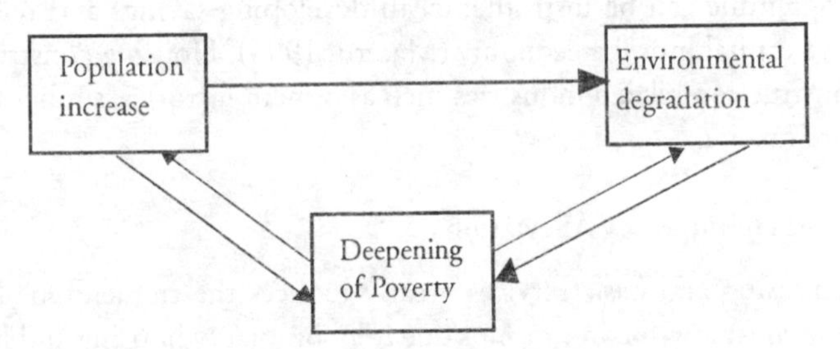

Figure 2.2: *The population-Poverty-Environmental Stereotype*

Urbanization and the Housing Problem

Like the general population growth, urbanization exacerbates environmental degradation and the magnitude of poverty. Urbanization and industrialization are major sources of environmental problems (Katima, 1999). The housing and environmental problems facing many people in urban areas can therefore be well understood and tackled if the causes, magnitudes and manifestations of the unprecedented urban growth are well understood.

Are the Urban Poor Poorer Than the Rural Poor?

According to the World Bank (1993), 85% of all poor Tanzanians live in rural areas. This is a phenomenon of all developing countries. However, when housing schemes for the poor are considered in developing countries, it is the urban poor who present grave concern. This is because overcrowding and living conditions are characteristics of the urban life and present much bigger problems than in rural housing. Furthermore, although in Tanzania, for example, population is growing by 2.8% per annum, urbanization rate is estimated at 9% per annum. This compels governments in all developing countries to put more efforts and allocate resources in an attempt to solve urbanization problems.

Although urban-rural poverty statistics place the urban poor in relatively better-off position, the urban poor may in fact suffer more in some poverty aspects. To quote World Bank (1990):

> Although urban incomes are generally higher and urban services and facilities more accessible, poor urban dwellers may suffer more than the rural households from certain aspects of poverty. The urban poor typically housed in slums and squatter settlements, often have to contend with appalling overcrowding, bad sanitation and contaminated water. The sites are often illegal and dangerous. Forcible eviction, floods, landslides and chemical pollution are constant threats.

As suggested by Kironde (1998), a given cash income might be considered adequate in a rural area where people grow their own food and maintain their own houses, but might be grossly inadequate in a city where accommodation has to be rented, and food bought. Fuel and water are other expenses for urban households, but it may be free or relatively cheap in rural areas. Transport from home to work is a further daily expense for many urban dwellers since, unlike in the rural areas, the workplace is usually far away from residential areas.

In developing countries, 60% of the population of many cities are without sewage connections, 50% of the households lack access to safe drinking water, and 90% of solid waste is not removed or dumped in safe disposal sites (McCarney, 1994). The urban poor do not only live in poor quality housing and environment, but when it comes to social amenities, they suffer more than the better-off urban dwellers. Urban housing situation in developing countries is therefore a paradox. According to Asiama (1990), resources such as land, housing finance, building materials and amenities are unavailable to the poor urban dwellers while the rich or better-off often take them for granted. The poor have to contend with living in slums and squatters with their squalid conditions, devoid of urban services and amenities, while the rich have well laid-out estates with all amenities conducive to the environment of their housing. Evidence (Anzorena, et al, 1998) suggests that in many cities, households with connections to water supply and sewers (predominantly middle and upper-income groups) pay less than the real cost of supplying and maintaining these systems - while households with no connections (predominantly low income households) often have to purchase water at many times the cost per litre paid by those with piped water. It can also be proved that in many countries, subsidized housing loans are available to middle or upper-income groups, or they can obtain tax deductions on such loans. Evidence by HABITAT (1996a) also confirms that low-income families pay much more for basic services provided informally than those served by existing trunk infrastructure (usually high and middle income groups).

However, the paradox of humankind does not end with the urban housing and services; it extends to the whole spectrum of human life. As Chambers (1997) puts it, in the present world, more people than ever before are wealthy beyond any reasonable need for a good life, and more are poor and vulnerable below any conceivable definition of decency. He further observes that the income taken home by the wealthy over-class is not twice, or 4 times or 8 times, or 16 times, but 32 times that of the poor underclass. Nevertheless, both classes are stable: the over-class has multiple interlocking privileges, securities and advantages which keep it on top; and the underclass has multiple interlocking disabilities, vulnerabilities and deprivations which hold it under. The question is how to help them converge, how to narrow the gap, how to enable the over-class to accept less, and how to enable the underclass to gain more.

The present work seeks to answer the question of how the better off (politicians, government bureaucrats, professionals, researchers, donor agencies, etc) can sacrifice part of their wealth, ideas and advantages to enable the poor urban households access better housing and related infrastructure for poverty alleviation.

THE URBANIZATION PROBLEM

Urbanization is not confined to Tanzania only, but other developing countries face similar problems. This mismatch between the rate of urbanization in developing countries and the housing supply is immense. While in 1990, there were about 2.5 billion people living in urban areas all over the world, it is expected that this number will double to 5 billion in the year 2025, with 90% of the growth occurring in developing countries (HABITAT, 1996b). Urbanization, particularly in developing countries, has resulted in a severe housing crisis with consequences that range from appalling housing conditions, a deficiency in or complete lack of essential services, continued exploitation of the poor in land and other shelter matters, and the growth of deprived settlements, amounting sometimes to homelessness (Aina, 1990). Kombe (1999) also alludes to this, saying that basic infrastructure services like water supply, sanitation facilities, storm water drainage and accessibility in urban centres are in most cases lacking or in pathetic situation. Simultaneously, overcrowding, unemployment and urban poverty have been increasing while public attempts to manage urban growth have not been successful.

In the developed world the most rapid urbanization took place over a century ago. For example, in 1989, it was estimated that 71% of the U.S.A. population was living in urban areas, while the ratios for Japan, Canada and Germany were 80%, 69% and 60% respectively (Button and Pearce, 1989). By 1995 more than 70% of the population in both Europe and North America was living in urban areas. Urban growth continues in these countries, but at a much slower rate compared to that of developing countries where roughly 150,000 people are added to the urban population every day. In fact, UNEP (1992) estimates that while the rate of urbanization in developed countries is growing at only 0.8%, that of developing countries is on average 3.6% per annum. It is estimated that currently there are about 1.8 billion people in urban areas of the developing countries compared to only 300 million in 1950. About 2.0 billion and 2.7 billion people are expected to live in urban areas in these countries by the years 2000 and 2010 respectively (Alile, 1994). Tables 2.2 and 2.3 give some statistics on urban population and level of urbanization.

Among the developing continents, Africa depicts the worst scenario. The rate of urbanization in Africa, which stands at 5.3% per annum, is the highest in the world (Ayogu, 1994). According to HABITAT (1993), it is estimated that currently Africa's urban areas have a population of about 240 million people. By the year 2010, Sub-Saharan Africa will have an urban population of 765 million people, which will be half of its total population. While in 1960 there were only two cities in Sub-Saharan Africa with over 500,000 people each, in 1980 there were 14 such cities, but by the year 2000, over 20 cities have more than 1 million people each, with Lagos having 8.3 million, Kinshasa 8 million and Johannesburg having 7.7 million people. Dar es Salaam, Nairobi, Khartoum and Addis-Ababa have over 3 million people. Although huge extension of the administrative boundaries has caused urban growth in many African cities, the major factor has been immigration (Pennant, 1990).

Table 2.2: *Urban Population and Level of Urbanization, by Region* (1950 - 2025)

Region	Urban Population (millions)					Share of Population living in urban areas (%)				
	1950	1975	1995	2000	2025	1950	1975	1995	2000	2025
L/America & Caribbean	69	196	358	401	601	41.6	61.3	74.2	76.6	84.6
Sub-Saharan Africa	20	70	184	233	661	11.3	21.0	30.8	34.0	51.4
N/Africa & Middle East	27	90	208	246	465	26.3	45.3	59.3	62.5	75.3
South Asia	11	33	82	105	284	9.9	16.8	25.4	28.4	47.6
India	62	132	251	292	630	17.3	21.3	26.8	28.6	45.2
East Asia & Pacific	36	104	223	264	486	16.8	27.0	39.3	42.7	59.0
China	61	160	369	443	832	11.0	17.3	30.3	34.5	54.5
Developing Countries	286	785	1675	1983	3957	17.0	26.3	37.4	40.5	56.9
Industrialized World	452	753	909	943	1108	54.1	68.8	73.4	74.7	82.4
World Total	738	1538	2584	2926	5065	29.3	37.7	45.2	47.5	61.1

Source: HABITAT (1996e)

Elsewhere other than Africa, it is estimated that urban population in Turkey, for example, is increasing at about 6%, while the overall population increase is about 2.3% (Parker, 1995). In 1987, 47% of Turkey's population was urban. According to the 1990 census, 55% of Turkey's population lives in cities. 70% of the population is expected to be urban by the year 2000 (Baykal, 1992). The rapid growth of urban poor, many of who have moved from economically non-viable farming communities that develop in areas unsuitable for residential use have put a large portion of the population of Turkey and many other developing countries at great risk. In Turkey, the informal slums often arise in land that poses severe earthquake damage risk (Parker, 1995). A good example is a recent (August, 1999) biggest earthquake that occurred in western Turkey, centering mainly on the northwestern industrial city of Izmit. That disaster left about 13,000 people dead and another 200,000 people were rendered homeless.

In Philippines, urban population was only 2.3% of the total population in 1980. This rose to 5.1% in 1990, while currently, it is estimated that the urban population is 42.7% of total population (Shubert, 1996). The housing deficit in the country is estimated at 156,000 units annually, while the central government has provided only 29,000 units over several years.

Urban areas grow more rapidly because they provide greater social and economic benefits than do rural areas on average. Among the important reasons for rapid urbanization are:

- The shift of job from agriculture to industry and service due to drought and severe drop in agricultural exports.
- Concentration of economic opportunities in urban areas.
- Civil wars, particularly in developing countries (Nhachungue and Dgedge, 1997). These have the effect of driving people from the rural areas to comparatively safer areas in cities.

Housing Shortage

In contrast to the high growth of urban population, there is a very serious deficiency in the housing supply to cater for this rapid urban expansion, particularly in developing countries. The problem is more serious among the middle and low-income groups. In Hong Kong, for example, the government has put much effort to construct public housing in a bid to provide decent accommodation for all. Yet, there are 693,322 households still living in private blocks, with more than a quarter of these sharing facilities with other households in the same living unit, often consisting of a bed-space, cockloft or small cubicle (Chan, 1994). As elaborated in chapter four, there is also a big housing problem in Tanzania.

According to a World Bank Report, it is estimated that in 10 years, some 400 million new dwellings will be required to house some 2.7 billion urban people who will be lacking adequate shelter. In Kenya, it was estimated that in 1989/90, the urban areas of that country needed a total of 117,652 housing units, out of which 50,454 were required for the city of Nairobi alone (Syagga and Kiamba, 1992). It is now estimated that Kenya's urban areas require 60,000 new housing units per annum. While demand for housing in Ghana stood at 141,000 units per annum in 1996, the delivery was only 38,000 units (25%) with a deficit of 103,000 units (Amoa-Mensah, 1997). It is also estimated that Malawi's urban population, which is estimated to be 1.9 million in the year 2000, will require 16,000 housing units every year.

In the city of Cotonou, Benin, it was estimated that housing requirements in 1965 was 22,000 units. However, only about 4,500 units were effectively constructed between 1961 and 1965, meaning that there was already a deficit of 17,500 units (Doutetien, 1999). In Nigeria, the shortage of urban housing is estimated at more than one million units, with about a quarter of the shortfall occurring in Lagos. In South Africa, the shortfall is 1,500,000 units; while in

Kenya the shortfall in 1987 was estimated at 280,000 units; Zambia had a shortage of 208,000 units in 1988, and Ghana had a shortfall of 375,000 units in 1993 (HABITAT, 1996e). While the housing demand in Zimbabwe in 1995 was about 670,000, the current demand is estimated at 1,000,000 units, but the private and public sectors are able to produce only 18,000 units every year, which is far below requirements.

As Halfani (1994) observes, East African countries are still faced with the problem of housing and overcrowding. Despite all the efforts of the past three decades, the countries have not succeeded in creating a self-sustaining organizational and technological framework for housing provision. There is a consistent failure to replicate the programmes of the 1970s. Deterioration of urban services is another critical problem that needs serious research attention. In East Africa as in other developing countries, most of the urban people live in sub-standard housing, characterized by overcrowding and poor sanitation, which is also accompanied by malnutrition, unemployment and low living standards (Syagga and Kiamba, 1992). As also observed by Ranson (1994), many parts of the developing world have a serious housing problem as manifested by homelessness, slums and poor quality housing, ostensibly contributing to hazards to health and well-being. For example, diseases, accidents and fires are all more prevalent in slum areas; psychological and social disturbances are also partly attributed to substandard housing. In many African cities and towns, there are no properly planned housing settlements. In Maputo, for example, proper housing accounts for only 10% of the total city area, while 70.5% of the city is for squatter population (Nhachungue and Dgedge, 1997).

Experience suggests that currently the biggest housing problem is the shortage of affordable and decent accommodation for the poor - the low-income majority. Over the last four decades, most official housing programmes have failed to reach considerable portions of this group, especially the lowest 20 to 40 percentiles (Tipple and Willis, 1991). But apart from the quantity aspect, the housing conditions and environments in most urban centres in the developing countries are appalling; with lack of social services and amenities exacerbating the problem. For example, as evident from Table 2.4, housing conditions in Tanzania are generally poor.

Many researchers, (Ondiege, 1992; Okoye, 1990 and others), have suggested that the main reasons for the housing problems in urban areas of the developing world include:

- High rate of urbanization;
- Lag in development of urban infrastructure that support housing development;
- Low purchasing power of the majority of the urban households; and
- Lack of appropriate building standards due to restrictive buildings by-laws.

Table 2.3. *Urban Population and Level of Urbanization in Selected Sub-Sahara African Countries (1975 - 2025)*

Country	Urban population (thousands)				% of population living in urban areas			
	1975	1995	2000	2025	1975	1995	2000	2025
Nigeria	14,676	43,884	55,751	146948	23.4	39.3	43.3	61.6
Ethiopia	3,061	7,371	9,516	37,929	9.5	13.4	14.9	29.9
Zaire (DRC)	6,860	12,766	15,865	52,129	29.5	29.1	31.0	49.8
South Africa	12,314	21,073	24,550	48,673	48.0	50.8	53.1	68.6
Tanzania	1,602	7,230	9,608	30,344	10.1	24.4	28.2	48.3
Kenya	1,775	7,817	10,347	32,616	12.9	27.7	31.8	51.5
Sudan	3,033	6,915	8,742	27,075	18.9	24.6	27.3	46.4
Uganda	933	2,670	3,504	13,818	8.3	12.5	14.2	28.8
Ghana	2,955	6,333	7,901	21,934	30.1	36.3	39.2	57.7
Mozambique	905	5,481	7,800	21,468	8.6	34.3	41.1	61.1
Madagascar	1,253	4,003	5,308	17,378	16.1	27.1	30.8	50.5
Cote d'Ivoire	2,168	6,211	7,869	23,611	32.1	43.6	47.0	64.1
Cameroon	2,022	5,938	7,521	19,504	26.9	44.9	49.3	66.9
Zimbabwe	1,202	3,619	4,502	10,874	19.6	32.1	36.0	55.4
Malawi	402	1,505	1,894	7,083	7.7	13.5	15.6	31.7
Angola	1,087	3,569	4,729	14,799	17.8	32.2	36.2	55.6
Mali	1,000	2,909	3,821	12,277	16.2	27.0	30.4	50.0
Burkina Faso	394	2,809	4,386	14,374	6.4	27.2	37.5	66.4
Zambia	1,686	4,071	4,807	11,467	34.8	43.1	44.7	59.9
Somalia	1,164	2,382	3,004	9,760	21.3	25.8	27.9	45.9
Niger	507	1,558	2,078	8,160	10.6	17.0	19.2	36.5
Senegal	1,643	3,512	4,280	10,505	34.2	42.3	45.1	62.2
Rwanda	175	483	610	2,367	4.0	6.1	6.7	15.0
TOTAL	69,925	183530	232756	660919	21.0	30.8	34.0	51.4

Source: HABITAT (1996)

Table 2.4: *Basic Housing Amenities in Tanzania (% Households)*

	Poorest	Better Off	All	Rural Poor	Rural All	Urban	Dar-es Salaam
Housing with non-earth floor	5.5	54.9	27.1	4.3	11.2	55.9	91.6
Houses with iron roof	20.1	71.9	45.0	17.5	29.9	75.0	94.2
Houses with no windows	25.5	7.4	14.8	27.8	19.3	'5.5	0.8
Houses with glass windows	1.1	3.4	2.3	1.2	2.0	3.2	1.8
House-holds with electricity	1.7	30.8	11.2	0.5	0.8	30.3	51.8
Kerosene as main lighting fuel	94.4	70.5	88.0	96.4	97.1	72.1	48.8
Wood as main cooking fuel	96.8	53.2	79.6	99.0	96.6	50.0	5.0
House-holds without toilet	10.2	2.4	5.3	10.9	6.6	2.6	1.3

Source: World Bank (1996), *Tanzania: Challenge of Reforms* Vol. II .

THE ENVIRONMENT AND HOUSING RELATED SERVICES

The severe economic crisis from the 1980's has had a serious impact on urban development and the capacity of urban management to maintain or improve the urban environment in many African countries. In many urban areas, environmental conditions, particularly in low-income settlements, have worsened, as economic problems have taken their toll on urban water, sanitation, low-income housing and transport programmes (Potts, 1994). The out-come of this large and fast scale urbanization in the midst of the crisis has been the spectacular growth of shanty towns (slum and squatter settlements), inadequate water supply and sewerage infrastructure, high rates of unemployment and proliferation of casualisation of labour, the proliferation of informal sector activities, crime, traffic congestion and so on (Misra, 1994).

A study of Allahabad city in India, for instance, revealed that the conditions of housing and environment, both in terms of quality and quantity in that city, are in deplorable state. About 80% of the population lives in substandard dwellings; 44% lives in one-room apartments; 31% in two-room apartments; 12% in three-room flats; 6% in four-room houses, and 2% in five-room houses. It is only a small proportion (3%), which enjoys the luxury of living in houses with five rooms and more (Misra, 1994). Environmental conditions in Allahabad are also appalling. Roads are congested with human and motorized traffic, piped water supply is often contaminated on account of leakage giving rise to several water-borne diseases. Air and noise pollution are increasing due to the multiplicity of 3-wheeled motorcycles that emit fumes, and smoke.

In Nigeria, despite the government putting much effort into various ways of providing housing, millions of the people live in poor and deteriorating housing conditions (Mutter, 1994). In 1985, it was estimated (Potts, 1994) that 27%, 33% and 67% of urban dwellers in Africa, India and East Asia respectively had no sanitation coverage, due to, among other things, poverty and relative powerlessness of urban governments, lack of security of tenure, difficult terrain, and ignorance. Potts (1994) also concludes that small, poorly ventilated dwellings promote the spread of communicable diseases, and overcrowding within them further increases the frequency of transmission of diseases such as upper-respiratory tract diseases, measles, tuberculosis, meningitis, influenza, mumps, diphtheria and whooping cough.

An interesting theory on the lack of attention to poor environment and other social services in urban areas is discerned by Peil (1994). He contends that since most of the population in urban areas come from villages where there is no electricity, piped water or sanitary services, and is struggling for survival, their expectations of urban services are not high, and neither them nor politicians pay much attention to the environment and services around them. Peil (1994) gives the example of West African countries where the environment leaves much to be desired, both at the domestic and the civic levels. For the low-income majority, housing is a necessity about which they can do little, and services are unreliable at best. Few urban residents own houses, and for most, the town is merely a "farm" like any other - to be used to produce a living. They have no particular commitment to the place where they are living and ignore the environment because it is not considered important or amenable to change.

3

HOUSING PROVISION AND IMPROVEMENT POLICIES

HOUSING FOR LOW-INCOME URBAN PEOPLE

This chapter reviews the policies and practices for providing and improving housing and related services and infrastructure to the poor urban people. More specifically the earlier conventional housing policies, and the changing philosophy and policy direction towards improving and financing housing and other related services are reviewed. The aim is to help in the conceptualisation of the severity and magnitude of the housing problem and poor urban services and the development of a notion that "partnership" is the only viable option in redressing the housing problem for poor urbanites in developing countries, like Tanzania.

Any low-cost housing scheme in any country has taken one or more of the following four types: Government, private, squatter or slum housing/settlement. While government and private housing are usually grouped under conventional housing, the slums and squatters are non-conventional in nature (see fig. 3.1).

Conventional Housing

The literal meaning of "conventional" is "being in accordance with acceptable standards." Housing is conventional if it is constructed through recognized institutions such as housing authorities and real estate developers, and if such construction is in accordance with established legal practice and standards. A major distinguishing characteristic of conventional housing is that it utilizes paid labour, is capital intensive and usually employs relatively sophisticated technology (Drakakis-Smith, 1981).

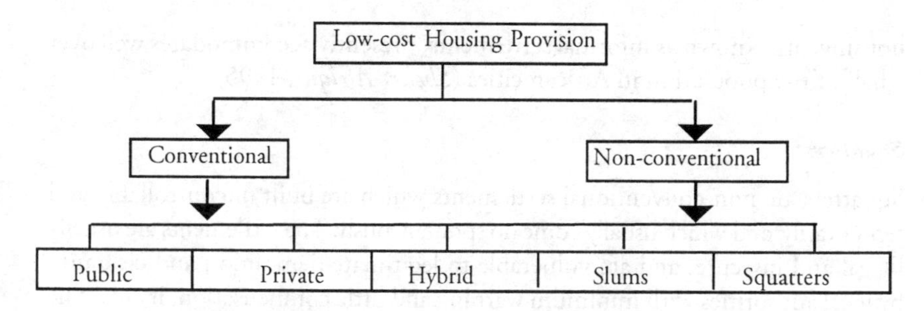

Figure 3.1: *Sources of Low-cost Housing*

Source: Drakakis-Smith (1981)

Public Housing

Public housing is one type of conventional housing. These are formal housing settlements provided by the central government. In many developing countries, the public does not substantially engage in provision of housing for the people. According to Dakakis-Smith (1981), the few housing projects undertaken by governments in developing countries are normally expensive projects that are designed to impress electorates rather than meet any real needs of poor households. Invariably, such projects are located in visually prominent townscapes and are in most cases high-rise apartment blocks that fulfill this psycho-political motive.

Private Housing

Conventional private housing is that which is constructed through normal institutional channels and is offered for sale or rent in the open market. Although in developing countries most of the conventional housing is undertaken by the private sector, these are usually expensive in relation to the financial ability of most low-income households. Sometimes the government may engage private construction firms to build houses for low-income households at market construction costs, but subsidize the prices or rents, which the earmarked households are charged to make the houses affordable.

Non-conventional Housing

Non-conventional housing is that type of housing constructed without complying with established procedures. Such housing is usually constructed outside the institutions of building industry, and is frequently in contravention of existing legislation. Non- conventional housing applies labour of individual households, although petty private building firms may sometimes operate therein. Squatters and slums are the widely known non-conventional housing. Non-conventional housing, also known as informal settlements, presently accommodates well over a half of the population in African cities (*Shelter Afrique*, 1995).

Squatters

Squatters are non-conventional settlements which are built uncontrollably and temporarily, and which usually come up spontaneously. The settlements are usually illegal and insecure, and are vulnerable to legitimate demolition and clearance by local authorities with minimum warning and little compensation, if any. The legal definition of squatting has been given as follows:

> What is a squatter? He is one who, without any colour of right, enters on an unoccupied house or land, intending to stay there as long as he can. He may seek to justify or excuse his conduct. He may say that this house or land was standing empty, doing nothing. But this plea is of no avail in law (Massawe, 1996c)

Slums

Slums are legal, permanent dwellings that have become substandard through age, neglect and/or sub-division into micro-occupational units such as rooms or cubicles. Quoting Steward (1972), Simime (1996) defines slums as areas where dwellings, predominate which, by reason of dilapidation, overcrowding, faulty arrangements or design, lack of ventilation, light or sanitation or any combination of these factors, are detrimental to safety, health or morals. Unlike squatters, slum formation is not usually illegal. Slums may therefore be formed from old buildings that the authorities cannot afford to decrease their already inadequate housing stock by demolition. In developing countries, dilapidation is more often due to the financial incapacity of landlords to maintain their property rather than any deliberate attempt at exploitation (Drakakis-Smith, 1981).

THE NATURE AND DEVELOPMENT OF INFORMAL (SLUM AND SQUATTER) SETTLEMENTS

Slums and shanties are frequently constructed at the edge of cities where land is relatively cheap, sometimes adjacent to industrial areas or just outside the administrative control of the city authority. These makeshift dwellings are normally constructed of salvaged materials, such as wood and corrugated iron. They often lack indoor water supply, drainage and sanitation, including provision for waste disposal, and proper access roads. Furthermore, indoor space requirements and air quality are poor, and inadequate building materials fail to compensate for changes in temperature and other climatic factors during the year. In these settlements, basic housing hygiene conditions are usually appalling and communicable diseases endemic.

There are, however, modern slums which consist mostly of slab-block or high-rise buildings frequently overlooking each other, and with little thought given to the planning, layout, internal design, maintenance and public health/ social consequences within the context of urban planning and healthy housing principles.

In South Africa, the term "informal settlements" designates unserviced shanty towns composed of rudimentary shacks in contradistinction to the fully serviced formal housing units constructed and managed either by the state or by private developers for renting or selling (Lupton and Wofson, 1994).

Slum housing is both widespread and presents an enormous challenge to public health. Despite the efforts being put by many developing countries to combat housing problems, these efforts are often slow and not always visibly obvious in the poorer areas where people still live in slums and squatters with terrible hygienic hazards. Studies have concluded that it is unrealistic for the large countries of South-East Asia, for example, to expect to solve their housing problems in the present decade, given the rate of urban population growth and the rapid increase in slum and squatter areas (Ranson, (1991). Even in Africa, the major source of urban growth is the rapid influx of immigrants from rural areas. In Mozambique, for example, rural migrants accounts for 66% of urban population (Ranson, 1991). In 1985, Maputo had about 1 million inhabitants, and an annual growth of 80%. This has increased overcrowding and facilitated the transmission of infectious and parasitic diseases.

Given the absence of significant subsidized housing schemes, effective demand for shelter is articulated in various sub-markets. These sub-markets range from squatter housing to legal and illegal low-income housing and higher income housing. The majority of the urban population, however, lives in slum and squatter settlements. For instance, in the major Asian cities, about 60-80% of the housing supply is provided and financed through informal sector mechanisms (Wegelin and Borgman, 1995). Studies in India, Korea, Philippines, Sri Lanka, Bangladesh and Indonesia suggest that the formal sector response has been inadequate in meeting shelter demand. In the Philippines, Bangladesh and other Asian countries, for instance, government assistance for housing construction and development favoured the middle- and higher-income groups, leaving the urban poor in a vulnerable situation. Appendix I shows types of housing markets in some selected Asian cities.

Results from studies done in Nairobi indicate that in aggregate, informal settlements occupy 5.84% only of all land area of Nairobi that is used for residential purposes, but they housed between 30- 40% of the city's population in the late 1980s (Alder, 1995; Lee-Smith, 1990). By 1995, it was estimated that

55% of Nairobi's population lived in these informal settlements (Alder, 1995). It was also found that the average density in the informal settlements is 250 dwelling units (or 750 persons) per hectare compared to 10-30 dwelling units (or 50 - 150 persons) per hectare in middle and upper-income areas (Alder, 1995). These findings mean that informal settlements are not isolated "pockets of poverty" which can be ignored in the planning and development of the city, but are settlements where the majority of the poor, and over half the city population, resides. They must therefore be fully integrated into strategies for urban management (Alder, 1995).

OTHER SHELTER RELATED SERVICES

Housing related social services affecting poor urban dwellers include land delivery systems, water supply, sanitation, garbage collection and health services.

Land Delivery Systems.

The issue of urban land tenure has received increasing attention in recent years (Payne, 1999) and is listed in the World Bank's latest Housing Policy Paper (1993) as among the most important factors affecting housing demand and the first priority in terms of demand side instruments. In Africa, land tenure is complicated by the existence of different legal systems such as customary practices, Islamic systems and imported European statutory systems (Payne, 1999). In some countries, several systems operate side by side, creating legal pluralism, in which people move between one system and another. In some African countries land tenure is characterized by traditional notions and beliefs that are often in conflict with efficient and economic use of land (Asiama, 1990).

Yahya (1990) shows that in Africa, when one wants to acquire land in urban area in which to erect a house, he has four options:

- He can approach local authority or the local chief or king's representative for allocation of a plot from communal reserves;
- He can be allocated land through government schemes to distribute serviced land for housing purposes;
- He can purchase or lease the land in the open market; or
- He can build illegally on someone else's land, be it public or private.

In Kenya, about 9,300 residential sites or plots are created annually. Out of these, only 10% are plots allocated by the Commissioner of Lands, the National Housing Corporation, Nairobi City Council and other local authorities (Yahya,

1990). The remaining sites are due to private sector efforts, of which 2,300 are illegal in the form of squatting and illegal sub-divisions.

Land management, which encompasses land allocation, land tenure and land use, is fundamental to solving the problems of informal settlements in urban areas. As suggested by Alder (1995), characteristics of a better and more equitable land system to benefit the poor and urban development in general include:

- Tenure system must ensure that residents directly benefit. Although rental system is preferred because of financial constraints, there should be a mix of ownership and rental tenure systems;
- There should be official standards for shelter and infrastructure, and these should be affordable, but must safeguard public health;
- Tenure system(s) must reduce the chances of "gentrification" i.e. should avoid the invasion of areas of low-income people by the more affluent groups;
- Tenure system must encourage and promote business investment;
- In order to provide shelter in significant quantitities and reduce rent levels, there must be rapid allocation of land to be developed in public-private partnership;
- There must be a balanced development of middle and low-income housing to prevent demand pressure on low-income housing by middle-income groups;
- Basic urban services must be extended to low-income settlements;
- Households must be provided with affordable credit to enable them renovate and expand shelter and for purchasing land.

Asiama (1990) documents evidence indicating that in many African countries, governments have made attempts to influence the ownership structures to bring them in line with the dictates of the modern economic and social conditions they find themselves in. For example, in Ghana, the government has reserved for itself wide powers of compulsory acquisition of land though it has been using such powers sparingly, and only in the public interest. In Nigeria, the Land Use Decree (1978) has vested all land in the state government in trust for the people, because it is deemed in the public interest that "the rights of all Nigerians to use and enjoy land in Nigeria... should be assured, protected and preserved." Similarly, in Tanzania, Ethiopia and Uganda, the state has absolute control over the ownership and use of land.

Poor land and tenure systems adversely affect low-income households in developing countries. Many of them fail to improve their housing because their settlements have developed illegally in the sense that either the land is illegally occupied, or it has been illegally sub-divided by landowners or developers. The houses themselves are usually illegal too, since they fail to meet building and planning regulations. As such, these houses or the sites cannot be used as collateral for loans. The households have also little incentive to invest in housing construction or improvement because there are always threats of eviction (Arrossi, *et al*, 1994).

Water Supply

While estimates by the World Health Organization (WHO) suggest that in 1988, 170 million urban inhabitants lacked safe and sufficient supplies of water (Arrossi, 1994), the World Bank estimates that currently about 220 million urban dwellers (13% of total urban population of developing countries) lack access to safe drinking water (Salewi, 1999). These figures are, however, greatly underestimated (Arrossi, et al, 1994) because of the criteria used to define what is an "adequate" supply and because of exaggeration by governments in the figures they supply to the WHO.

Inadequacies in water supply provision compel a high proportion of the population in most urban centres to collect water from open streams and wells which may be contaminated with waste, or purchase their water from private vendors who are subject to little quality or price control. It is estimated that between 20-30% of the urban population of developing countries get their water supply through water vendors who sell from tanks or carts (Arrossi, et al, 1994). This system is much more expensive than water supplied through piped connections, sometimes by about five times, for example in the case of Abidjan (Arrossi, et al, 1994).

The poor people are affected by lack of adequate water supply in several ways as follows:

- They are liable to suffer from diseases which can be carried in untreated water;
- Without water to maintain adequate hygiene, the risk of contracting disease increases; and
- The cost of purchasing water reduces the ability to purchase other essentials such as food, health care and education.

Available evidence suggests that many households in developing countries currently purchase water supplies from private vendors for which they have to pay a price many times that paid by households receiving piped water. An average cost of providing water in urban areas in developing countries is around US$ 120 per person saved. Capital costs for public standpipes are about half of this, although most of the reduction in cost occurs because of savings resulting from the lower level of water use, which in itself has health implications (Arrossi, *et al*, 1994).

Studies in various cities of developing countries (Hardoy and Satterthwaite, 1989) indicate that about one-third of the population in Bangkok had no access to public water and obtained water from vendors. In Calcutta, some 3 million people lived in "bustees" and refugee settlements that lacked portable water. Some 2.5 million others lived in similarly blighted and unserviced areas. A survey in 1980-81 in Dakar found that only 28% of the households had private water connections while 68% relied on public standpipes and 4.2% bought water from carriers. In Pikine, an outer part of Dakar, an average of 696 persons used one standpipe, with one neighbourhood having 1,513 people using one standpipe.

A survey in 1986-87 of 660 households in Dar es Salaam drawn from all income levels (Hardoy and Satterthwaite, 1989), found that 47% had no piped water supply either inside or immediately outside their houses while 32% had a shared piped-water supply. Of the households without piped water, 67% bought water from neighbours while 26% drew water from public water-kiosks or standpipes. Only 7.1% bought water from water vendors. In Jakarta, less than a quarter of the city's population had direct connections to a piped water system; some 30% depended solely on water vendors who sell water at five times that of piped water. These studies also found that in Karachi, potable water had to be brought more than 160 kilometres from the Indus and was available for only a few hours a day in most areas. One-third of households had piped water connections, and most slum dwellers and squatters had either to use standpipes or buy water from vendors at inflated prices.

A survey of 1,525 households in Makurdi and Idah in the Benue State of Nigeria, with respective populations of 144,000 and 47,200 in 1982, showed that only 49.8% of Makurdi residents and 30.4% of Idah residents had access to piped water in their own houses or compounds (Stren, 1990). Again based on a stratified random sample of 1,986 households in Ibadan, Enugu and Kaduna, it was found that on the average, close to one-third of the interviewees had no pipe-borne water connections to their homes (Stren, 1990). Of those with water connections, 27% of the Ibadan households, 40% of the Enugu households, and 39% of the Kaduna households had only a single tap on their homes. Most of those with water connections experienced various degrees of water supply interruption; while 34% of the Ibadan households, 27% of the Enugu households and 26% of the Kaduna households had perpetual dry pipes.

The number of people who suffer from poor water or waterborne diseases is immense. Quoting WHO, Buchan (1999) states that up to 50,000 people die daily from waterborne diseases, and that one in four hospital beds is occupied because of unsafe water. Mbuligwe (1999) presents horrifying statistics on water borne diseases from Water and Sanitation for Health (WASH) Project of the US Agency for International Development, which suggest that in the developing countries each year, there are 875 million cases of diarrhea, of which 4.6 million end in death, mostly among children. There are also 900 million cases of ascariasis, of which 200,000 cases end in death; and that there are 800 million cases of hookworm, 200 million cases of schistosomiasis and 500 million cases of trachoma. Eight million cases of trachoma end in blindness.

Sanitation

WHO also gives a seemingly low estimate that shows that 331 million people in urban centres lacked adequate sanitation in 1988 (Arrossi, et al, 1994). In reality however, many more people lack sanitation systems which are easily maintained and which ensure no contamination of food or water by faecal matter and a minimum of human contact with faecal matter. In informal and illegal settlements, provision of sanitation may be no more than pits dug into the ground or buckets. It is in these slum and squatter settlements, which are often overcrowded and under resourced areas, that the health consequences resulting from a lack of sanitation can be significantly worse than in other urban and rural areas. It is estimated that every year, 2.5 million children (5 every minute) die of diarrhea that could have been prevented by good sanitation (see Mashauri, 1999).

Improved sanitation results in better health and higher quality living environment. There are many different methods of providing adequate sanitation at a cost significantly lower than that of investing in conventional water-borne sewerage systems. Estimates for providing sanitation show (Arrossi, et al, 1994) that costs vary for each individual site according to the availability of water, sewage disposal, settlement density, ground conditions, and local social and economic factors, but may range as shown in Table 3.1.

Table 3.1: *Typical range of capital cost per household of alternative sanitation systems (1990 prices)*

Type of System	US$
Twin pit pour-flush latrines	075 - 150
Ventilated improved pit (V.I.P.) latrines	068 - 175
Shallow sewerage	100 - 325
Small-bore sewerage	150 - 500
Conventional septic tank	200 - 600
Conventional sewerage	600 - 1200

Source: Arrossi, *et al*, (1994), p.10

Again studies on the sanitation situation in developing urban cities (Hardoy and Satterthwaite, 1989) give shocking results. Bangkok, for example, had only 2% of its population connected to a sewer system so that human waste was generally disposed of through septic tanks and cesspools and their effluents. Similarly, wastewater from sinks, laundries, baths and kitchens was being discharged into storm water drains or canals. In Calcutta, the sewerage system was limited to only a third of the area in the urban core, while poor maintenance of drains and periodic clogging of the system had made flooding an annual occurrence. Of the five urban centres with sewage systems in Senegal, only the inner urban population generally had access to these facilities. In Dakar, nearly one-sixth of all human faeces is dumped outside proper toilet facilities.

Hardoy and Satterthwaite (1989) also show that in Dar es Salaam, only 13% of the dirty water and sewerage produced was being regularly disposed of. Out of the 660 households drawn in Dar es Salaam, 89% had simple pit latrines, while only 4.5% had toilets connected to septic tanks or sewers. Most households had to share sanitary facilities, and overflowing latrines was a serious problem, especially during rainy season, and provision of empty septic tanks or latrines was very inadequate. In Jakarta city, there were no waterborne sewerage system; septic tanks served only 25% of the population - others use pit-latrines, cesspools, and ditches along the roadside. Much of the population in Jakarta had to use drainage canals for bathing, laundering and defecation.

While the population of Nairobi was increasing at an estimated rate of 6% annually, the amount of refuse collected fell from a high of 202,229 tonnes in 1977, to 159,974 tonnes in 1983 - a decline of 21% over the six years. Thus, over the late 1970s and early 1980s, the Nairobi City Council was collecting, on average, almost 10% less refuse per capita every year (Stren, 1990).

Garbage Collection

It is estimated (Arrossi, et al, 1994) that 30-50% of the solid waste generated within urban centres is left uncollected and dumped in any available waste ground. The result is the outbreak of diseases, since piles of garbage serve as food and breeding grounds for disease vectors. Rubbish, causing stagnant pools that may overflow and sometimes carrying excreta also block water courses and open drains. During heavy rain periods, the blocked drains may result in serious flooding, with loss of life and property.

Similar studies by Hardoy and Satterthwaite (1989) showed that in 1987, around a quarter of solid waste generated in Bangkok remained uncollected and were dumped, mostly onto vacant land or in canals and rivers. Almost all Senegalese towns had no provision for removal of household and public waste, while in Dar es Salaam, only a quarter of the city's refuse was being collected. In Jakarta, around 30% of the garbage is not collected and ends up in canals and rivers and along the roadsides where it clogs drainage canals and causes extensive flooding during the rain seasons. In Karachi, only one-third of the solid waste produced in the city is removed.

Health Care

The study of health care is too diverse and it is not the intention of this chapter to dwell with general aspects of health care. We only intend to show the causal relationship between poor housing and health. Numerous studies have attempted to show some relationship between housing and its possible association with health, but these empirical evaluations of housing and health have proved difficult because of lack of reliable measurements (Ranson, 1991). However, even the World Health Organization (WHO) experts say that the lack of definite measurements does not denote the absence of a relationship between housing and health. By deductive method, a strong relationship can be established. Since the residential environment consists of many elements of the overall environment, with each element capable of exerting individual detrimental effects upon health and well-being, it can be deduced that the effects of the residential environment upon health is the sum of the individual factors.

Substandard dwellings without adequate water and sanitation offer a fertile ground for fleas, mosquitoes, flies, rats and other insects. For example in Latin America, according to World Health Organization (UNEP, 1992), the chagas disease (transmitted by bugs that live in cracks and crevices of poor-quality houses) infects about 500,000 people every year, 60% of them being children. Between 10% and 15% of chagas-infected people die during the fever that is typical of the acute phase of the disease. In Tanzania, frequent outbreak of cholera usually endemic in over-crowded and unhealthy poor settlements, particularly in urban areas is commonplace. Such communicable diseases account for a large proportion of illness and death in developing countries, where billions of people still do not have adequate shelter, access to safer water supplies, sanitation and refuse disposal facilities. In the mid-1980s, it was estimated that 17 million people (10.5 million being infants below the age of five) were dying in developing countries every year of infectious and parasitic diseases including cholera, malaria and schistosomiasis, compared to only 0.5 million in developed countries (UNEP, 1992).

It may not also be fully realized that unhealthy housing significantly contributes or causes stress-related diseases such as hypertension, migraine, depression, neurosis, alcoholism and social diseases manifested by pathologically derived antisocial behavior like crime, violence, mugging, vandalism, child abuse and mental or sexual disorders (Ranson, 1991).

As indicated earlier, ameliorated housing conditions greatly reduce the tremendous health burden facing most low-income groups. As suggested by Ranson (1991), improvements in death rates from infectious diseases such as cholera, typhoid and tuberculosis owe as much to improved standards of housing as to microbiology and antibiotics. Similarly, environmental conditions significantly affect health. According to WHO (1995), the major factor in health improvement in the UK and other developed countries in the 19th and 20th centuries, contrary to popular belief, was not advances in medical care and technology, but certain environmental, social and economic changes such as:

- A healthier physical environment;
- Limitation of family size;
- Increase in food supplies; and
- Specific preventive and therapeutic measures.

EARLY CONVENTIONAL HOUSING PROVISION POLICIES

Housing studies such as Shidlo's (1990) indicate that there are two main housing provision strategies, namely "supply-side" strategies and "demand-side" strategies.

"Supply-Side" Strategies

Under the supply-side approach, the government either undertakes construction programmes in which it builds its own housing for renting, or it gives subsidies to builders (formal or informal; for profit-making or non-profit making) or gives subsidies to consumers (low- or middle-income households). Unfortunately, where the state involves itself in construction, buildings are normally at too high an architectural standard for the poor, and without a clear understanding of the recipient's needs. As a result, such government housing has generally been too expensive, thereby offering very little flexibility in use, and often being in unsuitable locations (Shidlo, 1990). In Tunisia, public sector involvement in housing construction, upgrading and financing is much larger than in most other African countries. For example, between 1975 and 1980, the public sector constructed about 25% of all new housing units in Tunisia (Arrossi, *et al*, 1994). However, 75% of such state-aided housing was not affordable by low-income households. Evidence also abounds to the effect that many government accommodations are either purposely built for the upper- and lower-middle income groups, or if they are intended for the low-income groups, these poor people later move out and the middle- and upper-income groups move in. In many countries, it is the public sector employees, trade union members, or those with appropriate political links who benefit from government housing projects. Instead of reaching the most needy, these housing programmes benefit the upper and lower-middle sectors of the urban population.

"Demand-Side" Strategies

Under the demand-side strategies, the government leaves the role of providing housing to individuals and the private sector, so that the government only stimulates housing demand by subsidizing housing consumers by providing tax concessions, cheap or free urban land, and facilitating credit for house builders or buyers. Given the inability of most governments of developing countries to provide housing to the ever-growing urban population, this strategy, as shall be seen shortly, is the current focus.

Prior to the last one or two decades, many developing countries, like developed countries, had been pursuing state-centric housing policies, where governments were fully and solely involved in the design, construction and allocation of housing targeted towards the urban poor. Although in recent years there has been a change in direction in this policy towards "demand-side" strategies, other developing countries are still pursuing state-centric approaches to housing provision.

In Mexico (Connolly, 1990), there are three main kinds of "irregular settlements," namely unauthorized subdivisions of private property; invasions of either public or private property, and subdivision of agrarian community lands (ejidos). In few instances, local governments acquire land invaded by squatters for re-sale legally to the inhabitants. In Mexico, the government supports these irregular settlements, and in fact, there have been an increasing institutionalisation of irregular settlement formation and regularization.

In Brazil, the pre-1964 civilian government period can be characterized as an era of minimal intervention by the state in the housing market (Shidlo, 1990). The two decades of military rule that followed can be characterized as centralized state intervention in the housing market. The creation of National Housing Bank (BNH) enabled the military to co-opt the urban middle sectors and the trade unions. The majority of state housing was allocated to industrial states in the southeast region of Brazil who supported the regime until the early 1980s. The loss of public support in the latter states resulted in a shift towards allocating larger proportions of BNH budget to the loyal northeast states. The end of military rule in 1985 resulted in public criticism of the national housing policy and in the collapse of the BNH. The current civilian rule is characterized by a shift towards a decentralized housing system. In the early regimes in Chile (Kusnetzoff, 1990), the state housing policy was interventionist, but later there was liberalisation of the housing sector.

Another country, which pursued interventionist housing policies, was India (Bhattacharya, 1990). However, despite three decades of state intervention, the government failed to provide minimum shelter to the majority of the population since the policy lacked a comprehensive strategy and was guided primarily by the political party in power. Various housing policies enunciated by the government hindered, not only public contribution to housing, but also the ability of the private sector to participate in housing provision for the people. Unlike in Western societies where housing is treated as a commodity, in China and other socialist countries, housing is generally regulated by the state (Kim, 1990). In China, despite such regulation, the state has since early 1980s, been encouraging the urban population to build and/or buy their own houses. In Turkey (Keles, 1990), the private sector plays a major role in constructing housing to be purchased by households as owner-occupied dwellings. However, one of the most successful state interventionist housing provision system is found in Hong Kong. The government of Hong Kong's Special Administrative Region operates one of the most extensive public housing programmes in the world. In Hong Kong, public housing accommodates more than half of the total population. In fact, the state each year builds some 400,000 housing units, or 4.6 units per hour (Hui, 1999)!

In the late 1970s, the Zimbabwean state began to move from a collectivised housing provision system for the Black population to one fundamentally based on liberal policies. At this time, freehold tenure was made available to all blacks in urban areas. The political climate was changing and there was an increased need to provide low-cost housing, and the development of self-help policies and a shift towards the provision of housing on home-ownership basis. As such, the existing rental housing units were being sold to sitting tenants at considerable discounts (Teedon, 1990).

In Nigeria, despite the oil boom which emboldened the federal government to declare that it would now recognize housing as part of its social responsibilities, and participate actively and in large scale in its provision; and despite planning to provide 202,000 housing units in 1980, only 20% of this could be added to the existing housing stock (Okoye, 1990).

As evidenced by HABITAT (1996e), housing programmes in which the governments are directly involved in the design, construction and allocation of housing targeting urban poor have not worked well in developing countries as a result of the following weaknesses:

- Governments had been too concerned with producing formal housing programmes rather than facilitating inputs such as land and credit into the housing process;
- There has been a misallocation of resources in the form of subsidies to land, infrastructural provision and towards housing itself, which has gone to those better able to pay for such services than the poor;
- There has been a consistent failure among official land, housing and financial agencies to reach those who need assistance most of all;
- While there have been some successes in shelter programmes, however, these have generally been on a very small scale in comparison with the overall magnitude of the problem;
- Coherent and co-ordinated local shelter strategies have been the exception rather than the rule, which has made it very difficult to adopt consistent and effective policies towards the needs of the low-income groups.

THE NEW PARADIGM ON HOUSING PROVISION AND IMPROVEMENT

It has already been shown that 3.2 billion people, half of the world's population, were living in cities by the year 2000, with 70% of the urban population being in developing countries (Arrossi, et al, 1994). This rapid urbanization will not only exacerbate poverty and deteriorating environment, but will also cause huge gap between demand for urban infrastructure and services and the available supply. The most affected group will obviously be the urban poor who will lack adequate access to affordable and secure housing, sanitation services, education and health services.

Mismatch Between Urban Housing Demand and Government Capacity

It is now fully realized that governments in developing countries increasingly lack the capacity and resources to effectively address deficiencies in the provision and improvement of infrastructure, shelter and services. Realizing this fact, low-income groups in developing countries have started seeking alternative and creative solutions of their own.

It has also been observed that the direct and sole participation of governments in housing development in African countries, which has also been inspired by foreign or international agencies (Massawe, 1996b), has had a negative effect on housing provision. In Tanzania, and other African countries like Kenya and Cote D'Ivoire, government response to the crisis of shelter has been to involve itself directly in both construction of dwellings and financing home ownership.

Documented evidence reveals that this has not worked well, and the approach, in fact, runs smack against the spirit of the Structured Adjustment Programmes adopted in these countries (Ayogu, 1994).

Given the declining ability and effectiveness of direct and sole government involvement in housing development, many African governments and international institutions concerned with the shelter problem like HABITAT and Shelter Afrique have embarked on researches and seminars which have come up with enunciation and promotion of policies and programmes requiring the urgent need for greater private sector participation to address the housing problem in urban areas, including the involvement of community-based organizations (CBOs).

According to Drakakis-Smith (1981), governments' failure to meet housing challenges is a result of organizational inability of the public sector to carry out policy decisions. He contends that the allocation of funds for housing is futile unless logistical and technical requirements can be met at the same time. At present, the administrative planning and construction systems in most developing countries are unable to fulfil these requirements and, in an effort to cope with the accelerating housing shortages, many governments in the developing countries have turned to the successful technologies of the West. The resultant desire to replicate the West's building technology has led to large-scale imports of materials, techniques and personnel. Furthermore, most of the houses constructed in this way are too expensive and beyond the reach of the poor, even when subsidized. Such situation only serves to discourage further investment in low-cost housing provision.

Apart from the above "positive" housing policy of providing housing in line with Western styles, which Drakakis-Smith (1981) terms as an "alien" system, another positive housing system is what he terms "reactionary." Reactionary responses to housing problems are those in which the government is merely concerned with eradicating slum and squatter settlements because they disfigure and disrupt the city. There is usually no significant new construction for the displaced. A good example is the Dar es Salaam slum clearance schemes, and their little significance, in the 1960s and early 1970s. In other cases, the government usually hopes that demolition of squatters would check rural-urban immigration, and that the displaced would return to the villages. But to the contrary, the displaced and new migrants usually surface in another urban slum settlement to the chagrin of the urban authorities.

African governments, consisting of educated middle class and upper class people, would like to see everybody having a decent life. But this aspiration emerges out of a restriction on low standard accommodations. At its worse, it leads to demolition of the slums and squatters in settlements of the urban poor while high standard houses constructed in their place go to the officials themselves (Lee-Smith, 1990).

However, the third and best approach to the housing problem in urban areas is what Drakakis-Smith (1981) terms "indigenous" approach. This is the cheaper, more practical and more satisfactory way to improve the living standards of the urban poor, whereby energies of the people themselves are used in aided self-help schemes. It is argued that if the government prepares the land, provides basic infrastructural services and, possibly, cheap materials, then the residents themselves will build acceptable accommodation.

The aided self-help (indigenous) approach, which is now being advocated in the developing countries, is based on the premise that all non-conventional housing is a normal response to housing shortages and indicates the determination, effort and ability of the urban poor to invest in order to consolidate and ameliorate their life. In general, and as suggested by several scholars (Wegelin and Borgman, 1995), important changes in perception have been taking place globally in the area of housing policy and related services. These changes include:

- The view that the government is the provider of housing and other related social services for the poor has, by and large, been abandoned. This is partly due to the fact that the poor seldom have access to such schemes, and therefore have to settle for cheap rental housing in unserviced settlements, and partly due to the reliance, which is being increasingly placed by the poor on the informal construction sector as a more realistic alternative;
- It is increasingly being realized that investment in housing is productive, providing not only as a basic need, but also for promoting the local economy; and
- There is now an almost universal consensus that the role of governments is to provide an "enabling environment" for the private sector. The earlier governments' preoccupation with design, standards, building materials and other technical aspects of housing and related services has been replaced by an increasing emphasis on institutional and financial support mechanisms required to support the poor in housing themselves.

From Public to Private Sector Housing Policies

In view of the above, it is thus important to allow the private sector to have an increasing role in housing provision and improvements. Although the correct definition of private sector of the economy is the households as well as firms, in the context of housing regeneration, the term private sector applies not only to individual households, but also to property developers, financiers, CBOs, NGOs, and potential employers (McGregor, *et al*, 1992b). The private sector plays a major role in house construction in many countries, not only for rental, but also for purchase by households as owner-occupied dwellings (Keles, 1990), in the case of Turkey. In Scotland, 42% of Scottish housing investment comes from the private sector (Robertson, 1994).

The private sector has also been responsible for supplying low-income communities with a range of other basic services. For example, private expenditure on health care in Thailand is estimated at over four times the amount spent by the central government for this service (Arrossi, *et al*, 1994). In some cases the private sector has moved into the housing market because of government failure to provide the services. In other cases the government contracts the private sector to supply the services rather than supplying it directly. However, where the private sector is not contracted, i.e. where it involves itself for commercial reasons, it normally has little incentive to make major permanent investment in low-income areas, since there is no guarantee that demand for their services will continue given the usually illegal nature of these settlements which always present threats of its inhabitants being evicted.

According to HABITAT (1993), although Africa's shelter crisis is deep-seated, and although great problems still lie ahead, at least the continent has one very important asset: the African society has a long and valuable tradition of communal action. Advantage can be taken of this locally based dynamism by channeling it to self-help shelter improvement activities.

Partnership: The Only Viable Option in Redressing the Shelter Problem

Many countries have embarked on housing programmes that involve the central government as just one of the partners. Such strategies have been successful in countries such as Sri Lanka where, having realized the shelter need of its people, the government embarked on systematic housing programmes with the involvement of the central government, mortgage and investment banks, other public and private sector financial institutions and international agencies. As a result, several successful programmes have since been implemented to shelter several million households (Pallihakkara, 1992). In Bangla-desh, there is for example, the Slum Improvement Programme (SIP) initiated in five small cities in 1984 through UNICEF assistance to local governments. By 1996, the programme had been extended to cover 25 cities. The SIP covers walkways and drainage improvement, water taps or tube wells, primary mother and child-care and nutrition, non-formal literacy education, and savings and credit groups for women (Shubert, 1996).

Other shelter improvement programmes undertaken in partnership between the people, their community organizations and donor agencies are found in India and Pakistan (see Shubert, 1996). In India, there are programmes such as Scheme of Housing and Shelter Upgrading (SHASU), which is directed towards providing employment to urban poor people through housing and building activities. There is also Environmental Improvement of Urban Slums (EIUS), a scheme for improving the living conditions in the slum pockets through provision of water, drainage, community toilets, street lights and other services. In Pakistan, there is the Katchi Abadi Improvement and Regularization Programme (KAIRP) intended to regularize 2,320 settlements (or katchi abadis). These settlements have a total population of 5.5 million people. The programme is for improving settlements by providing water, sanitation, electricity and other social facilities. In Burkina Faso, there is the Ouagadougou Low Cost Sanitation and Public Information Programme (Ouayoro, 1994).

In South Africa, where the government's main problem seems to be the resettlement of millions of Africans displaced during the struggle for democratic rule, there are many housing and settlement programmes initiated and supported by the government in terms of subsidies and provision of infrastructure, but carried out jointly by the people, the government and other institutions. These include Transfer of Houses Programme, Upgrading of Informal Settlements, Consolidated Subsidy and Housing Support Centres, and High Density Housing and Institutional Subsidies (Narsoo, 1997).

Botswana has a Self- Help Housing Agency (SHHA) programme which was introduced in 1973 to assist the low income urban households to develop their own houses. Under the scheme, the government provides basic services such as earth engineered roads, communal water standpipes and a pit latrine to each plot (Kwelegano, 1997). In Kenya, having realized the inadequacies of the conventional mechanisms of housing delivery, the government has been emphasizing the need for non-conventional means for housing delivery even in its development plans. The government has supported many self-help programmes including sites and services upgrading schemes and dwelling schemes. The Pumwani, Kibera and Dandora estates in the city of Nairobi provide a good example (Syagga and Kiamba, 1992).

In Nigeria (Okoye, 1990), the Federal Government, World Bank and state governments co-operated to implement Site and Service Projects and Upgrading Schemes in several states. In these schemes the authorities provide and service the land with the necessary infrastructure and social amenities, while the individuals who are allocated the housing plots build their houses in accordance with approved plans of their own choice. The beneficiaries are assisted to obtain housing loans from the Federal Mortgage Bank (FMB), repayable in 15 years at 6% interest. They then build the core units under the supervision of the Project Implementation Unit. Each householder can later expand the core unit, putting additional rooms as per his needs and financial capability.

In India, the Home Development Finance Corporation (HDFC) of India, in collaboration with Kreditanstalt fur Wideraufbau (KfW), a Germany development bank, agreed to utilize up to DM 25 million out of the bilateral trade agreement with the government of India, for financing low cost housing projects for the economically weaker sections of society. Within this framework, HDFC has provided assistance to over 34,800 families to build their homes at 51 projects across India with a loan exposure of RS 411.7 million, of which RS.400 million was already disbursed by December 1997 (Mehta, 1997).

Nigeria's 1975-1980 Development Plan envisaged the construction of 202,000 housing units by the government. However, by the end of the plan period, only 14% of the planned units had been built, costing in excess of a billion US dollars (Sa-Aadu, 1997). Having realized the inadequacies of public provision of housing, the National Housing Programme in Nigeria now involves not only the central government, but also private organizations, individuals, and international agencies such as Shelter Afrique (Jakande, 1994). Organized self-help and co-operative forms of self-help have shown a lot of success in other countries including Mayotte Islands, Mexico, Columbia and Brazil.

Not only donor agencies, but also even rich nations these days insist on partnership in assisting poor countries. For example, the new U.K. Government approach to building partnership include:

> [Working] closely with other donors and development agencies to build partnerships with developing countries to strengthen the commitment to the elimination of poverty, and use our influence to help mobilize the political will to achieve the international development targets.... We shall pursue these targets in partnership with poorer countries [that] are also committed to them (U.K., 1997).

THE ROLE OF VARIOUS STAKEHOLDERS

As already pointed out, governments all over the world have played a major role in the provision of shelter to their citizens, but because of the rapid population and urbanization growth, governments are now overwhelmed. Governments can no longer engage in direct provision of housing. Rather, their role is now on policy, financial and institutional frameworks and structures that will enable people themselves to be directly involved in the provision of their own housing, with minimum subsidies from the central government. The last two decades have shown that the public sector does not have the capacity, both in terms of institutional and financial resources, to provide housing on a scale commensurate with demand. This failure to cope with demand is amply illustrated by the rapidly expanding informal settlements, which presently make well over a half of the population in African cities (Shelter Afrique, 1995).

Even the United Nations Centre for Human Settlements (HABITAT) in its global shelter strategy recognizes that the role of governments in dealing with housing problems lies not in massive public housing programmes, but in providing an enabling environment for people to improve and construct their own shelter.

HABITAT's Contribution to Shelter Provision and Improvement in Africa

Given that governments are handicapped in the public provision of housing in developing countries, international agencies concerned with shelter such as United Nations Centre for Human Settlements (HABITAT), Shelter Afrique (The company for habitat and housing in Africa) and its special organ - African Housing Fund (AHF) - have been very keen in assisting housing and shelter programmes in Africa in an effort to supplement governments' and peoples' efforts in ameliorating their living environment.

These agencies operate on a partnership basis, assisting where governments and/or other agencies and people (through self-help basis) are ready to participate. In this manner, HABITAT has done a commendable job in the sub-Saharan Africa (HABITAT, 1993). Examples of housing and shelter projects and programmes in Africa in which HABITAT has participated include the assistance to the government of Burkina Faso in a programme for making the country's small and middle-sized towns more attractive with bigger housing capacity so as to cater for the rapid urbanization as well as check out-migration of Burkinabè; support to Burundi government in the latter's efforts in training, improvement of social infrastructure and land development and support to ECOSAT - an agency created for training for social building and land development in Burundi.

Other projects supported by HABITAT include assisting the government of Cape Verde to redress the problem of rapidly growing urban areas. By 1987 HABITAT and the United Nations Capital Development Fund (UNCDF), with the government and peoples' efforts, were engaged in PROMEBAD (Project for the Improvement of Disfavoured Districts). In Chad, HABITAT has assisted in the development of N'Djamena city in a programme to rehabilitate water supply, electricity, highways and drainage networks as well as implementing land and housing census. In Congo, HABITAT has assisted the government in drawing up a plan of campaign for the production of housing to supplement the efforts by Real Estate Promotion and Management Company (SOPROG).

In 1987, the government of Ghana, with the support of HABITAT, initiated a project for Institutional Development, Training and Operational Studies to improve the capacity of the public sector to develop policies and strategies to address the question of housing delivery system by encouraging community participation by mobilizing women, youth, private developers, NGOs, community organizations and other grassroots organizations.

HABITAT also undertook a study of the development of plots of land at Koloma District and Enta in Guinea, a project which was co-financed by the Guinea government, UNCDF and UNDP. HABITAT also supported a scheme in Kenya that was initiated by local organizations trying to mobilize funds for improving or extending their houses. This revolving fund, which started in Mathare Valley in Nairobi was later extended to Kunati in Meru District and Chonyi in Kilifi District. HABITAT provided the initial capital of US $ 100,000. HABITAT has also participated in shelter projects in other countries such as Malawi (Rural Housing Policy and Institute of National Physical Planning), Namibia (National Shelter Strategy Formulation), Niger (Improving the Living and Housing Conditions in Urban Areas) and Senegal (Bureau for Aid to Social Housing Collectives - BAHSO).

Other countries in which Habitat's presence has been felt are Uganda (National Shelter Strategy) as well as Tanzania where the Sustainable Cities Project, Tanzania (SCP-T) is being supported by Habitat to enhance the environmental planning and management capacity of selected cities and municipalities.

Apart from Habitat, Shelter Afrique also insists on partnership in redressing the increasing housing deficit in Africa. One of its major objectives is "to promote through equity participation and technical assistance, investment in the housing sector and the development of viable housing institutions" (Shelter Afrique, 1994). Between 1986 and 1993, Shelter Afrique had participated or agreed to participate, as a co-financier in various housing projects in Africa including in Zambia (core housing), Nigeria (core housing), Gambia (building materials and community facilities), Uganda (squatter upgrading), Djibouti (feasibility study), Senegal (physical housing and infrastructure), Malawi (squatter upgrading), Cameroon (infrastructure), Guinea (sites and service infrastructure) and Burundi (PTA Bank headquarters). In 1996, after Tanzania was admitted as a member of Shelter Afrique, the latter agreed to participate in housing projects initiated by National Housing Corporation (NHC) in Arusha and Dar es Salaam, and another project by the National Shipping Agency Company (NASACO).

One of the strategies of the African Housing Fund (AHF), which was established for the purpose of improving shelter and living conditions of the poor in Africa, is "to work with the poor - in partnership" (AHF, 1995). In fact the AHF motto is "helping the poor to help themselves." AHF believes that the poor can, and must mobilize themselves if their housing projects are to succeed. They have the talents, the leadership skills, the determination and the will to improve their own lives. What they need is credit, land and training in the special skills required in their projects. AHF has, for the last ten years, participated in projects to alleviate poverty and improve shelter for the poor through provision of subsidized loans in various countries including Zambia, Kenya, Uganda, Burundi and Rwanda.

The Role of the Central Government

It has already been argued that the role of the central government in housing provision, and indeed, in improvement of housing and housing-related services, can no longer be that of direct involvement. Rather, the government should formulate a regulatory framework that facilitates a conducive legal and operational environment that can encourage and induce the private sector (individual households and their CBOs, local governments, NGOs, and other financiers and private property developers) to participate directly in housing provision and improvement. The role of the central government in housing provision and improvement should now be in the following areas.

Land Tenure System

The government must provide households with secure access to land, which entails a legal right to house sites. This includes legalizing land and sites in informal settlements. As alluded to by IUCN/UNEP/WWF (1991), one of the successful strategy for dealing with illegal urban settlements is to legalize them, arranging for fair compensation to owners, and accepting their way of building. Communities and individuals need secure access to the land and other resources necessary for their livelihood, and they must also get an equitable share in managing them, otherwise they will not be motivated to use those resources sustainably. Secure tenure generally promotes household investment in improving the house and more capacity to negotiate with local authorities for improved services (Vanderschueren, et al, 1996).

In many developing countries, land delivery systems, which include allocation and issuing of legal rights to land, is a cumbersome process and therefore discourages private investment in housing.

Support to Local Governments

Local governments all over the world are legally established. In Tanzania, local authorities are part of the country's constitution (Warioba, 1999). They are established under the Local Government (District Authorities) Act No. 7 and Local Government (Urban Authorities) Act No. 8 of 1982 respectively; and derive their authority from the instrument as approved by the National Assembly. Given such legal mandate, and realizing that local governments are nearer to the people, and therefore, know better their problems and capacity, the central government must strengthen these local governments by bolstering their capacity to plan, manage and finance programmes for improving housing and the environment of low-income urban people, including mobilizing people's efforts in participatory activities to improve their living places. For proper and effective implementation of local governments' functions, however, the central government must first properly define institutional responsibilities. This entails the division of powers between the central government and the local governments, and allocation of resources in the major areas of land management, housing and housing finance, infrastructure and services and so on (see Vanderschueren, et al, 1996).

Encourage Private Investment

The central government must also lay down a regulatory framework that encourages the expansion of the role of the private sector and NGOs in the provision of urban housing and infrastructure. The government may even privatise the provision of some urban services. In some developing countries, including Tanzania, investment codes, tax regime and general economic instability are still hindering both foreign and local private investors to invest in economic ventures, including the housing sector.

Access to Credit

Poor households have very limited capacity to save and invest in housing or environmental improvements. Despite their role and wide coverage, informal savings groups, often exclude the poorest. Formal banking and credit systems are also not accessible to the poor people because of the complex procedures, collateral requirements and high interest rates. The central government should therefore encourage the establishment of housing mortgage facilities for the poor, facilities which are currently very underdeveloped in poor countries. The government can also encourage and support commercial banks to create special purpose facilities for poor groups, in the style of Grameen Bank (Vanderschueren *et al,* 1996)

The Role of Local Governments

As pointed out by Wegelin and Borgman (1995), local governments (municipalities) are strategically placed to undertake local long-term planning in the area of urban poverty alleviation in conjunction with the private sector, NGOs and CBOs. With full support and autonomy from the central government, municipalities can generate and manage large-scale urban projects.

Sustainable urban development is only possible when local governments are given adequate powers and develop effective capabilities. They need to manage change in the context of an ecological approach so that cities can support more productive, stable and innovative economies while maintaining high-quality environment, proper services for all sectors of the community, and sustainable resource use. These conditions are most likely to be met if all interested groups participate, and if the central government is active, decentralized, representative and supportive of people's efforts. As suggested by Warioba (1999), a local government is not another central government-controlled department, but is a sphere of the state with some autonomy. Since it is a necessary link between the people and the central government, a sense of freedom and vitality is necessary.

In many developing countries, governments are increasingly realizing the relevance of municipalities and their role and importance as providers of basic urban services, including housing. In order to do this effectively, municipalities must assume legally enshrined policy-making and implementation powers to facilitate effective decision-making. They must be able to effectively manage existing resources, and mobilize additional resources including human resources in a participatory approach. It is also through local governments' support that initiatives at local levels by individuals, CBOs and NGOs can be positively felt. Concerning the provision and improvement of urban housing and other services for tne poor, municipalities can have a supportive role in the following manner (Wegelin and Borgman, 1995):

- In co-operation with central governments, local authorities can develop a city-wide housing sector programme in which low-income housing demand and supply form part of aggregate housing demand and supply.
- Local governments can convince the central government to allow modification of the regulatory framework related to land supply and building and planning regulations, so as to simplify procedures for greater flexibility in approved building standards and materials, and to provide opportunities for income generating activities by accepting multiple uses of dwellings.
- Municipalities could also encourage and facilitate the establishment and accessibility of local credit facilities that meet the demands of low-income groups (such as communally collateralized loans), to reduce the dependence of the poor on expensive formal and informal credit windows. In India, for example, the Housing Development Finance Corporation (HDFC) is now

lending, through NGOs, to slum dwellers to build or improve their houses at very low lending rates.

- Municipalities are also responsible for mobilizing resources for the provision of other services and amenities around the living areas of the poor such as water supply, drainage, flood protection, solid waste collection and disposal, local roads, public transport, street lighting and traffic management.

The Role of Households and Their Community Organizations (CBOs)

Vanderschueren, *et al* (1996), have suggested that strong and effective local governments are usually a result of strong communities that encourage the participation of low-income groups in various projects. Involving low-income households in participatory activities realizes the fact that, individually and given their poverty and often poor health, they cannot meet their households' requirements. The poor households and the organizations, which they form in participatory ways, can strengthen community organization and cohesion, which can result in strong capacity for low-income groups to negotiate with local authorities and external agencies and NGOs. People who organize themselves to work for sustainability in their own communities can be a powerful and effective force, whether the community is rich, poor, urban, sub-urban or rural (IUCN/ UNEP/WWF, 1991).

The involvement of households and their community-based organizations (CBOs) can be effective in the areas of environmental awareness, primary health care, primary education, and housing and related infrastructure services. Unfortunately, many local governments often do not recognize community organizations as having major role in community mobilization. In many instances, the municipalities fail to utilize and support such organizations in projects and programmes where they have an obvious comparative advantage. CBOs are in fact frequently beneficiaries of support from donor agencies and NGOs as they are seen as directly representing groups of residents and providing an organizational basis for community participation and management (Alder, 1995).

The involvement of community-based organizations in housing issues has not been prominent in developing countries as it has in developed countries, where housing associations, housing co-operatives and other local housing organizations have been established. In the developed countries, housing bodies have generally led to physical renewal of neighbourhoods (McGregor, et al, 1998). In Scotland, for example, the housing association sector provides accommodation for 3.25% of all households in the country (Kearns and Malcolm, 1992).

The Role of NGOs and Other Donor Agencies

As alluded to above, NGOs and other donor agencies prefer to deal with organized community organizations rather than the central government, when development programmes for the people are involved, because these CBOs represent the very groups of people, and provide an organizational basis for community participation and management. NGO and other donor involvement in community programmes is premised upon community participation, in which the affected people and their community organizations have a major role. NGOs and donors usually encourage low-income households and their organizations to make decisions about location and nature of their homes, the best methods of paying for their construction or improvement and for basic services, and choosing the best technology for providing these services, in terms of the quality of services relative to price. Assistance from NGOs and donors is basically concerning technical and credit provision with little grant options.

A good example of an NGO-supported programme whose principle is based on the belief that social and economic organizations should be created at the grassroots level is the Orangi Pilot Project (OPP) in Karachi, Pakistan (Hasan, 1994). This low cost sanitation programme enabled infant mortality to improve from 130 in 1982 to 37 in 1991 in the area. Morbidity rates also improved from 18.94 to 8.29 during the same period.

Low-income households and their communities are discouraged to depend on large external finance for executing their programmes. The less the external funds, the greater the possibility for poor households and their organizations to retain control (Anzorena, et al, 1998). Conversely, the more the external funds, the less the possibility for them to retain control. Moreover, the less the external funds, the more the chances of sustaining or expanding the initiatives when external funds are no longer available. The lesser the external finance, the lesser is the likelihood that wealthier groups will seek to hijack the programmes. And the lesser is the external finance, the greater is the chance of addressing dependency and forging a new kind of relationship between community organizations and external agencies.

In fact, in most developing countries, donor agencies are increasingly taking minor role in terms of the scale of funding made available for shelter and associated infrastructure and services. In recent years, shelter projects and housing finance have attracted less than 3% of the commitments of most donor agencies as shown in Table 3.2 (Arrossi, et al, 1994).

According to Arrossi, et al (1994), although infrastructure and services associated with shelter in developing countries still receive a higher proportion of funding for both multilateral and bilateral agencies, very rarely do these feature as high priorities for any agency. Three reasons explain this:

- In recognition of the fact that development assistance can never provide the scale of funding needed for urban development and that each country must develop its own capacity to fund urban development, largest donors, like the World Bank, have now changed their assistance direction towards funding national institutions concerned with funding urban development projects, rather than funding the projects directly.
- There has been a shift whereby it is the non-governmental organizations (NGOs) that are increasingly intervening in housing and related service provision and improvement in lieu of the withdrawal of large international donor agencies.

Table 3.2: *Proportion of aid and non-concessional loan commitments to shelter, basic services and other basic needs projects, 1980-91*

Agency	Proportion of total project commitments to						
Aid (concess. loans or grants) IDA	Shelter-related	Water, sanitation	Primary health	Basic education	Poverty reduction	% of total commitment for 1980-91	1990-91
• Africa	1.4	3.0	2.8	4.2	1.31	2.7	21.4
• Asia	1.5	4.7	3.7	2.3	0.31	2.4	22.2
• Latin Ame. & Carib.	2.0	5.8	4.7	2.8	6.3	21.6	41.1
A DB ('80-88)	0.7	10.5	2.2	2.4	-	15.9	-
ADF	1.2	2.0	1.0	1.8	0.3	6.4	8.4
IADB	2.6	15.9	1.4	3.0	1.3	24.1	29.5
CDB	1.3	4.8	-	-	0.5	6.4	3.9
AFESD	1.2	7.0	-	0.4	1.0	9.6	10.9
UNICEF	-	14.4	35.3	8.3	-	58.1	7.4
KFESD	0.9	8.0	-	-	0.9	9.8	8.0
OECF (1987-91)	0.9	3.2	-	0.4	-	4.5	3.7
Non-conc loans (IBRD)							
• Africa	2.5	8.2	1.4	0.8	0.1	13.0	12.6
• Asia	2.6	2.8	0.7	0.8	0.05	7.0	9.4
• Latin Am & Carib	3.7	4.8	1.8	1.1	-	11.3	15.5
ADB	0.3	7.5	0.3	0.3	-	8.5	-
ADF	1.6	5.3	1.4	-	-	8.3	1.3
IADB	1.5	6.4	0.3	0.4	0.7	9.3	12.7
CDB	1.1	7.4	-	-	-	8.6	8.5

Source, Arrossi, *et al* (1994: 28-29)

Key:
ADB = African Development Bank
ADF = Asian Development Fund
AFESD = Arab Fund for Economic and Social development
KFESD = Kuwait Fund for Economic and Social development
IAÐB = Inter-American Development Bank
IDA = International Development Agency
IBRD = International Bank for Reconstruction and Development/ World Bank
OECF = Overseas Economic Cooperation Fund (Japan)

- There is an increasing emphasis for governments of developing countries to build more capacity to manage urban development and put in place and maintain infrastructure and services.

Yet the World Bank has still been assisting and advising developing countries on urban human settlements issues. According to the World Bank, by 1982, thirty-five developing countries were implementing urban policies along the lines suggested by the World Bank (Campbell, 1990). Some 1.9 million households, or about 11.4 million people, benefited from World Bank shelter projects between 1972 and 1981, and between 1982 and 1986, a further 90 urban projects were under consideration for loans totaling US $ 4 billion. However, the World Bank (1992) has categorically stated that an increasing share of the lending programmes in developing countries will now be for environmental projects that address, in particular, management of natural resources especially soils, water and forests, urban water supply and sanitation, and pollution control.

While the World Bank has been gradually shifting from sites and services schemes towards upgrading in its shelter projects, its overall planning approach for the needs of lower income groups has had a strong influence on the urban policies of many recipient countries (Stren, 1990). In Africa, the major countries to have developed sites and services projects under the World Bank auspices were Senegal, Kenya, Tanzania, Zambia and Cote d'Ivoire. Most of the loan agreements attached to these projects oblige the recipient countries to carry out some reforms to improve the administration of their urban policies, although evidence on compliance in the implementation of these conditions is mixed.

FINANCING STRATEGIES FOR HOUSING AND SERVICES IMPROVEMENT

Despite the role of central governments, local governments, private sector and donor agencies in the provision of investment for shelter, infrastructure and services in urban areas, these efforts have failed to prevent the continuing deterioration of conditions of poor urban settlements in developing countries. There are two main reasons for this failure (Arrossi, et al, 1994). First, and as noted earlier, central and local governments, private sector and donor agencies lack adequate financial resources to significantly improve the shelter infrastructure and services of the urban poor. For the central and local governments, the lack of finance stems from historical perspective of the developing countries within the world economic order and the failure to prioritize investment in housing, basic services and infrastructure, and determining and distributing government expenditure. The low tax base and inefficient tax collection mechanisms also contribute to lack of finances. Many local governments in the developing countries have not been given adequate mandate and power by the central governments to raise taxes or have control and decision over the revenue collected in their municipalities.

As regards private sector, there is both shortage of credit for investment as well as lack of incentive to make long-term investments in the shelter, infrastructure and services, particularly in the settlements where land tenure is uncertain or illegal. Since local governments are also weak, the private sector has also failed to invest in settlement development because they are wary of the little or no support given by local governments.

The second reason for failure to significantly invest in housing and services, which is perhaps the more important reason, is the failure of the central and local governments to develop responses which match with local people's needs and priorities, and build on available local resources, both human and financial. According to HABITAT (1993) and Arrossi, et al (1994), what is now needed is a change in the current official "model" of urban development to one which works in partnership with these people, supports the investment flows the households make, try to solve some planning and technical constraints they face, and works with them to ensure that infrastructure and services are provided or improved with very limited per capita budgets.

This is extremely important given the failure of conventional housing finance to provide required finances for housing provision and improvement. As seen earlier, housing is the largest asset in the household portfolio. As such, virtually all house owners must pay for their units over several years because of the low levels of income compared to the price or cost of the housing unit. In Africa and other developing countries, this price-income ratio is considerably high (the price of a house is between six and ten times the annual income of the household). Additionally, traditional mortgage finance in these countries faces three basic dilemmas (Ferguson, 1999):

- Low and middle-income households usually can not afford the debt service required to finance the cost of a core minimum unit, even under the best circumstances, i.e. where there is stable macro-economic and financial regime; and where there is a functioning urban and land markets;

- Most low and middle-income households are self-employed, and cannot therefore meet the requirements of making monthly mortgage repayments as required by the traditional mortgage finance. Moreover, most of them have only para-legal rights on their house sites. Since these are not full legal titles to their property, they can not be accepted as collateral by the conventional mortgage finance system, though they are good security;
- Even when conditions are proper, commercial financial institutions have little interest in mortgage finance.

In recognition of the failure of conventional housing finance institutions either to expand greatly the number of housing units built or to benefit poorer households, some governments have been trying new approaches. For instance, the Philippines government has introduced a community mortgage scheme to ensure that even households with no legal tenure and with few resources are also considered for formal credit systems (Arrossi, *et al*, 1994).

The new financing strategies or innovative credit schemes have therefore been enunciated in various developing countries as a consequence of failures of the existing formal or informal credit institutions. Since the formal credit institutions act as intermediaries between those from whom they take deposits and those to whom they provide loans, they have to apply exclusionary eligibility criteria and unnecessary bureaucratic procedures which deny credit to a high proportion of individuals and poor households who can not make regular repayments and who have no acceptable collateral. Informal credit, which is usually supplied by friends, relatives and professional moneylenders, is also problematic. Such credit has problems of restricted availability of funds and/or the high costs of repayment.

Innovative credit schemes, which have been successful in many countries (see, for example, Arrossi, et al, 1994, and Vanderschueren, et al, 1996), are based on mobilization of urban households and their community groups through savings and credit schemes, or by encouraging and supporting commercial banks to create special purpose facilities for poorer groups. Municipalities may also encourage the establishment (without themselves being directly involved in credit provision) of community-based credit unions or banks, and facilitate some links between such groups and the formal banking system. The establishment of such credit schemes does not, however, remove the possibility of some low and middle-income households accessing formal mortgage finance through systems as recommended in chapter five, if they can meet the lending criteria. Appendix II shows recommendations by UNCHS (Habitat) on sustainable financing strategies for effective housing finance and urban infrastructure finance for poor countries.

4

POVERTY IN TANZANIA: A SITUATION ANALYSIS

INTRODUCTION

This chapter reviews Tanzania's socio-political and economic background and brings into perspective the poverty situation in the country. Several attempts by the country to eradicate poverty are briefly highlighted, including policy-oriented researches undertaken in this area. The chapter concludes that despite these attempts, policy makers and researchers have not properly and adequately addressed the question of urban housing poverty and its possible alleviation.

POLITICAL AND ECONOMIC BACKGROUND

The United Republic of Tanzania, which is the largest and currently the most populous country in East Africa, covers an area of 945,000 square kilometres with a population currently estimated at 32 million people, and grows at 2.8% per annum. The country comprises of Tanzania mainland and Zanzibar islands, and is considered to be one of the poorest countries in the world. Official World Bank estimates of 1995 show that the country's per capita income is US$ 130. However, these data exclude household and informal sector data. In fact, household surveys suggest that per capita income of Tanzania in 1996 was close to US $ 200 (World Bank, 1996a); while Bank of Tanzania (BoT) estimates that by July 1999, per capita income was US $ 250. Tanzania's economy of is heavily dependent on agriculture, which accounts for over 50% of Gross Domestic Product (GDP).

On the political front, Tanzania had since independence in 1961, followed a single-party socialist policy that emphasized on the predominance of the public sector in economic development. It was not until the mid 1980s when the country started liberalizing its economy with a shift from a centrally planned and confined socialist economy to an open or de-confined market economy which emphasizes the development of the private sector as the engine of economic growth. In 1992 the country adopted a multiparty democracy allowing for the multiparty general elections of 1995.

Immediately after attaining independence in 1961, Tanzania (then Tanganyika) declared war against three development enemies, namely: ignorance, disease and poverty. Various plans and programmes were enunciated and implemented which aimed at expanding and strengthening social services, such as education, health, water, communication and transport, agriculture and the economy at large. Consequently, the country registered some impressive performance on the social front, like a literacy rate, which was about 90% in early 1980s, though it has now come down to 68% (URT, 1998) and improved access to health and education services. In general, during the first decade of independence, Tanzania's economy performed quite well until the mid 1970s when the economy plunged into serious economic problems. These problems included inappropriate economic policies, unfavourable terms of trade, adverse climate and non-performing parastatals. As a result, among other economic adversities, the GDP growth declined from an average of 5 % per annum between 1970-76 to less than 2% between 1977-86. The number one economic enemy - inflation - also rose from an average of 5% between 1966-70 to 34% in 1995, with the real per capita income declining by more than 15% between 1965 and 1986. By 1995, the overall budget deficit had reached 11.5% of the GDP. The balance of payments also deteriorated, with the current account deficit increasing from US $ 321 million in 1975 to US $ 644 million in 1995.

The factors contributing to the decline of Tanzania's economy prior to 1980 were both external and internal. External factors included the global recession of 1974, which had a significant impact on Tanzania as a developing country. Prices of primary commodities decreased, while those of manufactured imports rose remarkably. This was compounded by the oil crisis of 1973 and 1974. The country thus faced budgetary constraints, whereupon it relied heavily upon foreign capital support. Other factors were the collapse of East African Community in 1977; the war with Iddi Amin's Uganda in 1979; and the droughts, which hit the country in 1973, 1974, and again in 1975.

Internally, there were also problems of lack of comprehensive economic development policies, despite the Arusha Declaration with its policy of Socialism and Self Reliance, which enabled the public sector to grow suddenly as a result of putting the "commanding heights of the economy" in the public sector. The 1972 decentralization policy also increased the burden on scarce administrative resources, and caused negative results of ineffectiveness.

Since 1984, however, Tanzania has been implementing various economic reform policies under the World Bank and International Monetary Fund (IMF) inspired Structural Adjustment Programmes. These reforms culminated into the launching of the National Economic Recovery Programme (ERP) in June 1986. Since then, the country has witnessed a remarkable improvement of the economy characterized by trade liberalisation, financial sector reforms, parastatal sector reforms and privatisation and the lifting of price control in almost all locally produced as well as imported goods. Interest rates have also been liberalized as a consequence of reforming financial sector and foreign exchange regime. But above all, inflation has gradually fallen from 36.9% and 26.9% in December 1994 and December 1995 respectively, down to 13.8% in March 1997 and 12.1% in June 1998 respectively. Of course the initial desire of the government to reduce the same to 5% by June 1998 was too optimistic. Economic growth rate, measured by GDP, has also increased from 3% in 1994 to 3.9% in 1995. Droughts and El Nino conditions, however, caused GDP to fall again to 3.6% in 1996/97 and 2.8% in 1997/98. By March 1999, the GDP was estimated at 4.0% despite droughts that had caused acute food shortage throughout the country. By the end of June 1999, GDP was expected to rise further to 4.3% according to the Bank of Tanzania (BoT) sources. The budgetary deficit had also narrowed and government recurrent savings improved from 2.7% of GDP in 1994/95 fiscal year to 1% in 1997/98. According to the latest BoT reports, the total GDP of the country by July 1999 was 7.5 billion US dollars, resulting in a per capita income of US$ 250. Inflation had also gone down to 7.5% by the end of July 1999, while foreign reserves at BoT had reached 587 million US dollars. Table 4.1 gives some selected macro-economic performance indicators in Tanzania, while Table 4.2 illustrates how the inflation rate has been falling since June 1995 due to macro-economic and financial reforms in Tanzania.

Table 4.1: *Selected Macroeconomic Indicators in Tanzania*

	1994/95	1995/96	1996/97	1997/98
End of Period Inflation	27.7%	22.7%	16.4%	12.1%
Average headline inflation	34.7%	25.3%	16.7%	14.9%
Real GDP growth, at factor cost	2.6%	4.1%	3.6%	2.8%
Total Expenditure/GDP ratio	29.2%	23.65	17.8%	21.7
Revenue/GDP ratio (excluding grants)	22.0%	25.1%	17.3%	15.2%
Revenue/GDP ratio (including grants)	25.9%	26.8%	19.8%	18.4%
Current Exp./GDP ratio	27.1%	23.3%	16.9%	16.5%
Development Exp./GDP ratio	2.1%	0.3%	0.9%	5.5%
Deficit (excluding grants)/GDP ratio	-7.2%	1.4%	0.4%	n.a.
Deficit (including grants)/GDP ratio	-3.3%	3.2%	n.a.	n.a.
Current Savings/GDP ratio	-5.1%	1.7%	0.5%	-1.2%
Exports of Goods & Services to GDP ratio	22.2%	20.9%	18.0%	16.0%
Imports of Goods & Services to GDP ratio	40.5%	34.3%	29.6%	26.7%
Current account/GDP ratio (including grants)	-14.5%	-9.6%	-8.7%	-7.6%
Annual depreciation of T.shs./USD	16.1%	2.9%	0.7%	-7.6%
Lending Interest Rate	37.3%	33.8%	25.8%	22.0%
Deposit Interest rate	32.3%	13.9%	10.0%	10.9%

Source: BOT Economic and Operations Report for the year ended 30th June 1998.

Table 4.2: *Fall in Inflation Rates: June 1995 to August 1999*

Month	Inflation Rate (%)	Target Rate (%)
June, 1995	27.4	
June, 1996	23.0	
January, 1997	14.0	
February, 1997	13.8	
April, 1997	17.2	
June, 1997	16.4	15.0
October, 1997	15.8	
December, 1997	15.4	
March, 1998	13.4	
June, 1998	12.1	10.0
October, 1998	12.3	
December, 1998	11.2	
January, 1999	9.10	
March, 1999	8.80	
June, 1999	7.70	
July, 1999	7.60	
August, 1999	7.40	

Source: PPF Annual Seminar Reports, 1999

Tanzania realizes that it is only through improving macro-economic policies that the country can expect to increase its economic growth, and hence reduce poverty among its people. Evidence (World Bank, 1996a) gathered in several African countries demonstrates that poverty was more likely to decline in those countries that improved their macro-economic balances. In such countries, there was remarkable economic growth which depreciated the real effective exchange rates. There are, however, claims that macro economic reforms, especially reducing expenditure, have increased poverty, for example, the poor no longer get free education and health services.

But the findings (World Bank, 1996a) also highlighted three causes for policy concern:

i) Many African governments have yet to display a real commitment to macro economic reforms;
ii) The poorest of the poor have not benefited from recent growth in some countries; and
iii) The prospects for the poor are not rosy unless there is more investment in human capital and better targeting of social spending.

In fact, the World Bank (1998) has advised that poverty alleviation efforts would be more successful if donors directed their assistance to countries with the right policies. Reporting that an increase of about US $ 10 billion in aid disbursements would lift seven million people out of poverty, the World Bank cautioned that such aid would be wasted if disbursed to countries with unsound policies and institutions. Even Economic Commission for Africa (ECA) warns that in order to meet the UN target of reducing poverty by half, by the year 2015, Africa needs to raise her gross domestic product (GDP) rates to an average of 7% per year for the whole region, compared to an average of 4.5% growth realized during the 1995-98 period.

POVERTY SITUATION IN TANZANIA

Despite the apparent positive economic indicators as a result of change in economic development policies as illustrated earlier, poverty remains pervasive in Tanzania. The country is still among the poorest countries in the world, and as Mkapa (1994) put it, "much poor than we would like it to be." As Table 4.3 demonstrates, Tanzania is among the few countries in sub-Saharan Africa with over 50% of the population living below the poverty line. In fact 36% of all Tanzanians live in abject poverty (URT, 1998).

Table 4.3: Poverty Profile: Selected African Countries

Country	National poverty headcount as % of population	% of population below 2/3 of national mean per capita income 1991-1995		% of household income on food
		Urban	Rural	
Benin	33	n.a.	n.a.	n.a
Burundi	36	n.a.	n.a.	n.a.
Cameroon	40	n.a.	n.a.	55
Gambia	64	21	73	59
Ghana	31	26	45	39
Guinea Bissau	49	29	65	n.a.
Kenya	42	12	69	54
Lesotho	49	n.a.	n.a.	n.a.
Mauritania	57	n.a.	n.a.	n.a.
Mauritius	11	n.a.	n.a.	n.a.
Nigeria	34	32	52	67
Rwanda	51	n.a.	n.a.	n.a.
Tanzania	51	20	52	70
Togo	32	n.a.	n.a.	n.a.
Uganda	55	16	46	63
Zambia	86	16	75	75
Zimbabwe	26	n.a.	n.a.	n.a.

Source: *African Development Indicators*, World Bank, 1997

Realizing this fact, Tanzania's development policies aim at poverty reduction through sustainable economic growth by promoting the role of the private sector and strengthening government capacity to manage the economy and provide essential services. Pertinent issues addressed by the National Development Programme are poverty reduction, macroeconomic management, financial sector reforms, planning and budgetary reforms, civil service reforms, parastatal reforms, private sector development, agriculture development, tourism and mining development, human resources development, rehabilitation of infrastructure, energy sector development and environmental protection.

According to the World Bank (1995), Tanzania is the second poorest country in the world with the standard dollar estimate of per capita income of US $ 130 in 1995. The per capita income is obtained by dividing the Gross National Product, GNP (the aggregate of material benefits and services consumed or used for capital investment in a year), by the population of a specific country. However it must be cautioned that the use of official GDP estimates of per capita income is subjective and usually underestimates national income and expenditure. There are other measures, which have given more encouraging results. For example:

a) According to the World Bank Report (1993), a household survey in 1991 puts the per capita expenditure in Tanzania at US $ 281.
b) The United Nations Development Programme (UNDP) utilizes Human Development Index (HDI) to measure poverty. Using this indicator, UNDP ranked Tanzania higher than 34 other countries in the world in 1995, though according to the conventional per capita income based on official average income as measured by GDP, the World Bank (1995) ranked Tanzania the poorest country in the world, save for Mozambique. HDI is a social indicator that takes into account adjusted real GDP per head, life expectancy and educational attainment. It recognizes the fact that average per capita income and per capita expenditures are not good measures of welfare. Human Development can be stated thus:

$$HD = f(eo, lt, Y)$$

Where,

HD = Human Development
eo = life expectancy at birth
lt = literacy rate
Y = per capita income

c) Another welfare indicator is the United Nations International Comparison Project (ICP). Using ICP, the per capita purchasing power parity (PPP) equivalent GDP for 1990 was estimated at US $ 540 for Tanzania.
d) Since per capita income and GDP use prices in official markets which do not capture the reality of prices in extensive parallel markets in Tanzania, the

official per capita income and the deflator implicit in estimates of real GDP are likely to be underestimated, thereby overestimating the growth rates of real income in Tanzania shillings. For example, the World Bank (1993) estimated the annual per capita income at T.shs. 55,369 in 1991 (see Table 4.4) and per capital expenditures at T.shs. 61,564 (see Table 4.5).

Table 4.4: *Per Capita Income in Tanzania Since 1969 (in 1991 Prices)*

	1969	1976/77	1979/80	1982/83	1991
Rural	6,620	6,860	8,570	10,280	36250
Urban	74,980	23,890	n.a.	n.a.	100,222
Tanzania	n.a.	n.a	n.a.	n.a.	55,370

Source: World Bank (1993), World Development Reports, African Development Indicators: Social Indicators of Development.

NB. To convert the figures to 1991 prices, the inflation rate implicit in the GDP deflator was used.

The above positive indicators do not however imply that the welfare of Tanzanians is high. Many previous studies (Jazairy et al, 1992, Tinios et al, 1993, Sarris and van den Brink, 1993) had revealed that the majority of Tanzanians are very poor. Obviously determination of poverty extent in a country depends on data about the living conditions of the poor as reflected in a poverty profile. But as admitted even by the World Bank (1996), constructing a poverty profile that can be relied upon to guide policy options is often difficult.

Table 4.5: *The Distribution of People by Adult Equivalent Household and Per Capita Annual Expenditure, 1991*

Quintile	Annual Expenditure per Adult Equivalent mean				Annual per Capital Expenditure [mean]			
	All	Rural	Poor	Very poor	All	Rural	Poor	Very poor
Poorest : 1	11,887	9,613	6350	4347	7362	5942	4045	2679
: 2	29,300	23,576	16,234	12,544	18,068	14,463	10,149	7781
: 3	50854	39742	23831	17,610	31848	24,483	14,626	10,965
: 4	86,380	64,598	32,056	22,891	56,422	41,952	19,824	14,156
Richest : 5	279,968	247,516	42,474	28,208	193,750	158,103	27,294	20,065
Richest/ Poorest	24	26	7	6	26	27	7	8
ALL	91,500	77,200	24,000	17,100	61,600	49,620	15,200	11,00

Source: World Bank (1993).

The data and methods used can also matter greatly to the policies chosen. The World Bank (1996) cautions that at their worst, poorly devised poverty profiles can misdirect scarce resources, say, to cities when poverty is worse in rural areas, and vice versa.

The conceptual, methodological and factual shortcomings above notwithstanding, the latest World Bank Poverty Profile (1993) can be relied upon on the question of poverty situation in Tanzania. This profile categorizes the level of well being (poverty) of households under three groups:

i) Very Poor Households (Hard-core Poor)

These are households that are unable to afford even the basic needs recognized by the society. Such basic needs are essential food diet relating to local eating habits and nutritional requirements with the addition of a few non-food items necessary for survival. The cost of obtaining these needs was estimated at T.shs. 31,000.00 for 1991, using a basket of market prices. Thus the hard-core poverty line was T.shs. 31,000.00

ii) Poor Households (Soft-Core Poor)

These are households with less than 50% of the mean "adult equivalent" income. The poverty line was calculated to be T.shs. 46, 173.00 per adult equivalent. This is referred to as the soft-core poverty line.

iii) Better-Off Households

These are households that are above the soft-core poverty line of T.shs. 46,173.00. In measuring poverty, the World Bank (1993) used the three groups mentioned above. The World Bank also used incidence (headcount) to measure how many households were below the poverty line; severity (extreme), to measure how many of them were extremely far below the poverty line, and depth, to measure how far below the poverty line these households were.

Headcount (Incidence of Poverty)

According to the World Bank, an average of 51.1% of all Tanzanians live in households classified as poor, and 35.9% hardcore poor households (see Table 4.6).

Extremity of Poverty

The Foster Greer-Thorbecke index of severity of poverty was estimated at 15.6% for upper poverty line and 9.4% for hardcore poverty line, indicating a greater severity of poverty in both distributions (see Table 4.6).

Depth of Poverty

According to the World Bank, if perfect targeting were possible, the minimum amount of transfer payments required to raise all the poor to the soft-core poverty line would be T.shs. 11,497.00 annually per person and T.shs. 4,867.00 per annum to raise people to the lowest, hard-core poverty line of T.shs. 31,000.00. The total national transfer required would be T.shs. 306 billion (US $ 1.5 billion) and T.shs. 130 billion (US $ 0.64 billion) respectively. In general, the poor are poorer in the rural areas, so it would cost more in total to bring the rural poor up to the poverty line than the urban poor (see Table 4.6).

Table 4.6: *Three Different Poverty Indices and Two Poverty Lines, by Location of Households*

Locations of Households	Headcount (Po)		Depth (P1)	Severity(P2)	Pop. Share		
	Soft	Hard	Soft	Hard	Soft	Hard	
Villages	59.1	44.1	29.9	19.6	19.2	11.8	73.5
Urban, outside DSM	39.3	17.9	15.1	6.9	7.8	3.6	17.4
Dar es Salaam	9.3	4.38	03.1	1.19	1.4	0.41	9.1
All Tanzania	51.1	35.9	24.9	15.7	15.6	9.4	100.0

Source: World Bank, 1993

Notes on Table 4.6
1. *Headcount*: Counts the number falling below each poverty line.
2. *Depth*: % of poverty line income required to bring everyone below it to the poverty line.
3. *Severity*: More heavily weights the extremely poor: It would be smaller if most poor were near the poverty line and larger if many were much poorer than the poverty line.
4. *Soft*: Soft-core poverty line (of T.shs. 46,173 p.a.)
5. *Hard*: Hard-core poverty line (of T.shs. 31,000 p.a.)

Other World Bank (1993) revelations on the poverty situation in Tanzania were that 59% of Tanzanians living in rural villages are poor (10.9 million people), while 30% of all Tanzanians living in urban centres are poor. However only 9% of Dar es Salaam residents are categorized as poor. In general, 85% of poor households and 95% of hard-core poor respectively, live in rural areas. Expenditure on food for Tanzanians is high, at an average of 73.1%, indicating that Tanzania has a low standard of living (Table 4.7). It was also revealed that 83% of all households in Tanzania are engaged in agriculture. Out of these households who depend on agriculture as their source of income, 59% are poor households. In the urban, 14% of all Tanzanians are self-employed. Of these, 34% are poor.

Poverty profile for Tanzania based on "calories" or "food basket" concept is as shown on Table 4.8 below. This table compares the income required to purchase a minimum food (and other basic essentials) basket in rural and urban Tanzania.

Table 4.7: *Expenditure Types and Food Sources*

% Share of Expenditure by item	All Tanzania	Better-off	Poor	Very Poor	Rural	Urban	DSM
Food	73.1	70.8	75.6	77.2	77.4	63.6	69.3
Health	2.60	2.80	2.10	2.10	1.90	4.30	2.90
Education	0.66	0.70	0.61	0.62	0.57	0.90	0.80
OthersSource of Food	32.6	25.7	21.69	20.08	20.12	31.2	37.0
Expenditure(%) Market Purchases	66.8	65.9	67.8	64.8	58.3	82.1	87.2
Home Production	33.1	34.0	32.2	35.1	41.7	17.9	2.98

Source: World Bank (1993)

OTHER MANIFESTATIONS OF POVERTY IN TANZANIA

Apart from differences in terms of income and expenditure between the poor and the better off households, the World Bank also found stark differences in their access to water, housing conditions, durable goods and education. In general, 40% of all Tanzanians spend more than 15 minutes to reach the nearest water source (with 26.1% of rural people using 30 minutes). Generally only 33% of all households in Tanzania live in houses without mud walls, while 53% of houses have no corrugated iron roof. For the poor, these values are 21% and 68% respectively. The World Bank also found out that the literacy rate in Tanzania was 68% (61% for women and 76% for men). 80% of illiterate people live in rural areas. 70% of illiterate Tanzanians are women.

With regards to education, it was found that the poor have less education. In fact 34.9%, 32.2% and 19% of the hard-core poor, poor and better-off people respectively have no education at all, while only 1.3%, 2.2% and 11.3% of the hard-core poor, poor and better-off respectively have attended secondary education.

As repeatedly pointed out, apart from low income, poverty is manifested by other factors such as illiteracy, inadequate clean and safe water supply, poor health services, high mortality rates, malnutrition, environmental degradation, unemployment and homelessness or poor housing. The government of Tanzania (URT, 1998) has also highlighted the gloomy situation regarding these manifestations which accentuate poverty in the country.

Table 4.8: *Calorific Defined Poverty Lines for Tanzania Mainland - TShs /capita (1991)*

	Annual income required to purchase (T. Shs.)			
	All	Rural	Urban (non Dar)	Dar es Salaam
1900 calories		25,613	28,969	50,866
% of households	50.5	55.6	28.9	23.0
% of population	43.6	50.1	21.2	16.2
2000 Calories		27,721	33,186	54,950
% of households	54.4	59.3	34.6	26.5
% of population	47.6	54.1	26.4	18.3
2100 Calories		29,831	37,777	59,138
% of households	58.1	63.2	37.1	29.7
% of population	51.4	58.2	29.2	20.4

Source: Cooksey, (1994.4).

Illiteracy

One of the signs of poverty in Tanzania is the low level of literacy and numeracy. While in the 1980s the literacy level was about 90%, currently literacy rate is measured at only 68%, testifying to the worsening trend of poverty and to the reversal of gains made earlier in human development efforts (URT, 1998). Among the low-income families, the literacy rate is 59% that is 9% lower than the national average. In the 1980s, the gross enrolment rate for primary school pupils was 90%, but by 1996 the rate had gone down to 77.8%.

Inadequate Clean and Safe Water Supply

Availability of clean and safe water supply and sanitation services is one of the basic indicators of human development. Common diseases like malaria, diarrhoea and respiratory infections are closely associated with poor or inadequate water supply, improper hygiene and lack of sanitary means of excreta disposal. In Tanzania, coverage of water supply in urban areas is 65% and in the rural areas is 46%. The weighted average is therefore 50%. However, if non-functioning water schemes are accounted for, then the weighted coverage is further reduced to about 30% (URT/UNICEF, 1994).

For the majority of Tanzanians, water is therefore not within easy reach. Only about 11% of households have water services at the door. About 38% have to walk up to 15 minutes in order to reach a water source; while about 27% of households spend up to 30 minutes walking to a source of water. The rest have to spend more than 30 minutes to reach a source of water (URT, 1998). As also suggested by Mpuya, *et al* (1990), women and girl-children are the most adversely affected by lack of water because culturally and traditionally they have the role of fetching water. As for urban centres, Hoek-Smit (1991) reports that about 30% of the urban population in Tanzania has no portable water. These findings concur with other studies which indicate that in 1993, for example, 63% of the urban population had access to piped water, while the remaining 37% depended on shallow wells, traditional wells, rivers/streams and rain water (Uronu, 1999). The 1988 survey, however, showed an improvement in that 68% of urban population was now accessible to piped water.

According to Uronu (1999), despite the rapid urbanization in Tanzania, the International Drinking Water Supply and Sanitation Decade (IDWSSD) Programme (1981-91) and Tanzania Water Supply and Sanitation Programme (1971-99) concentrated more on rural water supply and sanitation programmes and neglected the urban water and sanitation schemes, resulting in infrastructural collapse in these urban services. A survey of 10 years (1990/91-1999/2000 Budget Survey) indicates that only 1.9% of the national development budget goes to the urban water and sewerage sub-sector (Uronu, 1999).

Poor Health Services

Poor health services reflect the extent of poverty of the country. For example, according to the Health Statistical Abstract (1997), the ratio of population per health facility in Tanzania is 7,421; there is one hospital bed per 1,000 people, and one physician per 23,188 people, while about 30% of the people live more than 5 kilometres from the nearest health centre.

High Mortality Rate

According to the Health Statistical Abstract (1997), the average life expectancy at birth of a Tanzanian is 50 years compared to a life expectancy of 77 years in developed countries and 62 years in other developing countries. The infant mortality rate (IMR) is 96 per 1,000 live births compared to 7 in developed countries. The under-five mortality rate is 158, while maternal mortality is between 200 and 400 per 100,000 live births. Comparable figures for developed countries are 9 per 1,000 for under-five mortality rate, and 95 per 100,000 live births for maternal mortality rate. These high mortality rates in Tanzania are a clear indication of poverty.

Malnutrition

Many Tanzanians suffer from malnutrition, particularly under-malnutrition. Many also suffer from micro-nutrient deficiencies due to nutritional illiteracy, especially as it relates to the use of fruits and vegetables and proper methods of planning cereal-based diets. According to Tanzania Demographic Health Survey (1996), malnutrition among under-fives shows stunting to be 43.4%, under weight 30.6% and wasting 7.2% (URT, 1998). Adult malnutrition especially maternal malnutrition is widespread. Indicative of maternal malnutrition is the high prevalence of low birth weight.

Environmental Degradation

Environmental degradation, which is caused by over exploitation of land resources, perpetuates poverty. Poverty has forced smallholder farm households and pastoral groups to intensify exploitation of land by way of survival. This has led to widespread soil erosion. Furthermore, in the absence of alternative sources of energy, firewood remains the dominant source of domestic fuel all over the country. Cutting trees for firewood has led to widespread deforestation and drought, thereby increasing the danger of desertification, subsequent food shortages and malnutrition.

Unemployment

High incidence of unemployment is among key distinguishing features of poverty. Largely because of poverty, the Tanzanian economy has not been able to generate enough employment opportunities to meet the needs of the labour force. A labour force study conducted in 1990/91 gave an estimated 8.9 million economically active people aged between 15 and 64 years of whom about 10.7% were unemployed (Kombe, 1999). While the population growth rate of Tanzania is estimated at 2.8% per annum, the proportion of the economically active labour force has been growing at the rate of over 3.0% since 1978 (Wangwe and Tsikata, 1999).

In 1992, the government estimated that 700,000 people were entering the labour market every year, out of whom only 30,000 got employment in the formal sector (see Kombe, 1999). However, while the formal sector can absorb only 8.5% of annual increase in labour force, the informal sector has a capacity to employ about 62.5% (URT, 1997e). A recent report (ILO, 1999), which confirms the 1991 Informal Sector Survey, shows that Tanzania is one of the countries whose urban informal sector absolves more than 50% of the employable labour force.

Poor living conditions in the rural areas serves as a centripetal force pushing the young from rural to urban areas where most of them remain unemployed. The near 30% of youth unemployment reflects, in part, the inability of the economy to create sufficient employment opportunities for the growing population, but also the inability of the rural areas to create gainful employment opportunities and incentives to retain youths after graduation from primary schooling. Alongside this situation is the growing problem of street children who are a manifestation of worsening poverty. Some social indicators for Tanzania as compared to other sub-Saharan African countries are shown in Table 4.9.

Table 4.9: *Social Indicators for Tanzania and Sub-Saharan Africa*

	1980		1985		1990/91	
	Tanzania	SSA	Tanzania	SSA	Tanzania	SSA
Per Capita income (1991 US $)	284	582	309	391	110	340
Infant mortality per 1000	122	127	117	118	115	105
Life expectancy at Birth (years)	47	47	48	49	48	51
Average daily Calorific intake (Kilo-calories per Capita)	2244	2107	2229	2040	2206	2120
Primary School Gross enrolment Rate	93	70	72	68	63	69

Source: World Bank, (1993)

GOVERNMENT'S POVERTY ERADICATION POLICIES

It would be a misconception to think that it was the World Bank, or any other foreign institution, which enlightened Tanzanians or the government for the first time about the severity and impact of poverty in Tanzania. Far from it, Tanzanians knew the extent of their poverty even before independence in 1961.

Early Responses to Poverty

Immediately after independence, the government of Tanganyika, and later, Tanzania, embarked on development plans and strategies that were geared towards alleviating poverty among its people. The post independence clarion was "Freedom and Hard Work" so that the three national enemies, namely: poverty, ignorance and disease could be eradicated. Although poverty here was separated from ignorance and disease, the latter two are not only inseparable with poverty, but they are almost synonymous with it (Mkapa, 1994). It can therefore be summed that the number one agenda of this country immediately after independence was the eradication of poverty (which included also ignorance and disease).

The country embarked on an ambitious goal of development with enviable successes from the infrastructural point of view. It established an extensive and successful infrastructure of social services, especially in health and education. Many health centres and government hospitals were established where people could get free medical services, with the back-up of subsidized religious hospital services. Education for all also became the post-independence policy, a policy whose components later included Universal Primary Education (UPE) and Adult Education Programmes.

Cognizant of the fact that agriculture was the backbone of the national economy, the government established a comprehensive network of agricultural extension services to boost agricultural output. An extensive network of agricultural research institutes to revolutionalise rural agricultural production in terms of methodology and technology was established.

Alleviating poverty amongst Tanzanians has apparently meant raising their income which would be reflected in increased economic growth of the country. Even steps taken by the government to alleviate urban poverty have mainly focused on employment creation. Various policies in relation to income and employment were promulgated including wages, incomes, rural development, investment and price policy of 1967 and national policy on productivity, incomes and prices of 1981. All these policies were aimed at, among other things, raising public sector employment (it rose from 160,005 in 1967 to 239,261 in 1972. i.e. by 49.5% - Mtatifikolo, 1994), creating a fast momentum for reducing income differentials among groups, regions and between rural and urban areas, promoting socialist production and distribution, raising efficiency in resource allocation and utilization, and speeding up national economic growth.

Other measures taken by the government to alleviate poverty through employment creation included the enactment of the Human Resources Deployment Act of 1983 (Nguvu Kazi), the formulation of National Employment Policy (1997) and the National Youth Development Policy (1996). Through the Human Resources Deployment Act, the government embarked on resettlement projects of emigrants from urban areas to engage in agricultural activities in selected rural areas. However, the policy has had little impact, largely because it subjected people to state coercion rather than voluntary participation. In fact the policy was abhorred, not only by the affected people, but even the International Labour Organization because it appeared to contain elements of human rights violation. The latter two policies are new schemes that are yet to be fully operationalized due to scarce resources.

A seemingly successful programme created by the government with the support of UNDP and other donors is the National Income Generation Programme

(NIGP). The programme creates employment and income through mobilization of resources for supporting micro-enterprises, small-scale business ventures, petty trade, farming, construction and improvement of economic infrastructure such as roads, drains and markets. By improving infrastructure, NIGP has been promoting labour-based technology (LBT), which has been successfully tested in Hanna Nassif ward in Dar es Salaam.

In a wider context, since early 1980s the government embarked on various economic reforms so as to stimulate and sustain national economic growth. Two economic recovery programmes (ERP I: 1986/87 - 1988/89 and ERP II: 1989/90 - 1991/92) were launched, both aimed at raising GDP growth, reducing inflation, restoring internal and external balances in the economy and improving social services delivery. In early 1990s, the government issued the Policy Framework Paper, 1991/92 - 1993/94, which recommended reforms in the civil service and parastatal sector. The civil service and parastatal reforms were intended to reform expenditure to effect savings and thereby contribute towards enhancing incomes and possibly alleviating poverty (Mtatifikolo, 1994).

New Thrust in Poverty Eradication

The above policies devised by the government to restructure the country's economic pillars enabled Tanzania to witness some improvement in economic growth. The above policies notwithstanding, poverty remains pervasive in Tanzania. To be sure, the government has not lost hope on poverty eradication as it believes that eradication of poverty is a realistic prospect, not a naïve dream. Poverty eradication can, and must, be pursued relentlessly if social standards are to be upheld. Addressing the North-South Conference for Sustainable Development in Berne in 1998, the first President of United Republic of Tanzania, the late Mwalimu Julius K. Nyerere said:

> Universal social standards are not possible, and certainly would not be compatible with justice, unless they are linked to, and conditional upon, the parallel implementation of a deliberate, coherent and internally consistent anti-poverty programmes, both nationally and internationally.

In a bid to tackle poverty, the government made a deliberate resolve to vest the Vice President's office with all poverty-related issues. Through this high profile office, a wave of new anti-poverty initiatives may be activated by all sectors of society involving individuals, civil society organizations, religious groups, the business community and non-governmental organizations (NGOs).

Furthermore, the government of Tanzania has formulated a national policy on poverty eradication and its Long-Term Development Perspective (Vision

2025). Through the national poverty eradication strategy (URT, 1998), the government has set the goal of reducing abject poverty by the year 2010, and eliminating it by year 2025. This strategy outlines areas of strategic interventions by different stakeholders and defines roles and responsibilities of those actors so as to ensure its effective implementation. Other international institutions and donors have also pledged their support through various ways in the government's endeavour to reduce poverty among the people. For example, the UNDP's sixth country programme (1997-2001) focuses on six major programmes to support Tanzania, among which include poverty eradication and sustainable livelihood. Realising that some 1.3 billion people on earth live in absolute poverty, the World Bank has identified two shifts in its implementation strategy. First, a shift from describing poverty to formulating strategies for reducing poverty; and secondly, a shift from counting poverty-focused projects to assessing their impact on the poor (World Bank, 1998). Tanzania is poised to gain from this new strategy of the World Bank.

As a new initiative, the government of Tanzania has recently prepared a Poverty Reduction Strategy Paper (PRSP). PRSP is a medium term strategy for reducing poverty in Tanzania developed through broad consultations with national and international stakeholders in the context of the enhanced Highly Indebted Poor Countries (HIPC) initiative.

However, the government does not seem to have well defined, articulated and visualized policy and institutional framework for implementing housing provision and improvement programmes in an effort to alleviate urban poverty, despite some action plans mentioned in both the national poverty eradication strategy and national human settlements development policy.

Research on Poverty Alleviation in Tanzania

Since poverty eradication is multi-dimensional and multi-sectoral aspect requiring various policy actions, it is imperative that all stakeholders in the whole process of poverty eradication understand the appropriate policy options available to the government and other actors. This can only be achieved through research on poverty issues, dwelling particularly on past and present policies, and recommending appropriate policy options. However, hitherto, not much research has been carried out in this context. There remains a huge untapped research area calling for an urgent need to build and strengthen research capacity (Bagachwa, 1994).

Commenting on the prevalence of poverty in Tanzania despite the early realization of the seriousness of this scourge and the need for research on poverty eradication, the President of United Republic of Tanzania, Benjamin W. Mkapa

(1994), who was then the Minister for Science, Technology and Higher Education, had this to say:

> I believe that the war against poverty has slowed down because in the flourish of the early successes we may have attacked on too many fronts all at the same time with inadequate preparation for intervention. I believe that in planning, strategizing, executing, supervising, monitoring, co-ordinating and setting out specific sectoral goals we may have been poorly informed and hasty of decision and action. Interventions were well intentioned and called for. But the ground may not have been well set and the implementation may have been impatiently pursued.
>
> This is where the role of research in policy-making and implementation becomes very important. Important in the sense that it provides the opportunity to prepare the ground, review the assumptions, to re-evaluate the strategies and to correct the approaches to making the interventions in social development. For, research provides for analysis of past action. Through research findings we can learn what went wrong, or what is going wrong with plans. And we can use the research findings to make adjustments or change course realistically and scientifically.

In realization of inadequacies in the local research capacity on poverty alleviation, the Research Programme on Poverty Alleviation (REPOA) was established in 1993 - initially sponsored by the Government of the Netherlands, but under Tanzanian management. The overall objectives of REPOA are (REPOA, 1995):

- To build an effective and autonomous poverty research network with local to global connections;
- To deepen the understanding of poverty issues among grassroots organizations, local researchers, research bodies and policy and decision makers;
- To contribute to the development of policies aimed at combating poverty both locally and more generally; and
- To forge linkages between poverty research and interested parties, including decision makers in government, NGOs and grassroots organizations, business, academic and donor communities.

REPOA has already identified five priority areas of interest to constitute the core research issues on poverty eradication in Tanzania for the coming years, namely:

Link Between Poverty and Public Policies

Realizing that macro-economic policies are of fundamental importance to poverty and its reduction, research issues under this theme, according to REPOA, would include analysis of the implications of the past and present economic reform policies for income distribution and poverty. These would involve analysis of causes of past policy failures; the performance of the state including government capacity/weaknesses, and the roles of NGOs, Parliament and local governments in implementing poverty-related programmes.

Link Between Poverty and Environment

The study of environmental degradation and its link to poverty though poorly understood, is of great significance to the question of eradicating poverty. Issues for research here, as outlined by REPOA, would include relationship between population growth, migration and the environment; poverty and poor environments, conflicts resolutions relating to pastoralists rights; the impoverishment of peasant farmers, and the dynamics of integrating traditional and modern agro-ecological practices. Other areas would include institutional aspects of poverty and the environment, especially the regulatory role of the relevant ministries and institutions related to the environment; the role of local governments and NGOs, and the impact of biotechnology on the environment and agricultural output.

Technology and Poverty Alleviation

Promotion of more sustainable patterns of development must include a consideration of technology. REPOA has outlined various research issues under this theme including ways of cultivating a science and technology-oriented culture; identification of industries in which Tanzania has a comparative advantage; the search for a relevant techno-economic development policy and building of institutions that would constitute an enabling technology environment. Other areas include the role of indigenous knowledge in grassroots problem solving; technology for sustainable energy use; the implications of modern bio-technology, and modern information technologies.

Gender and Poverty Alleviation

Though gender studies usually examine the relationship between men and women, the impact of economic reforms and adjustment has been uneven and those who have suffered most have been women and children, particularly among the poor. Research issues under this theme, include focus on differentiation among women, especially the interface between gender and class, changing patriarchal ideologies, forms of control and forms of cultural expression as well as women's resistance. Other issues include property rights, the effects of rural-urban migration on gender relations, the changing position of old people, the impact of liberalisation on the work-load of rural women and equal education opportunities among boys and girls.

Socio-Cultural Determinants of Poverty

The focus in this theme would be the study of behavioural motivations and constraints affecting the poor. Some of these constraints are economic in nature, while others are social and cultural.

In January 1994, REPOA in collaboration with other leading research-oriented institutions in Tanzania organized a workshop for research on poverty alleviation in Tanzania. This was a first step towards the operationalization of the REPOA progamme. In this workshop various papers were presented which provided the background for discussion. The papers reviewed and analysed previous and current development in as far as the five focal research areas mentioned above were concerned. The papers also defined specific areas that warranted further research. Subsequent to this workshop, several other workshops and studies have been conducted on the question of poverty alleviation.

HOUSING FOR THE POOR: THE ABSENT CENTRE OF CURRENT POVERTY ALLEVIATION RESEARCH

The government's focus on poverty alleviation, and indeed even REPOA's identified themes for research on poverty, seem to have paid little attention to the issue of housing provision as means of poverty alleviation. The five themes identified by REPOA for research initially did not link poverty and housing conditions of the poor. Even the areas proposed for further research under each theme did not explicitly touch on the plight of the poor (particularly urban poor) regarding poor housing conditions and their associated problems such as diseases, malnutrition and other health hazards. Undoubtedly, these problems exacerbate the poverty situation in Tanzania.

Although Mtatifikolo (1994) dwells very well with public policies on poverty eradication since independence, much of the thrust in his analysis revolves around policies, which are related directly to income generation and distribution. While policies such as Economic Recovery Programmes were also geared towards improvement and revitalisation of infrastructure and social services, and although housing provision is one of social services, no specific housing policy for the poor is analysed. Mtatifikolo (1994) concludes his analysis by providing eight possible policy agendas for research on poverty alleviation. Unfortunately all the proposed agendas lack the explicit (even implicit) reference to low-cost housing policies as means for eradicating poverty among the (urban) poor.

There is a very close linkage between environment, housing and poverty. In his analysis of relationship between poverty and environment, Mascarenhas (1994) briefly mentions the problem of urbanization, but this is only intended to explain the impact of population distribution on the environment. How the rapid urbanization has caused environmentally unsafe squatter and slum settlements, which exacerbate poverty among the poor urban do not explicitly come out in his analysis. The sufferings of the poor from environmental disasters caused by, or taking place in, unplanned or poorly planned housing settlements need to be in the agenda when linkage between poverty and environment is made.

Technology is a fundamental requirement for the successful advancement of civilization (Chungu and Mandara, 1994). Technology can be treated as a substitute indicator for development since the two are highly correlated. The importance of technology in improving housing standards and housing related infrastructural services in the poor households' communities should have been one of the agenda items for research on poverty alleviation.

Women play a major role in ensuring safer housing conditions in any household. Healthy housing and their environment therefore depend, to a large extent, on how women (whether in male-headed households or, and particularly, in female-headed households) participate in the improvement of housing and living conditions. In proposing areas for research on gender and poverty alleviation, Mbuguni (1994) at least talks of characteristics/strategies of female-headed households. However, this seems to be in relation to merely the linkage to issues of defining the households in the Tanzanian context. Research needs to go further on the issues of women contributing physically, and through ideas, to the planning and maintaining of housing requirements for the households. What can women, for example, do to mobilize self-help efforts among neighbourhood women for the improvement of their housing environments? The issue of women and housing conditions is crucially and particularly important in female-headed households. It should be realized that female-headed households form a rising proportion of households. It is estimated that one-fifth of all households in the world are female-headed households (HABITAT, 1996c).

Omari (1994) discusses the socio-cultural factors influencing poverty in Tanzania, and poses several research agendas on this theme. However, his analysis does not cover the social and cultural factors that influence housing standards and various ethnic living cultures and habits, extended families etc. Such factors may contribute to overcrowding and the urge (or lack of it) for improving or extending housing accommodation.

Subsequent to the REPOA workshop of 1994, there have been some attempts to study and assess poverty alleviation issues in Tanzania. However, not much research/study has been carried out hitherto, which links housing conditions (and their environment) with poverty alleviation. Various researches and studies on poverty alleviation have so far concentrated on general policies (Richey, 1996; Kweka, 1996), policies on agriculture (see Wambura, 1996; Ponte, 1996; Kyulule and Kihiyo, 1996), gender issues (Chamwali, 1996; Makombe, 1996; O'Riordan et al, 1997; Diyamett et al, 1998), the role of technology on poverty eradication (see Mutagwaba et al, 1997; Kilonzo, 1996; Bangu, 1996; Shitundu and Luvanga,

1998). Jambiya, et al (1997) and Temba (1996) have also highlighted the linkage between environmental degradation and poverty. Temu (1996) and Kashuliza *et al* (1998) have dealt with the role of finance and financial markets in poverty alleviation, while Kamuzora and Gwalema (1998), and Liviga and Mekacha (1998) have worked on social and population problems and how the two affect poverty.

It is however encouraging to note that subsequent to the first REPOA workshop of 1994, urban poverty has been explicitly recognized in the REPOA agendas. Within the REPOA priority areas of interest which will constitute core research issues in the future, REPOA has now specifically mentioned the question of urban poverty (REPOA, 1995). According to REPOA (1995), Tanzania's population will be 40% urban by the year 2000. It is believed that although the majority of poor Tanzanians will continue to be rural, there is likely to be an increasing concern with urban poverty issues. These issues include: access to social services (health, water, education), housing and transport, formal and informal employment, pollution, waste management, energy consumption, marginality and crime; urban governance and democracy.

Despite such recognition, no further attempts have been made by REPOA to encourage and promote actual research works on urban poverty, particularly housing poverty. The aim of this book is to fill this gap.

5

HOUSING AND SHELTER PROVISION POLICIES IN TANZANIA

INTRODUCTION

The Tanzanian constitution recognizes shelter as one of the basic human needs (others being food and health). In fact, housing development was one of the major concerns of the government immediately after attaining independence in 1961. But even before independence, the colonial government of Tanganyika had put some importance on urban development and housing. In this chapter, having documented urbanization trends in Tanzania and the consequential urban housing shortage and poor social and infrastructural services, we shall review some attempts by the public to redress housing and its associated problems since independence. The main argument is that as a result of policy mis-directions, very little achievements have been registered from the public housing policies and programmes enunciated so far.

POPULATION AND URBAN HOUSING TRENDS IN TANZANIA

Population and Urban Growth

Currently the population growth rate in Tanzania is estimated at 2.8%. With that growth rate, the current population of about 32 million people is expected to reach some 56 million people in 20 years. With an estimated urbanization rate of 9% per annum (one of the highest in Africa), one in every two Tanzanians is expected to be living in urban areas in twenty years time (Mahanga, 1998; Kombe, 1999).

Rapid urbanization in Tanzania, as in other developing countries, has been fueled by high rates of natural population increase in the urban areas and slow adoption of family planning (birth control) measures (Kombe, 1999). This is exacerbated by rural-urban migration. The 1978 and 1988 population census reports indicate that rural-urban migration accounts for a bigger percentage of the population increase in urban areas than natural increase in the urbanization process in Tanzania.

Commenting on why people move from rural to urban areas the first President of Tanzania, the late Mwalimu Julius K. Nyerere, had this to say:

> Unfortunately, the life of the urban minority has become a matter of great envy for the rural majority. Life in the towns has come to represent opportunities for advancement, a chance of excitement, and the provision of social services, none of which is available in the rural areas .... Most of all, there is an almost universal belief that life in towns is more comfortable and more secure, ... that the rewards of work are better in the urban areas and that people in the rural parts of the country are condemned to poverty and insecurity for their whole lives (Mwalimu Julius K. Nyerere, 1968)

But Nyerere hastened to discount such beliefs and views, and continued:

> The vast majority of our town dwellers live extremely poor and in most cases they are on the whole worse off, both materially and in the realm of personal satisfaction, than the people in the rural areas could be ...and for most people, the ever present threat of unemployment, and consequent real hunger in the midst of apparent wealth, introduces evils which can be excluded from life in the rural areas if this is based on the traditional principles of African society.

Despite Tanzania being one of the least urbanized countries in Africa, the rate at which it is being urbanized is frightening. As opposed to the average urbanization rate of 5.3% in Africa, Tanzania is being urbanized at the rate of 9% per annum. In fact between 1980 and 1991, annual urban population in Tanzania grew by 10.1%, which was the highest among the low-income economies, according to the World Bank (Kombe, 1999). In 1967, the 21 urban centres with at least 5,000 people each had a population totaling about 700,000, equivalent to 5.7% of total population of the country. By 1978 and 1988 the proportion of total urban population had shot to 12.8% and 27.7% respectively (see Table 5.1). In fact, it is estimated that this has risen to 40% by the year 2000. This sharply contrasts with some neighbouring countries' statistics. For example, the rate of urbanization in Uganda is not that terrifying. It is estimated that currently only 11% of the Ugandan population lives in urban areas (Tibenda, 1997). Yet Uganda needs to build 20,000 housing units per annum in the urban areas alone (Habitat, 1993).

Given the above scenario in Tanzania, there is a very great demand for housing in urban areas. The gap between the supply and demand for housing has been widening over time. It is estimated that at the end of the First Five Year Development Plan (1964-1969), there was a shortage of 21,000 houses in urban areas. The shortage grew to 25,000 houses at the beginning of the Second Five Year Development Plan (1969-1974), and shot to 300,000 housing units in 1982. The growing housing shortage is confirmed by overcrowding in urban areas (see, Table 5.2). Assuming that overcrowding means more than two persons per room, the percentage of families in overcrowded homes is 34.4% in Dar es Salaam city, 34% in Mwanza, 37.4% in Arusha, 37.2% in Moshi, 38% in Dodoma, 24.7% in Kigoma and 28.7% in Kilosa. The cumulative shortfall for units of conventional housing in urban areas is currently estimated to be more than 1,500,000 units. With this trend, the deficit will rise to 2,200,000 by the year 2000 (URT, 1999a).

Table 5.1: *Growth of Regional Centres, Total Population and Urban Population: Tanzania Mainland (1948 to 1988)*

Centres/Year	1948	1952	1957	1967	1978	1988
Dar es Salaam	69,227	99,140	128,742	272,515	737,836	1,360,850
Mwanza	11,296	13,691	19,877	34,855	109,480	223,013
Dodoma	9,414	12,262	13,435	23,569	45,637	203,833
Tanga	20,619	22,143	38,053	60,935	102,560	187,155
Morogoro	8,173	11,501	14,507	25,263	61,890	177,760
Mbeya	3,179	5,566	6,932	12,469	75,948	154,844
Arusha	5,320	7,690	10,038	32,348	55,240	134,708
Shinyanga	2,596	2,596	2,907	4,732	20,448	100,724
Moshi	8,048	9,079	13,726	26,696	52,223	96,838
Tabora	12,768	14,011	15,561	20,994	67,392	93,506
Sumbawanga	n.a	n.a	n.a	10,422	28,389	91,972
Songea	612	990	1,401	5,403	17,944	86,880
Iringa	5,702	8,013	9,578	21,946	57,182	84,860
Kigoma	1,106	1,351	16,255	21,369	49,900	84,647
Singida	n.a	3,125	3,938	9,540	29,252	80,987
Mtwara	4,125	14,382	15,266	20,414	48,366	76,632
Musoma	2,962	4,937	7,707	15,415	30,976	68,536
Bukoba	3.247	3,570	5,297	8,186	20,431	47,009
Lindi	8,577	10,784	10,315	13,351	27,019	41,587
Kibaha	n.a	n.a	n.a	n.a	2,217	37,638
Total National Population	7,480,500	8,785,613	8,788,500	11,958,000	17,036,449	22,533,758
Total Urban Population	197,266	269,841	361,072	677,780	2,203,000	6,250,173
% Urban Population	2.6	3.1	4.1	5.7	12.9	27.7

Source: Bureau of Statistics, Official Population Census 1948 to 1988, Dar es Salaam

Table 5.2: *The National Housing Corporation Keko "Star" Blocks of Flats: Overcrowding Evidence*

Block No.	No. of Units	Rooms per Unit	Authorized Occupants	Actual No. of Occupants	Occupants per Room
A	32	1	32	160	5
	16	1.5	16	80	5
B	48	2.5	48	300	6.3
C	32	1	32	160	5
	16	1.5	16	80	5
D	32	1	32	160	5
	16	1.5	16	80	5
Total	168		192	1020	5.3

Source: Kabwogi (1997.128)

Land Delivery Systems and Poor Urban Infrastructure and Services

Tanzania and many other African countries have a complicated land tenure system as a result of the co-existence of different legal systems, together with several extra-legal forms, such as customary practices, Islamic systems and imported European statutory systems (Payne, 1999).

As regards land allocation/acquisition, evidence suggests that in many developing countries, urban land can either be obtained formally or informally, and that the informal sector provides much more land to land seekers (including the majority of the poor) than the formal sector (Kironde, 1998). For instance, it is now estimated that over 70% of Dar es Salaam's population lives in unplanned areas, where, invariably, land is obtained through informal means. It means that the official land allocation system has been outstripped by the acquisition of land through informal means like buying (Kironde, 1998; Hoek-Smit, 1990). The majority of landowners in Tanzania got the land through informal ways. Quoting UNCHS (1996), Kombe (1999) aptly concludes that informal land parcelling and transactions emerge where there is an effective demand for building sites that official or formal system cannot satisfy. As if that is not enough, most housing in urban Tanzania is constructed without reference to planning authorities even in planned areas, resulting in the construction of substandard structures. Only 35% of houses in urban Tanzania comply with existing regulations (URT, 1999a). Poor infrastructure for most neighbourhoods is another impediment to proper housing development. As evidenced by Table 5.3, the proportion of urban population in unplanned settlements varies from 40% to 75% depending on the size of the urban area. Dar es Salaam has the highest proportion (75%) of its residents living in unplanned settlements. Houses constructed in unplanned settlements account for 60% of all urban housing development.

Table 5.3: *Proportion of Unplanned Settlements in Selected Urban Centres in Tanzania*

Name	Jurisdi -ction area (Km).	Built-up urban area in Hectare	Un-planned Area in Hectare	Ratio unplanned to built-up (%)	Popln. unplanned area	Popln. in unplanned area (%)
DSM	1,393	14,878	5,197 (1992)	35	1,400,000	70
Mwanza	1,277	8,675	944 (1996)	11	213,646	58
Arusha	9,200	9,198	3,493 (1992)	40	76,332	68
Mbeya	184	4,400	1,843 (1990)	42	114,380	86
Morogoro	110	5,345	275 (1996)	5	63,000	44
Dodoma	2,618	4,733	681 (1994)	14	42,001	45
Tanga	360	4,025	356 (1992)	9	57,703	38
Iringa	162	5,980	679 (1990)	11	26,848	38
Tabora	117	6,278	683 (1996)	11	92,175	82
Moshi	77	5,679	346 (1992)	6	16,715	16

Source: Quoted in, Kombe (1999)

Rapid urbanization has inevitably increased pressure on the already over-strained urban infrastructure and services, much of which has not been maintained or expanded to cope with this rapid urban growth. In addition to the failure to provide commensurate and adequate infrastructure and services, there has been a failure, on the part of the administrative machinery, to provide for a planned housing delivery system at a time when demand is growing rapidly. As put by Kombe (1999), lack of infrastructure services adversely affects individual or households health, property value and the overall amenity of an area. Quoting Habitat (1996), Kombe (1999) continues to assert that a satisfactory level of infrastructure services in a town and a country in general, is a critical factor in attracting investment.

The inadequacy of the formal shelter delivery system to cater for the urban population has led to an extensive development of squatter or unplanned settlements. Studies indicate that nationally about 70% of the urban population live in unplanned settlements and that about 60% of the urban housing stock is found in these settlements (URT, 1999a). A more disturbing situation is the rate at which these settlements have been growing. For example, the total number of houses in the unplanned areas of Dar es Salaam was about 50,000 housing units in 1974. The current figure is estimated at 200,000 housing units. Studies also indicated that about 65% of all residential housing constructed in urban areas in 1980 was in unplanned settlements, and that in the same year, developers in unplanned areas constructed about 10,000 dwellings in the various regional centres compared to less than 2,000 that were constructed in planned areas

Table 5.4: *The Condition of Infrastructure Services in Selected Urban Centres*

Urban Centre	Dar es Salaam	Arusha	Tanga	Dodoma	Morogoro	Iringa
Solid Waste	1800 tons are generated per day, only 241 tons are collected	200 tons generated per day, 112 tons collected. 44% not collected	225 tons generated per day, 135 tons collected, equivalent to 65%	350 tons generated per day, 42 tons collected and disposed	260 tons generated per day, only between 20-26 tons(10%) collected	45 tons generated per day, only 23 tons are collected (47% not collected)
Water Supply	Water demand is 90 million litres per day, supply is only 40 million litres per day	35,000m^3 supplied/day against 42,000m^3 demand (12% not met)	Demand is 40,000m^3, supply is only 26,000m^3/p er day	Demand is 37,500m^3, supply is only 14,700m^3 per day (40%)	Demand is 30,000m,^{3} supply is only 14,500m^3/ day (48%)	Demand is 12,000m^{3}su pply is only 8,500m^3 Per day
Storm Water drainage	1,700 km, mostly built in 1950s and largely un-maintain e-d	Data not available	Data not available	Data not available	Data not available	2/3 of the roads do not have drains
Roads	1,200 km, out of this 450 paved. Only 10% are in good conditio n	Data not available	896 km of roads. Only 93 is tarmac, 659 gravel, 144 earth	Data not available	Data not available	Out of the 292 km, only 26 km are tarmac
Liquid Waste	Only 5% of the city area is sewered, 20% lacks elementa ry sanitatio n facilities, 80% use on-site sanitatio n	Only 14% of the town is sewered	75% of liquid waste uncollected	Data not available	About 82.4% use pit latrines	4.21 million lit/day, 42,000 litres are collected daily
Formal and Informal Housing	Planned housing 40%, unplanne d housing 60%	Over 50% population live in 76.7% unplanned area, only 23.3% planned	Data not available	Unplanned housing 27%, planned housing 73%	Planned housing 43%, unplanned 57%	Data not available

Remarks: Predominant problems in the urban centres:

1. Inadequate capacity to manage solid and liquid waste
2. Insufficient water supply
3. Poor accessibility including poor maintenance of roads and insufficient storm water drains
4. Urban sprawl – rampant development of informal settlements

Source: Quoted in, Makombe (1999)

As evident from Table 5.4, physical and social infrastructure in urban settlements is either missing or is in very poor condition. Common phenomena in these places include unhealthy water supply systems, overcrowding, lack of land for circulation routes and community facilities, and poor environment characterized by poor sanitation and uncollected garbage. For example, it is estimated that the current daily rate of solid waste generation in Dar es Salaam is about 2,000 tonnes of which only 11% is being collected and disposed of at dump site (Halla and Majani, 1997). The remainder is dumped along the streets and open spaces, including cemeteries. As regards sanitation, about 20% of residents in Dar es Salaam have no proper sanitation facilities (Halla and Majani, 1997). Ageing sewers that cause leakages through bursting exacerbates the poor sanitation condition. In areas with on-site sanitation facilities and where the water table is high, overflowing of pit latrines and septic tanks is persistent. Further, inaccessibility in some densely built-areas constrains pit emptying.

Lack of Housing Finance

Another major constraint to increasing the supply of housing in Tanzania is the near complete lack of formal long-term mortgage finance. After the collapse of the only formalized housing finance institution in Tanzania, the Tanzania Housing Bank (THB) in 1995, due to poor capital base; poor funds mobilisation strategies; poor lending criteria; poor record keeping; mal-administration, and corruption, Tanzania has no formal housing finance system. As shall be seen later, this has made house construction a difficult undertaking for most households, especially those in the low-income category. Currently in Tanzania, housing is financed from personal and family savings over a long period of time, which immensely retards the supply of housing.

COLONIAL HOUSING PROVISION POLICIES

The aim of urban development and housing policies during the colonial era in Tanganyika was to facilitate political control and exploitation of natural resources for export to Europe and to provide housing to colonial administrators and civil servants. During this period, planning policy was based on racial segregation of the towns into separate areas for Europeans, Asians and Africans.

To support these policies, the British colonial government passed a series of planning legislations such as the 1919 Sanitation and Control of Development Rules for Dar es Salaam Township. The scope of the 1919 rules was expanded in 1920 into Township Ordinance that empowered the Governor to proclaim townships and to appoint townships authorities who could make township plans and exercise limited powers of controlling development. With regards to housing development, the colonial government in Tanganyika introduced a scheme called Colonial Development and Welfare Fund after the Second World War, intended to provide accommodation relief to urban dwellers. The scheme was terminated at the eve of independence. Another scheme established in 1957 was the African Urban Housing Loan Scheme intended to encourage civil servants and business people to construct housing units of better quality. This was, however, unsuccessful since it lasted for only three years when about 600 units had been built.

Yet another scheme before independence was the Urban Roof Loan Scheme introduced in 1960 with the aim of providing finance for roof improvements using corrugated iron sheets. The scheme was also a failure, largely because the corrugated iron sheets were placed on already dilapidated roof timber frames which collapsed soon after re-roofing (Kabwogi, 1997).

In as far as Urban Development in general was concerned, East Africa Royal Commission on Land and Population was formed in 1952 which came up with a report on urban development in 1955 covering all three East African countries.

CURRENT SOURCES OF HOUSING SUPPLY IN TANZANIA

Currently there are four systems for the provision of housing in Tanzania, viz. private housing, government housing, institutional or employer housing and housing provided by the National Housing Corporation.

Private Housing

With private housing, individuals construct dwelling houses. Urban private housing is divided into formal or planned and informal or unplanned housing. Planned housing is where houses are built in planned and surveyed areas as approved by relevant authorities i.e. ministry responsible for lands and city, municipal or town councils. Unplanned housing is where houses are constructed in unplanned areas that have not been conventionally surveyed. These are the squatter dwellings.

Private housing can further be categorized into houses for renting or owner-occupation. In the first case, individual private landlords build houses for renting purposes either in planned or squatter areas. Owner occupation is where an individual builds a house for his own use. Where the house has surplus capacity/ rooms or where the owner wishes to get supplementary income from tenants, s/ he normally lets some rooms to other tenants so that the house is both owner-occupied and rented.

The level of private housing in Tanzania is significant (Kabwogi, 1997). In Dar es Salaam, it accounts for 75% of the total housing stock. According to another study (Hoek-Smit, 1990), about 50% of privately owned housing units in Dar es Salaam are occupied by more than one household, and about two thirds of the households are room renters.

Government Housing

This is where the government constructs houses for its civil servants under service tenancy. Government housing schemes in Tanzania started before independence when the colonial government in Tanganyika constructed houses in urban areas for its foreign employees. After independence and thus the departure of colonial masters, these houses were allocated to senior local civil servants, who by virtue of their positions were entitled to government accommodation. On retirement or termination of government services, employees surrender such accommodation. The present stock of government houses is very small and concentrated in Dar es Salaam and the Regional and District headquarters because no new houses have been constructed since independence. In fact it can be rightly argued that government housing may be heading for extinction.

Institutional/Employer Housing

Institutional or employer housing is mostly owned by public organizations, which include educational institutions, banks, and other large national corporations. The purpose of such housing is to provide accommodation to employees at subsidized rents. Similar to government housing, this accommodation is tied to a job and is surrendered to the employer upon leaving employment.

Previous studies indicate that institutional/employer housing stock accounts for 15% of Dar es Salaam's total housing stock (Hoek-Smit, 1990), and is far greater than that owned by the government. However, as a result of the recent privatization of most of the public corporations, the restructured institutions are scrapping the policy of such organizations owning and maintaining company houses. The argument for such a change of policy is in line with the new market-oriented business efficiency, whereby such activities are seen to be outside the ambit of their business lines and are sources of higher operational costs. Instead, most of these organizations have devised housing allowance schemes, whereby workers, according to their positions and entitlements, are given allowances and required to find their own housing accommodation.

As a result of the new policy, almost all large public corporations including financial institutions, but with the exception of educational institutions, have sold, or are in the process of selling their stock of staff houses, either to their staff or through public open tender. In due course, as is the case with government housing, employer housing may no longer exist.

National Housing Corporation's Housing

The last system of housing provision in Tanzania is through construction of dwelling houses by the National Housing Corporation (NHC). Houses built by NHC have been for renting as well as for outright sale although of late, the corporation hardly engages in construction of residential houses for renting. Instead almost all new houses being built are for outright sale. We shall later review the performance of National Housing Corporation, and shall note that despite its contribution to alleviating the housing problem to the urban dwellers of Tanzania, its impact to the housing deficiency in the country is marginal.

POST-INDEPENDENCE SHELTER AND RELATED POLICIES

After independence in 1961, the government realized the acute problems of urbanization and shelter for its people, and also noted the inadequacies of housing schemes started by colonial administrators, which basically focused on the colonial civil servants and foreign businessmen. During the first five year Development Plan (1964-69), the government estimated that housing demand was 517,619 units, while the then existing stock was 217,575 units i.e. 42% of total housing demand. (Of course currently the situation has worsened since supply of housing is only 20% of the country's total demand). The government therefore gave top priority to the development and provision of housing.

Among government policies, legislations and schemes which were directed towards urban and housing development and financing since independence included:

- Establishment of the National Housing Corporation by Act No. 45 of 1962;
- Establishment of the Revolving Housing Loan Fund through Staff Circular No.8 of 1962 and No. 4 of 1965;
- Promulgation of Growth Pole Policy in 1969;
- Nationalization of Buildings in 1971;
- The Squatter Up-grading and Sites and Services Schemes introduced in 1972;
- Establishment of Tanzania Housing Bank (THB) by Act No. 34 of 1972;
- Establishment of the Ardhi Institute (now the University College of Lands and Architectural Studies) in 1972;
- Establishment of Building Research Unit (BRU) in 1971;
- Establishment of Housing Co-operatives;
- Decentralization of Government Administration and Shift of National Capital to Dodoma;

- Sustainable Dar es Salaam City Project;
- Promulgation of National Housing Development Policy in 1981;
- Enactment of New Land Act in 1999; and
- National Human Settlements Development Policy, 1999.

These government initiatives, including their successes and failures are briefly reviewed hereunder.

The National Housing Corporation

The National Housing Corporation, which is the largest formal sector property developer and the biggest landlord in Tanzania, was established by Act No. 45 of 1962 with the objective of providing and facilitating the provision of houses and other buildings in the country by providing loans for building purposes or undertaking construction of housing itself. During the first decade (1962-1975) of NHC existence, the government provided subsidies to the Corporation which were used to construct houses in urban areas, with 60% of construction undertaken in Dar es Salaam where large slum areas existed and where the housing shortage was more critical.

However, NHC did not take off on a sound financial footing. While the corporation expected to get T.shs. 100m from the government and another T.shs.260m as grants from donors between 1964 and 1969, only T.shs. 69.4m and T.Shs.19.4m was obtained respectively. As a result, between 1962 and 1970, the NHC constructed 8,272 housing units only as opposed to the planned construction of 25,800 units between 1964 and 1969. By 1975 a total of 14,485 units had been constructed throughout the country at an average of 1,114 units per year. Although during the second Five Year Plan (1969/70-1974/75), the corporation targeted to construct 2,000 units per year, it was only during 1968/69 and 1971/72 that this target was reached and surpassed (see Table 5.5). The houses built by the NHC during this time were low cost (90%) and medium cost (10%), with 70% of these replacing slum houses. This followed the government policy aimed at providing finished public housing for low-income families to modernize traditional built environments of the urban areas by demolishing squatter settlements through the Slum Clearance Program (Kanyama, 1995). Through this scheme, 3,400 slum structures were pulled down.

The slum clearance scheme did not however solve the housing problem to any significant extent. Although it solved to some extent the quality aspect of the housing problem by building physically better houses, it did not solve the quantity aspect of the problem (the main problem) since, despite destroying many slum houses, only a few were built in their place at an average of 400 units per annum (Kabwogi, 1997).

Meanwhile, in 1973 the Tanzania Housing Bank (THB) came into being, and following this development, NHC's role of providing housing loans was delegated to THB with NHC now being required to borrow from THB for its housing schemes in order to supplement government subsidies and NHC own funds. The other source of funds was the loans and grants extended to the government of Tanzania by the government of the Federal Republic of Germany (FRG) - funds which were also provided in the form of equipment and technical personnel. Sources of T.Shs. 265 million used by NHC to construct 14,485 houses between 1962 and 1975 were as follows:

- Government subsidy 40%
- Grants/Loans - FRG 10%
- TPHF/THB loans 37%
- NHC own funds 13%

In the mid-1970s, the economic recession forced the government to backpedal in granting subventions to NHC, thereby lowering the building capacity of the corporation. As opposed to the period from 1962 to 1975 when the corporation built 14,485 units through the assistance of the government (see Table 5.5), from 1975/76 to 1989/90, the corporation could only build 1,694 houses.

Stren (1990) contrasts the Kenya's National Housing Corporation established in 1967 with Tanzania's NHC. While the Kenyan NHC operated through tendering procedure with private sector contractors, the Tanzanian NHC hired a large staff and built directly. But over the first five-year plan (1964-1969), about 70% of the 5,705 low-cost houses built by the Tanzanian NHC were replacement units, built on the site of the former 'slum' dwellings that had been demolished in Dar es Salaam. Although the Kenyan NHC managed to maintain a relatively high level of production of conventional housing units throughout the 1970s, from a low of 317 in 1976 to a high of 4,085 in 1979, the Tanzanian NHC built an average of less than 100 units per annum between 1975 and 1980, particularly after the government had stopped subsidies. Among the problems cited for the dismal performance of Tanzania's NHC were mismanagement and corruption, inability to keep costs down and unavailability of low-interest funding from the Treasury (Stren, 1990).

The government's failure to provide subsidies to the NHC, which was now directed to borrow its development funds from newly created THB marked the beginning of the decline of NHC (Kironde, 1985). These bank loans were given at commercial interest rates. As if this was not enough, NHC was also forced to charge low rents since the Rent Restriction Act (1964) controlled rent determination, that limited rents to a maximum of 14% of the historical cost of construction.

Until 1984, the Rent Restriction Act did not provide for rent reviews. Given the fact that the government was no longer granting subventions to the corporation, and given high borrowing cost for loans provided by THB, the low rents charged by NHC forced NHC into serious financial distress. This was exacerbated by non-timely payment of rents by its tenants including government departments. The ability of the corporation not only to construct new houses, but also to repair the existing stock of houses dwindled significantly. It was not until 1990 when the government decided to merge NHC with Registrar of Buildings (RoB) that the corporation got a new lease of life since RoB had many centrally located rental buildings that fetched reasonable rents.

Table 5.5: *Housing Units Constructed by National Housing Corporation*

1962/63 to 1974/75			1975/76 to 1989/90		
Year	Units	Cost (Tshs)	Year	Units	Cost (Tshs)
1962/63	51	22,697,858	1975/76	454	27,035,012
1963/64	11	5,000,000	1976/77	150	14,200,000
1964/65	1,014	17,164,520	1977/78	184	5,000,000
1965/66	1,220	17,411,440	1978/79	285	11,800,000
1966/67	1,208	17,582,684	1979/80	102	5,600,000
1967/68	1,504	18,917,032	1980/81	99	2,200,000
1968/69	2,350	18,344,045	1981/82	36	12,400,000
1969/70	875	22,026,047	1982/83	42	11,763,418
1970/71	1,340	30,691,632	1983/84	58	14,384,612
1971/72	2,064	28,182,149	1984/85	46	14,400,000
1972/73	1,242	24,328,581	1985/86	32	21,700,000
1973/74	1,241	23,200,000	1986/87	45	16,400,000
1974/75	340	19,314,758	1987/88	33	29,600,000
			1988/89	53	130,300,000
			1989/90	75	150,900,000
TOTAL	14,485	164,860,746	TOTAL	1,694	467,683,042

Source: NHC Annual Reports

In 1984, a new Rent Restriction Act was passed which allowed rents to be revised based on 14% and 18% of the value of residential and commercial property respectively, although revised rents according to the new Rent Restriction Act were still below economic market rates (see Table 5.6).

Despite the low rents charged by the NHC compared to private landlords, it is unfortunate that the government, for some political reasons, has not adequately and forcefully supported the corporation on the issue of rent regulation and rent levels. On several occasions, there have been political and legal statements and decisions in support of the unrealistic and flimsy complaints and contentions of the tenants who challenge NHC rents. A recent report by the University College

Table 5.6: *NHC rents compared to market rents, 1991.*

Type of accommodation	Typical NHC rents (T.shs.)	Typical market rents(T.shs)
One room fully serviced	9-100	1,200-1,500
One bedroom plus a sitting room, fully serviced	60-200	2,000-2,500
Two bedrooms plus sitting room, self contained:		
• Low cost	68-500	4,500-6,000
• Medium cost	250-800	15,000-20,000
Three bedroom plus sitting room, self contained:		
• Low cost	250-1,000	16,000-25,000
• Medium cost	300-2,400	30,000-45,000
• First class construction	1,200-3,600	45,000-150,000

Source: Institute of Housing Studies and Building Research (1997: 81)

of Lands and Architectural Services (UCLAS) on NHC activities has summed the position very well when it concluded that NHC is still entangled into the bureaucratic and political imbroglios that prevent it from operating as a commercial entity. There is need for a policy, which is not at the mercy and caprice of the politicians.

On the other front, from 1994, the government allowed NHC to sell some of its low-cost and medium-cost residential units to its sitting tenants. By 30th June 1999, some 4,140 requests for buying these units had been approved by the Board of Directors out of which only 1,559 units (39% of the offers) had been sold, earning the corporation a total of T.shs. 1,727,366,677.85. The terms for the sale of these houses are 25% down payment, with the balance paid within one year thereafter, free of interest. After the first year, the balance is charged market lending interest rate for one year, whereupon the offer is withdrawn, and advance payments (except interest) treated as rent paid in advance. The low income of most households and lack of credit facilities like mortgage finance is responsible for the fact that only a few people have managed to buy, not only the units being sold to sitting tenants, but also the few other new houses being constructed by NHC.

Revolving Housing Loan Fund

The colonial government in Tanganyika provided housing to its foreign employees by constructing its own houses in urban areas. After independence, the government's role, activities and the size of its civil service expanded significantly while government quarters did not increase in number. This created a big housing shortage for its civil servants. As a means of curbing this problem, the government, through Staff Circular No. 8 of 1962 and No. 4 of 1965, established the Revolving Housing Loan Fund to finance renovation, construction or purchase of houses for its employees.

However, given the typical problems of government subsidies and the fact that a specialized institution to mobilize financial resources for housing development (THB) had been established, the Revolving Housing Loan Fund was abolished in 1972 and all borrowers transferred to the newly established THB. But it did not take long before operationalization of this fund under THB also failed, largely because:

- The loans issued by the Bank carried high and frequently increasing interest rates. This, coupled with low income capabilities of most civil servants, made it difficult for most civil servants to qualify for adequate loans, and even those who qualified, failed to repay them as required, creating huge arrears and sometimes legal action against them.
- THB was required to operate on commercial principles and therefore was often biased towards big business enterprises at the expense of civil servants and other individuals. This situation worsened from the end of 1980s due to rising default rates on the bank's portfolio arising from an increase in unemployment and rising inflation rate, which in turn, eroded borrowers' ability to meet their mortgage obligation (Dev Consult, 1995).

In recognition of the above fundamental constraints of the housing finance system, the government in 1995 re-introduced the Revolving Housing Loan Fund for its Civil servants. The main features of this facility are:

- The Fund should serve all permanent and pensionable civil servants (Central Government).
- The Fund will initially depend on contributions from the Treasury.
- Collateral will be the property being constructed.
- The Fund should be able to serve about 500 applicants annually in order to have impact.
- The Fund will be used to develop housing in both urban and rural areas throughout the country and will, inter-alia, cover the following conditions:
    - Construction of a new house on surveyed land with Certificate of Title in urban area;
    - Rehabilitation to an existing house with Certificate of Title in urban area;
    - Construction/rehabilitation of a house in a registered village;

- Purchase of an existing house in urban or rural area that meets the first two conditions mentioned above; and
- Redemption of high interest loans from THB.

Loans from this Fund are initially given at an interest rate of 3% per annum. By 1998, the government had released only 300 million shillings to the Fund, which was used to provide housing loans to only 160 civil servants, with a backlog of 611 applications (URT, 1999a).

Growth Pole Policy

The 'growth pole policy' was a major urbanization policy initiated and incorporated into the Second Five Year Development Plan (1969-1974). The Plan acknowledged that urbanization was inevitable and also defined a long-term urban development policy through the 'growth pole strategy.' One of its aims was to reduce the primacy of Dar es Salaam by directing investment and migration towards nine growth poles, namely: Morogoro, Tanga, Moshi, Arusha, Mwanza, Tabora, Dodoma, Mbeya and Mtwara. Implementation of this policy could not succeed well because of lack of co-ordination in the location of industrial projects and lack of public resources for investment in the selected growth poles.

Nationalization of Buildings

The Registrar of Buildings (RoB) was established under the Acquisition of Buildings Act No. 13 of 1971, an Act which empowered the President of the United Republic of Tanzania to acquire non-owner occupied residential and commercial buildings worth more than T.shs. 100,000/= or US $ 5,000 at 1971 prices, in the public interest. A total of 2,900 buildings valued at over US $ 32 million were nationalized. The rationale behind this move was derived from an attempt to break the monopoly enjoyed by the Asian landlords in the urban housing market, but once achieved, the government made little effort to maintain or expand public housing (Campbell, 1990)

The major functions of the RoB were to manage, maintain and repair the acquired buildings/properties, and to collect rent from the tenants in those properties. However, the RoB went also into construction activity of residential and commercial buildings (see Table 5.7). Most of the residential buildings constructed by the RoB in regional capitals were medium and high cost structures that were un-affordable by low-income earners (Kyessi, 1996). The total number of rental units administered by the RoB nationwide before its dissolution in 1990 was 13,250. In 1990, the government decided to repeal the Acquisition of Buildings Act of 1971, which established the Registrar of Buildings, and through

No. 2 of 1990 transferred all properties of RoB to the reconstituted National Housing Corporation. Under this Act, NHC continued to be charged with the responsibilities of providing and facilitating the provision of houses and other buildings in Tanzania for use by members of the public for residential, business, industrial or other purposes.

Table 5.7: *Construction by the Registrar of Buildings 1971-1987*

Year	Commercial		Residential		Total	
	Units	CostT.shs	Units	CostT.shs	Units	CostT.shs
1971	04	1,823154	60	4,433,300	64	6,256,454
1972	02	9,876,421	12	8,236,835	14	18,113,256
1973	14	7,521,422	37	4,788,844	51	12,310,266
1974	01	299,436	--	--	01	299,436
1975	03	4,980,122	11	458,700	14	5,438,822
1976	--	--	--	--	--	--
1977	--	--	--	--	--	--
1978	01	38,400	36	6,916,948	37	6,950,348
1979	17	11,673,155	47	11,863035	64	23,536,190
1980	04	2,770,471	46	11,691,645	50	14,462,110
1981	--	--	06	1,235,145	06	1,235,145
1982	04	1,047,614	49	14,475,145	53	15,522,750
1983	--	--	--	--	--	--
1984	--	--	14	5,185,010	14	5,185,010
1985	01	1,340,558	--	--	01	1,340,558
1986	--	--	175	15,584,985	175	15,584,985
1987	--	--	72	105,850,000	72	105,850,000
Total	51	41,365,752	565	190,719,585	616	232,085,337

Source: Kyessi (1996)

Having sold some of its houses to sitting tenants, the National Housing Corporation boasted of a stock of 18,464 residential and commercial renting units by July 1996. According to 1992 estimates, these buildings were valued at US$ 350 million, out of which 71.43% valued at US $ 250 million were located in Dar es Salaam.

Sites and Services and Squatter Upgrading Programme

As an approach to human settlements development in urban areas, the government in 1972 introduced a scheme called Sites and Services and Squatter Upgrading Programme. This programme was a result of the realization by the government of the fact that people had a responsibility of providing for their own housing while the government's role was to facilitate the efforts of the people towards that end. The government undertook to upgrade squatter areas by providing them with essential services such as water supply, electricity, roads, schools, health centers, sanitation etc. The programme also provided surveyed and serviced plots to the low-income groups for housing purposes and those who were displaced during the upgrading process.

However, the rapidly expanding but unserviced areas that housed many poor people were being incorporated into an urban agglomeration which had neither the organization nor the finance to develop and administer them (Campbell, 1990). For example, the timing of the Squatter Upgrading Scheme and its enlarged scale (four years after it was set out in the Five-Year Plan) indicated a desire to defuse growing worker militancy in the squatter areas (Campbell, 1990). Since this decision coincided with the shift to a nationally coordinated Ujamaa policy with its consequential costs, the government looked for external sources to secure necessary finances.

During the first decade of the Sites and Services Programme, 5 towns - Dar es Salaam, Mbeya, Morogoro, Tabora and Iringa - had been covered. The project was in general, successful in the sense that it increased the housing stock, improved infrastructure and provided community facilities that led to improved health and better security. However, its implementation arrangement could not be sustained because it was beset by the following problems:

- To a large extent, the project, especially the sites and services aspects, benefited the middle income earners instead of the targeted low income category;
- Difficulties in administering cost recovery and cost sharing schemes including poor administration and recovery of housing loans;
- Over-dependency on external donor finance and technical assistance could not allow sustainability of the programme; and
- It applied top-down planning principles at inception and implementation stages. This was a result of the then non-existence of local authorities.

Collapse of the Tanzania Housing Bank and New Thrust in the Re-establishment of Housing Finance System

The Rise and Fall of the Tanzania Housing Bank

The Tanzania Housing Bank (THB) was established by an Act of Parliament No. 34 of 1972 and became operational in 1973 as the only formalized housing finance institution in the country. Before then, the history of housing finance in the country can be traced back to the colonial period, although the growth of housing finance institutions during this period was slow and erratic (Massawe, 1996d). During this period, there were several building societies that were mainly formed by members of various communities, such as Ismailia Community (Ngalomba, 1992). Apart from such societies, the colonial government established the African Urban Loan Fund in 1954. This fund was financed from a revolving loan fund. Through this fund, Africans were encouraged to build houses of improved standards (Ngalomba, 1992). It was intended for those who had the ability to accumulate a small down payment, but who were considered too large a risk for loans from the building societies.

In 1961, the First Permanent Building Society was established. The Society was registered in Northern Rhodesia (now Zambia) but operated in East Africa also. This building society was undertaking savings and deposit mobilization and lending for housing and construction in urban areas.

As East African countries were preparing to gain their independence, the society ceased its lending operations in East Africa and remained with its savings and deposit mobilization functions. In 1963, the East African branches of this society were restructured and a separate institution called First Permanent East Africa Limited, was formed, shareholders being East African countries with the participation of the Commonwealth Development Corporation. The headquarters were moved from Lusaka to Nairobi.

In 1968, the company closed its business in Tanzania after being taken over by the Permanent Housing Finance Company of Tanzania Limited (PHFC), with the government of Tanzania and the Commonwealth Development Corporation as equal shareholders. Lending activities that had been stopped resumed, but the maximum loan was fixed at T.shs. 75,000 (Nnunduma, 1996). However PHFC had two undesirable limitations:

- It restricted financing of housing construction in urban areas where only few urban elite benefited;
- Management agreement between the government and Commonwealth Development Corporation helped to ensure the continuation of foreign domination in housing finance policy.

As a result, the government in 1972 nationalized PHFC and established THB, which took over assets and liabilities of the former. THB's objectives included mobilization of savings for housing development, provision of technical and financial assistance for owner-occupied housing and provision of finance for commercial and industrial buildings development. But THB had a weak capital base with a share capital of only T.shs. 400 million held by three shareholders as follows:

	T.shs. (million)	Percentage
Government of Tanzania	186.0	46.5
National Insurance Corporation (NIC)	120.8	30.2
National Provident Fund (NPF)	93.2	23.3
TOTAL	400.0	100.0

The Tanzania Housing Bank issued three types of mortgage loans. The unsubsidized mortgages were issued from its own funds (main fund), whereas the subsidized mortgages were issued from the Special Forces Fund and the Workers and Farmers Housing Development Fund. By 1995, just before its demise, THB had issued about 16,400 mortgages from its main fund (DevConsult, 1995).

The Workers and Farmers Housing Development Fund was established to make low interest mortgage loans to workers and farmers in both rural and urban areas. Its source of funds was a 2% housing levy charged on the wage bill of employers with more than 10 employees and channeled to THB. However in 1985, these contributions were redirected to the Treasury and the Fund started operating as a revolving fund. Before the suspension of the contributions to THB, a total of T.shs. 1,144,659,000 had been received by the bank, out of which T.shs. 927,865,000 had been disbursed to 21,067 beneficiaries, with the number of mortgages issued dwindling in the last years due to lack of resources, lack of acceptable security in respect of rural loans, very high default rate (82% in 1993) and lack of appropriate legal procedures to deal with the chronic defaulters in the case of unsecured mortgage loans (DevConsult, 1995).

The Special Forces Fund was established in April 1987 to finance purchase of building materials for the employees of the Tanzania Peoples Defense Force, Police Force and Prisons Department. Before suspending government contributions to the Fund, about T.shs. 35,000,000 had been received by the Fund, with only 316 individuals benefiting after a total disbursement of T.shs. 38,740,000. The maximum loan was set at T.shs. 170,000 at an annual interest rate of 4% (DevConsult, 1995).

Given the lack of resources, very few individuals benefited from THB loans. For example, between 1990 and 1992, THB received 176 loan applications but only 44 were approved (Bagachwa, 1995). A study in 1980 (Magembe, et al, 1980) also indicates that hardly 10% of individuals building houses in Dar es Salaam during this period obtained loans from THB. Out of a sample of 95 people interviewed, only 6 people used purely THB loans, while 11 responded that they used a combination of THB loans and own savings. Others (see Table 5.8) used non-THB sources.

In total, between 1973 and 1990/91, THB financed only 40,327 units (or 2240 units per annum) with loans to the tune of T.shs. 3,154.6 million (Kironde, 1996). Apart from the failure to satisfy demand for housing finance, THB faced serious default problems. It is estimated that THB had loan recovery rate of only 22% (Bagachwa, 1995). Of course, there are other critics who blame the poor performance of THB partly on the government itself, which wanted people of different income groups to borrow from THB to build conventional houses, while due to their low income, the needs of some of them could have been better met simply in the sites and services schemes. In these schemes they could have been helped to improve their own housing conditions in situ, rather than being "forced" to borrow large loans for building complete houses, while they had no ability to repay such loans (Massawe, 1996d).

It was therefore no wonder when the government declared THB bankrupt and liquidated it in 1995. Apart from default problems, other factors which caused the collapse of THB were a weak capital base, dependency on short-term borrowing to finance long-term assets, poor record keeping, poor collateral, mal-administration and corruption.

Table 5.8: *Gross Statistical Distribution of Housing Finance Sources*

Source	Number	Percentage
1. Own Savings only	61	64.21
2. THB loans only	06	06.31
3. THB loans and own Savings	11	11.60
4. Compensation only	02	02.10
5. Compensation and own savings	03	03.15
6. Employer's loans	01	01.05
7. Pension and own savings	03	03.15
8. Inheritance	01	01.05
9. No response	07	07.38
TOTAL	95	100.00

Source: Magembe *et al*, (1980)

Re-establishment of Housing Finance System in Tanzania

The collapse of the Tanzania Housing Bank in 1995 was a major setback to the country's efforts towards housing development, because this was the only formalized housing finance lending institution in Tanzania. Even before the collapse of THB, and particularly after its demise, there has been a growing concern on the part of the government, other institutions and professionals on the urgent need to establish a mortgage finance facility in Tanzania. It must be emphasized that an institution of affordable finance for housing is an absolute necessity if low-income households are to be helped to acquire shelter.

In mid 1997, the Ministry for Lands and Human Settlements Development in collaboration with National Housing Corporation commissioned a study, which was undertaken by Shelter Afrique, on how the country can establish a mortgage facility for housing finance. The final report of the Shelter Afrique study was presented to the government so that it could work out the modalities of establishing a workable housing mortgage facility in the country in collaboration with other relevant institutions like Parastatal Pensions Fund (PPF), National Housing Corporation (NHC) and other interested local and international agencies. It is disheartening to note that the government is apparently not serious in implementing the recommendations for re-establishing this facility, because more than three years have gone by since the Shelter Afrique's report was presented, but no positive steps have been taken.

From an empirical study by Mahanga (1998), there is already a relatively conducive economic, legal and financial environment in the country to allow the establishment of a workable and sustainable housing finance system. Various recommendations for establishing a sustainable housing finance system in Tanzania put forward by Mahanga (1998) and Diamond (1998) are as follows:

1) The government and relevant institutions should ensure that the conducive economic, legal and financial reforms, which are currently being implemented in Tanzania, are enhanced and sustained to allow a robust housing market development.
2) Although a specialized primary housing finance institution is desirable and may be established, other commercial banks should also be encouraged and motivated to undertake mortgage lending for housing.
3) To deal with the problem of liquidity which normally characterizes primary housing finance operations, Tanzania should introduce a form of liquidity facility, such as secondary mortgage market or other forms of secondary finance facility that would be able to tap funds from domestic capital markets, either directly from pensions, social security and insurance funds, or through the stock exchange.
4) The current government's efforts to establish a mortgage finance facility in which its institutions like PPF, NSSF and NHC would be the owners or shareholders of the new institution, should be a short-term take-off strategy for the purposes of providing initial working capital and laying down institutional and operational framework for the institution. In the long run, these public institutions should hold minority shares, if any, in the institution

and leave private sector to own and operate the system. Available evidence suggests that governments all over the world lack dispassionate judgment and incentive to run commercial activities. Moreover, there is currently a global shift from public to private enterprise setting, with minimum interference from the government. By PPF, NSSF and the like (which are public organizations), having majority shares in the new institution, the latter would also effectively be a public institution. This should be avoided. PPF, NSSF and NIC should mainly participate in the housing finance institution as institutional investors by channeling their long-term funds to long-term mortgage lending through secondary market operation.

5) Realizing that the household sector is a net supplier of savings to the rest of the economy, households should be given incentives to save with financial institutions. The first incentive in this regard would be to establish a housing finance system, since access to mortgage finance provides a strong incentive for people to save. Further, financial institutions should be innovative in the design of appropriate instruments that would induce households to save more. Such instruments should have characteristics that protect the saver against wealth erosion. In this way savings by individuals will be a source of funds for housing finance.
6) The current lending and interest rate policy in Tanzania motivates financial institutions to invest more in short-term deposits, Treasury bills and Government bonds, rather than in long-term securities. To foster innovation and appropriate risk taking by financial institutions, the Government and the Bank of Tanzania should discourage the current desire of financial institutions in short-term deposits/bonds and Treasury bills. This will require a change in macro-economic policy that induces banks and other financial institutions to redirect part of domestic savings into long-term mortgage finance.
7) In case liquidity facilities are established in Tanzania, such institutions should issue mortgage bonds, which should then be sold to investors - including long-term institutional investors - for housing finance. The use of mortgage bonds is a very promising way of attracting capital into the housing sector.
8) A secondary mortgage market, when started, should rely on securitization of originated mortgages which should then be sold to long-term investors in order to raise funds. The use of securitization is, in fact, a special case of funding through mortgage bonds. However, unlike the mortgage bond system, securitization requires considerable expertise in structuring the instrument, the pricing of mortgages, the legal aspects and the marketing procedures to sell the mortgage-backed securities (MBS).

9) In view of the current levels of salaries, particularly in the government service, the government should make deliberate efforts to increase levels of salaries for its civil servants to enable them afford housing loans. It is, of course, realized that such a move need to go hand in hand with higher productivity to avoid possible inflation which may render salary increases worthless.
10) The government should encourage and facilitate the development of informal sector activities, because such activities help households to augment their incomes.
11) Cognizant of the low-income levels of most Tanzanians, property developers, such as the National Housing Corporation, should put more emphasis on the construction of affordable low-cost houses. Consideration should be put also on semi-finished (core) houses, which are sold and left to be finished by buyers at their own pace as their income flow allows.
12) Interest rate in mortgage loans is considered to be the cost of the loan, because at higher levels of interest rates, the payments are higher and the amount households can afford to borrow (can afford the repayment on) is lower. Therefore, the new housing finance institutions should structure interest rates in such a way as to make the loans affordable to the mortgagors. Because fixed interest rates results in diminution of the real value of repayments to the detriment of the lender, house finance institutions will wish to use adjustable interest rates. While such adjustable interest rates should be set at about the current bank lending rates (to attract investment in housing finance), housing loans should be indexed for inflation or wage levels.
13) Another likely obstacle to the affordability of households is the owner's equity or advance payment requirement. Housing finance institutions are likely to demand between 20% and 30% of the value of the house as owner's equity. For example, this may translate into not less than T.shs. 2 million for a low-cost house of between Tshs.10 million and T.shs. 15 million. Many mortgage loan seekers may not afford the amount. Therefore, some guarantees should be made available to households. These may include guarantees from employers for their employees, or from pension, social security and insurance funds against workers contributions or insurance policies.
14) A system that allows proper underwriting of the loan should be put in place. This is a process of assessing the ability and willingness of the borrower to repay. The underwriting process should include confirmation of borrower's employment and income, assessment of stability of employment and prospects for retrenchment, willingness of employers to deduct repayments at payroll, past history of debt repayment including outstanding debts, and criminal record. Where a borrower has no formal sector income, there should be

ways to develop evidence of his income or confidence in repayment capacity and willingness.

15) Repayment of housing loans is tied to easy and reliable access to the house itself as a collateral. There should be a clear and effective policy that turns houses into reliable collateral for long-term loans. This will require appropriate provisions in the new Land Act. The Act should create and enforce property rights. Foreclosure or other such provisions in the Act should enable the lenders easy access to the collateral for sale and/or recovery of the loan should the borrower default/fail to repay.

16) Reasons for defaults in repaying mortgage loans as per findings by various research studies should be carefully studied and analyzed by the housing finance institutions in the offing. These findings are as follows:
   - Default is directly influenced by the age of the borrower. The older the borrower is, the greater the chance of defaulting;
   - Default is inversely influenced by the annual income of the borrower. The lower the income, the greater the likelihood of the borrower to default;
   - Default is inversely associated with amount of equity (down-payment) provided by the borrower. The lower the equity, the greater the likelihood of default;
   - As monthly repayments increase, the magnitude of default also increases;
   - Default is directly related to number of years set for repayment, such that the longer the repayment period, the greater the likelihood of default;
   - The higher the level of lending rate, the higher the magnitude of default;
   - Default is positively related to market value of property, such that the higher the market value, the greater the likelihood of default;
   - There is direct relationship between default and cost of construction of the property, such that the higher the construction cost, the greater the probability of default;
   - An inverse relationship exists between default and the expected rental income for the property (in case of loan taken to acquire a house for rental). The higher the expected rental income, the lesser the probability of default; and
   - The loan-value ratio is positively related to default. The higher the loan-value ratio, the greater the likelihood of default.

Building Research Unit (BRU)

The Building Research Unit (BRU) was established by the government in 1971 with the objective of researching into better ways of enhancing housing development in Tanzania. Apart from conducting research in different building materials, the Unit also organizes lectures, seminars and exhibitions so as to disseminate researched information, particularly to rural construction units, supervisors of self-help housing and village governments, rural artisans and the public at large.

The Building Research Unit had, in collaboration with local agencies, embarked on housing improvement campaigns (Better Housing Campaigns or Nyumba Bora), which covered 39 districts in the country. It also built demonstration houses based on local conditions (see, for example, Kirobo, 1977).

University College of Lands and Architectural Studies (UCLAS)

As a move towards equipping the country with expertise in land management, building economics and shelter issues in general, the government established Ardhi Institute, which has now been elevated to a constituent college of the University of Dar es Salaam by the name of the University College for Lands and Architectural Studies (UCLAS). Ardhi Institute was upgraded to a higher learning institution in 1972 with the aim of training and researching in architecture, town and rural planning, quantity surveying, land valuation, building economics and public health engineering. Professionals trained from this institution work with local authorities, the central government and the private sector in the development of the human settlement sector.

Lack of working tools and funds, and declining national economy have, however, contributed towards the failure of the country to fully utilize graduates from this institution, and some of them have in fact turned to other types of jobs (Kyessi, 1996)

The Centre for Human Settlements Studies (now Institute for Housing Studies and Building Research), at the Ardhi Institute, was started in 1978 with the mandate of offering continuing education in the form of short courses, seminars and conferences, research and consultancy services in the area of human settlement. Again, lack of funds for research and training has hindered effective functioning of the institute.

Housing Cooperatives

As early as 1962, the Government of Tanzania (then Tanganyika) began to mobilize people to build better houses through mutual self-help approaches. However, the first housing co-operative which was known as Mwenge Housing Co-operative was formed in 1971, and since then many housing co-operatives have been started all over the country. By June 1988, the Ministry of Local Government, Co-operatives Development and Marketing had already registered a total of 72 housing co-operatives in the whole of Tanzania (Ndatulu and Makileo, 1989). Housing co-operatives have, however, not been successful in the country because of the following reasons:

- Lack of clear government policy on how these housing co-operatives should operate;
- Institutional constraints especially when it comes to allocation of scarce surveyed plots and building materials;
- Inadequate assistance from the government;
- Lack of finance and human resources mobilization strategies;
- Poor administration;
- Lack of competent and honest leadership.

As Ndatulu and Makileo (1989) have argued, poor implementation of co-operative housing policy has left most of them as nothing but a group of mixed gathering of individuals simply seeking shelter, with disregard to the improvement of physical infrastructure and services. An example is the Mwenge Housing Co-operative where, after the initial installation of infrastructure by the Dar es Salaam City Council, individual members have been practicing urban horticulture, disregarding altogether the improvement of physical infrastructure through community participation. Eventually, trenches have been blocked with silt; access roads are un-serviced, and garbage is disposed haphazardly in open spaces, resulting in the spread of diseases and creating public nuisance.

Decentralization of Government Administration and the Shift of the National Capital to Dodoma

The government decentralized its administration and decision making (devolution of power) to regional and district levels in 1972. Alongside the decentralization, local governments and urban authorities were abolished in that year until 1978 and 1982 when Urban Local Authorities and Rural District Councils respectively, were re-introduced. The absence of urban authorities between 1972 and 1978 exacerbated the state of urban infrastructure and services.

But as suggested by Rweyemamu (1974), the effect of decentralization was not a devolution of power and responsibility to the regions and districts, but a de-concentration of government offices out of Dar es Salaam. This step was also the death knell of urban administration as the locus of decision-making shifted to Regional Councils where concerns for broader development issues ended even the maintenance of basic urban programmes like water supply, sewage and roads. At the same time, local government staff were reallocated and funds for urban development diverted resulting in high levels of unplanned 'shanty town' development.

The absence of urban administration led to the deterioration in the level of basic services, and failed to ensure that settlement corresponded to the basic urban plan. Squatting rose sharply to an average of 5,000 dwelling units per year between 1969 and 1972, before declining to around 3,000 units per year in the late 1970s (Campbell, 1990). In general, by the mid-1970s, approximately 44% of Dar es Salaam population was living in squatters and by 1979, eleven persons lived in every squatter house compared to only about 8 persons per house in 1972, a rise in the occupancy rate by 40%.

In 1973, the Government decided to shift the national capital from Dar es Salaam to Dodoma as a measure of reducing congestion in Dar es Salaam and promoting growth and development of the hinterland and other parts of Tanzania given that Dodoma is in the centre of the country. The capital transfer programme has, however, not been successful to date because of financial and management problems.

The Sustainable Cities Programme, Tanzania

The Sustainable Dar es Salaam City Project (SDP), which is now known as the Sustainable Cities Programme (SCP) -Tanzania, was launched in 1992. It aims at managing the growth and development of the rapidly growing city of Dar es Salaam, the biggest industrial and commercial centre in the country, in a sustainable manner. The project, which is in lieu of the Master Plan approach, aims at strengthening the local capacity to plan and manage the development of the city in a participatory manner by all actors and stakeholders with necessary co-ordination and in partnership with developers in services and infrastructure provision. The concept is currently being replicated in other municipalities in the country with the UNDP (Habitat) assistance, after which SDP is now known as Sustainable Cities Programme, Tanzania.

The introduction of SDP has increased public awareness on the role and contribution of various stakeholders and the private sector as a whole in the planning, development and management of human settlements. In addition, it has made the planning system more transparent and accountable to urban residents than before. Further, it has brought in more integration of various sectoral and community participation from planning, implementation and management (URT, 1999a).

The National Environmental Policy

The National Environmental Policy (URT, 1997a) was promulgated in 1997, and it underscores the fact that the survival of man depends on his harmonious relationship with the natural elements. The policy emphasizes the need to manage the environment and its natural resources in ways which enhance the potential for growth and the opportunity for sustainable development of present and future generations. Environmental degradation leads to widespread poverty and vice versa. Environmental protection and conservation is an integral part of sustainable development and is indeed a social and economic necessity.

The policy document further reiterates two points. First, sustainable development means achieving a quality of life that can be maintained for many generations because it is socially desirable, economically viable and environmentally sustainable. Secondly, development is sustainable if it takes place within nature's tolerance limits.

Of particular significance to our study, the National Environmental Policy appreciates that urbanization is a major issue in the transformation of human settlements; and that a growing proportion of Tanzanians will soon live in urban centres, which are more and more subject to drastic crisis, poverty, environmental decline, inadequate urban services and access to serviced land and shelter.

National Land Act, 1999

Before the enactment of the new Land Act in 1999, one of the contributing factors to housing problem in Tanzania has been the system of land tenure. Tanzania's land policy, in terms of legislation, institutional framework and land management delivery system go back to the colonial period. The main enactment which regulated land tenure in the country was the Land Ordinance, Cap 113 of 1923. The revised Land Ordinance, Cap 113 of 1962 nationalized all land. Section 3(1) of the Ordinance declared the whole of Tanganyika (whether occupied or not) as public land. Under that Act, unimproved land had no official value and could not be charged for or taxed. Individuals could hold government rights of occupancy for a period of 33 years, 66 years or a maximum of 99 years and pay annual land rents to the government during the period. Customary land tenure was also recognized. People could occupy land in unsurveyed areas without paying land rents. According to the ordinance these were dubbed "deemed rights of occupancy."

Although officially land in Tanzania had no value, there had long been a land market and prices had been, and are still, very high, particularly in Dar es Salaam where there is an acute shortage of developable land. As can be noted from Table 5.9, over 50% of land in urban areas was purchased (in Dar es Salaam it is 69.4%).

High land prices increase housing costs, worsening the housing problem. As a result, some people fail to acquire plots and resort to building in disaster prone areas such as areas with frequent floods. On the part of the government,

Table 5.9: *Percentage of Land Tenure by Area*

Land Tenure	All	Urban	Dar es Salaam
Inheritance	0.30	0.40	0.60
Public Authority	21.3	16.6	7.30
Clearing	19.8	11.7	11.9
Purchased	45.5	50.0	69.4
Other sources	5.60	10.0	4.60
Reason not given	7.40	14.3	6.00
Total	100.0	100.0	100.0

Source: *Tanzania: Challenge of Reforms* Vol. II, World Bank 1996,

experience shows that an official survey and registration process was taking an average of 4 to 5 years from the time an official offer has been made to the allottee (Devconsult, 1995).

Having recognized the problems of Land Policy in Tanzania, the government adopted a new National Land Policy in 1997, following of which the Parliament endorsed the resultant new Land Act in 1999. The Land Ordinance Cap 113 has now been repealed. The new land policy and Act have paved way for an open and properly functioning land market system.

Following the new Land Policy and Act, the allocation of land for residential and institutional uses whenever possible will be on a cost recovery bases, and prime residential, commercial and industrial land will be allocated in a transparent manner such as open tender or auction. Further, land is now considered to have value although a landholder can only transfer the right of occupancy and not ownership. Special taxes will be imposed so as to deter speculation. Disposition of land in the form of sale and mortgages will be allowed to transfer obligation to meet prescribed development conditions. Since land is now recognized to have value, compensation for acquired land will be based on the concept of opportunity cost and will include, among others, the market value of the property. Such compensation should be paid promptly, otherwise interest at market rate will be imposed.

National Human Settlements Development Policy

As noted earlier, housing development in the country is still individually/privately dominated such that individuals initiate about 98% of housing development in the country. In urban areas, the proportion of individual contribution is about 90% on average, while in Dar es Salaam city it is approximately 75%.

Despite so many programmes and policies enunciated by the government as seen above, the critical dilemma of the government initiatives was that the institutions established and the programmes enunciated worked incoherently for lack of clear national policy on housing or human settlements development.

It was not until 1981 when the government at long last endorsed a National Housing Development Policy (NHDP), which however, could not be effectively implemented. Realizing the shortcomings of the NHDP, the government has already prepared a National Human Settlements Development Policy, a draft of which was awaiting final government approval at the time of publishing this book.

According to the draft policy, the development of human settlements in the country had not been sustainable because it had not combined socio-economic development with environmental conservation and protection, thereby aggravating urban and rural poverty.

The policy recognizes that human settlements development and shelter delivery are inseparable and require a coherent and comprehensive policy, which links them in a common framework. The need to develop a National Human Settlements Development Policy arises from the Government's resolve to address and reverse the deterioration of human settlements' conditions in the country. The government thus intends to facilitate adequate delivery of shelter and the development of sustainable human settlements in the country. The policy aims at harnessing existing initiatives in shelter delivery and infrastructure investment by various actors in the public, private, informal and community sectors as well as guide the rapid transformation of the settlements pattern (URT, 1999a).

The policy highlights goals, objectives, policy statements and action plans for every stakeholder and actor in the whole issue of human settlements development. These include the central government, local governments, private sector, community-based organizations (CBOs), non-governmental organizations (NGOs), and, not least, the affected people.

As with past policies and programmes, the author is however skeptical with the new policy, since it does not clearly address the questions of the capacity and priority of the government in the mobilization of all stakeholders, regularization of institutional frameworks and the whole issue of sustainability. Given the country's poor economy and so-called national priorities, it is doubtiful whether the government is soon going to be serious with urban settlements problems. Although the role of provision and improvement of housing in urban areas should now be left to private sector, individuals and their communities, the government still has monumental task of facilitating these efforts through provision of basic infrastructure, mobilizing stakeholders and instituting legal and administrative frameworks.

6

HOUSING RELATED SERVICES IN DAR ES SALAAM

Using mainly secondary data and information, we shall in this chapter review the situation of housing and related services in the city of Dar es Salaam, which apart from being the largest urban centre in Tanzania, was also the case study area for the research for this book. The aim is to attempt, eventually, to confirm research findings from the said study so as to come up with supportive conclusions and recommendations.

ADMINISTRATIVE BACKGROUND OF DAR ES SALAAM

The city of Dar es Salaam (within which the study area of Yombo Vituka is situated) lies on the East African coast between longitude 39° and 39°33' East and between latitudes 6°34' and 7°10' South of the Equator. The city has the characteristics of tropical coastal climate. Rainfall ranges between 750 mm and 1,000 mm in a year and the temperature between 24°c and 30°c. The relative humidity ranges between 67% and 96%.

Dar es Salaam is still the administrative capital of Tanzania, although the government had since 1973 decided to shift the national capital to the central town of Dodoma, and few administrative functions such as the National Assembly and at least one ministry (Ministry of Local Government and Regional Administration) have at the time of publishing this book effectively moved to Dodoma. Dar es Salaam, which is also the major port, commercial and industrial centre in Tanzania has an estimated population of 2,500,000 people or 25% of the country's urban population (URT, 1997b). However, other reports (see, for example, URT, 1996) give an estimate of 3,000,000 people as the population of the city by 1995. The population density of the city is between 50 and 300 inhabitants per hectare, or between 20 and 120 people per acre. Almost 75% of the city is in squatter areas. According to the 1988 population census, the crude death rate of Dar es Salaam is 14.3%.

Like other urban centres, the rapid urbanization facing Dar es Salaam (see Table 6.1) is attributable mainly to rural-urban migration and natural growth. As can be observed from Table 6.1, by the turn of the century, the city is anticipated to have 3,500,000 people.

Table 6.1: *Dar es Salaam Population Changes*

Year	Population	Annual compound rate of change (%)
1867	900	--
1874	10,000	41.1
1913	34,000	3.20
1943	450,000	0.90
1952	99,140	9.00
1967	272,515	7.00
1978 (census)	843,090	10.8
1988 (census)	1,360,850	4.90
1992 (estimate)	2,300,000	7.20
2000 (projected)	3,500,000	7.20

Source: URT (1997b)

The boundaries of Dar es Salaam have been fixed and changed several times; in 1933, 1935, 1948, 1961, 1966, 1968, 1978 and 1984. There have also been several administrative changes in the city set-up during the last fifty years. Dar es Salaam had been a township until 1949 when it became a municipality. In 1961, Dar es Salaam became one of the districts in the Coast Region under the City Council. In 1972, the Municipal Council, like other urban authorities, was abolished in the wake of Decentralization Policy. The Dar es Salaam Municipal Council thus lost its municipality status, and the district became a region with three distinct districts of Ilala, Kinondoni and Temeke, which were administered by respective District Development Councils (DDCs). The Dar es Salaam City Council (DCC) was established in 1978. At this stage it included only urban wards until 1984 when it encompasses also the rural wards as shown in Table 6.2.

Due to mismanagement, the Government, in 1996, dissolved the Dar es Salaam City Council and appointed an interim City Commission. The Commission initially was to operate for one year, but its term of office was later extended to the year 2 000. The appointment of Dar es Salaam City Commission has tremendously improved the management of the city in terms of planning and revenue collection. Revenue collection increased by almost ten times per annum compared to the era of Dar es Salaam City Council. Infrastructure in general has also improved as a result of proper governance and better management of the city's resources.From the year 2000, when the Dar es Salaam City Commission went out of office, the city's governance is through three distinct districts that are independent and autonomous municipalities plus the Greater Dar es Salaam City Council to oversee common city infrastructures and functions of a general nature.

Table 6.2: *Dar es Salaam districts and their wards*

KINONDONI URBAN WARDS	ILALA URBAN WARDS	TEMEKE URBAN WARDS
Mzimuni	Kariakoo Mbagala	
Magomeni	Mchafukoge	Miburani
Ndugumbi	Gerezani	Mtoni
Makurumla	Kisutu	Temeke
Manzese	Kivukoni	Kurasini
Kigogo	Jangwani	Keko
Mabibo	Upanga East	
Ubungo	Upanga West	
Kinondoni	Ilala	
Mwananyamala	Mchikichini	
Msasani		
Tandale Kawe		
RURAL WARDS	RURAL WARDS	RURAL WARDS
Kunduchi	Buguruni	Yombo Vituka
Kibamba	Vingunguti	Charambe
Goba	Kipawa	Kigamboni
Bunju	Tabata	Kibiji
Mbweni	Ukonga	Samagila
	Kinyerezi	Vijibweni
	Pugu	Kisarawe
	Msongola	Trangoma
		Chamazi
		Kibanda

Source: DCC Ward Map, 1995

The Dar es Salaam city has an estimated Gross Regional Product (GRP) of T. Shs. 316.5 billion (or equivalent of US $ 592.7 million) at 1994 prices (URT, 1997b). In 1994, the GRP per capita of Dar es Salaam city was estimated at T. Shs. 197,107 (or US $ 397.1). These figures imply that economically, the city accounts for 19.1% of the GNP of the whole country.

According to the informal sector survey, in 1993 the percentage of the employed population whose activity is part of the informal sector is approximately 56%. Table 6.3 indicates the trend of Gross Regional Product of Dar es Salaam city during 1992 - 1994.

Table 6.3. *Gross Dar es Salaam Regional and National (Domestic) Products*

Year	GRP of DSM (Bil. shs)	GRP of DSM (Mil.US$)	GDP of TZ (Bil.shs)	GDP of TZ (Mil. US$)	% of GRP to GDP
1992	200.9	485.3	1,031.0	2,492.7	19.5
1993	243.8	504.8	1,289.0	2,668.7	18.9
1994	316.5	592.7	1,660.0	3,108.6	19.1

Source: National Accounts of Tanzania 1976-1994, Bureau of Statistics, 1995.

Population Growth and Housing Problem in Dar es Salaam City

The last census for Dar es Salaam was carried out in 1988. Since then estimates for the city's population and its annual growth have been done through different studies. These studies give varying estimates since they are based on different perceptions and criteria. For example, while some reports (see, for example, URT, 1995) give a population of 1,821,151 people in 1995, others (see, for example, URT, 1997b) estimate a population of 2,500,000 people; yet other studies (see, for example, URT, 1996) give an estimate of 3,000,000 people in the same year of 1995.

In spite of these estimate differences, the population of Dar es Salaam city (for both urban and rural wards) is currently around 2,500,000 people. This figure is in line with estimations by the last planning study of Dar es Salaam of City Master Plan prepared by Marshall Macklin Monaghan in 1979 (The MMM Master Plan), which estimated that the population of Dar es Salaam in 1999 would be 2,461,000 people (see Table 6.4).

As demonstrated in Table 6.4, the city of Dar es Salaam has gone through various periods of relatively rapid growth due to rural-urban migration in the 1960s, followed by periods of consolidation and/or decline such as during the late 1980s. Nevertheless, the growth rates for Dar es Salaam have historically exceeded those for the Tanzanian mainland as a whole as depicted by Table 6.5.

Table 6.4: *M.M.M. Master Plan Projections of Dar es Salaam Population*

Year	Population	Growth Rate
1979	932,000	--
1984	1,269,000	6.37%
1989	1,642,000	5.29%
1999	2,461,000	4.13%

Source: URT, 1995

Table 6.5: *Actual Population and Growth Rates*

	Dar es Salaam		Tanzania Mainland	
Year	Population	Growth Rate	Population	Growth Rate
1884	11,500	-	-	-
1948	79,611	3.1.%	-	-
1967	349,559	6.7%	11,958,654	3.2%
1978	851,522	8.4%	17,039,499	2.8%
1988	1,360,860	4.8%	22,533,758	

Source: URT, 1995

As documented by URT (1995), the factors that contributed to the restricted growth rate in the late 1980s were a direct result of the rapid population growth experienced during the 1960s. Some of these factors are:

- Acute shortage of existing housing and consequently higher rents;
- Stiff competition for land resulting in insufficient surveyed and serviced plots both for residential and industrial development;
- High compensation costs involved in acquiring land for development;
- Overcrowding and rapid growth of squatters and slum areas;
- Health hazards and high incidence of crime;
- Government policies of nationalization of properties which discouraged private investment in housing industry, coupled with poor performance of public housing sector;
- The emergence of Dodoma as an administrative centre, shifting emphasis away from Dar es Salaam;
- Inadequate supportive infrastructure such as roads, water supply, electricity and solid waste management as well as social amenities such as schools and hospitals;
- Recent policies such as structural adjustment programme and trade liberalization has made other urban centres in the country equally attractive for trade and business, and especially given that land is easily available in other urban centres;
- The increasing rate of unemployment and recent redundancies in the government;
- Urban sprawl into peri-urban land, thereby creating long travelling distances and high transport costs.

The rapid urban growth rate of Dar es Salaam has compounded housing problem in the city, where the overcrowding levels confirm housing shortage. Assuming that overcrowding means more than two persons per room, the percentage of families in overcrowded homes represent 34.4% of all households in the city (URT, 1999a). The average number of persons living in one house is 11 (URT, 1994b). A recent report covering eight residential areas in Ilala and Temeke districts in Dar es Salaam (URT, 1997d) also indicated that in almost 26% of all houses surveyed, there were more than 5 inhabitants; while rooms with 3 people or more accounted for almost 47%. The survey also found that about 58% of all households had only one room each (see Table 6.6).

Table 6.6: *Characteristics of Household in selected areas in Dar es Salaam*

Household Occupancy		Rooms per Household		Room Occupancy	
Persons per house	%	Rooms per house	%	Persons per room (excluding single person households)	%
Single person	21.4	No room(s)	2.5	<1 person	2.5
2 persons	15.3	1 room	57.6	1 person	18.4
3 persons	15.3	2 rooms	18.2	2 persons	32.3
4 persons	13.1	3 rooms	9.60	3 persons	22.0
5 persons	9.90	>3 rooms	12.1	>3 persons	24.8
>5 persons	25.9				

Source: URT (1997d)

LAND USE AND LAND DELIVERY SYSTEM IN DAR ES SALAAM

Land Use Plan

According to the proposal by MMM Master Plan of 1979, population densities for residential areas in Dar es Salaam should have been between 12,500 and 13,800 persons per km^2 which include low density, medium density and high density plots in the ratio of 1:2:7 respectively. However, from Table 6.7, it is evident that the actual densities are much higher than those proposed by the MMM Master Plan, and since the ward areas shown in Table 6.7 are total areas including all lands such as hazard lands, open spaces, industrial and institutional, the population densities for strictly residential areas are even higher than those indicated in Table 6.7, evidencing the extent of overcrowding.

From the 1992 aerial photography, one easily observes major departures from MMM Master planning in relation to the envisaged urban structure, the extent of urban sprawl, the proposed planned areas and the densities. The departure is explained by the fact that the basic assumptions of the MMM Master Plan on infrastructural development and development control have proved difficult to implement. Master plans require interpretation by qualified staff.

However, due to the shortage of sufficiently qualified manpower to effect implementation, the problems of controlling the Dar es Salaam Master Plan have been enormous (Kihunrwa, 1981). Since the Master Plan (and particularly before the City Commission was appointed in 1996) there has been little or no infrastructural development. All annual development budgets of both the central government and the City Council have tended to emphasize the rehabilitation of existing services. Moreover, the City Council could not push the establishment of an effective mechanism for development control (URT, 1995). The result has been a concentration of residential development along the major transportation axes of Bagamoyo, Morogoro, Pugu and Kilwa roads. Tables 6.8. and 6.9 illustrate Dar es Salaam's land use by ward and by land typology respectively. Table 6.10 shows projected land development up to the year 2002 based on an estimated population of 2,000,000 in the year 2002.

Table 6.7: *Population - Historical Data*

Ward	Area (km2)	1967 Census	1967 Pop. Density/ km2	1978 Census	1978 Pop. Density/ km2	1967-1978 growth) rate(%)	1988 Census	1988 Pop. Density /km2	1978-1988 growth Rate (%)
KINONDONI DISTRICT									
1. Magomeni	1.4	10,604	7574.3	14256	10183	2.7	16994	12139	2
2. Makurumla	3.3	12,079	660.3	29422	8916	8.4	53991	16361	6
3. Ndugumbi	1.1	9,810	8918.2	24146	21951	8.5	32736	29760	3
4. Tandale	3.0	4,219	1406.3	24699	8233	17.4	58413	19471	9
5. M'nyamala	6.0	13,070	2178.3	44614	7436	11.8	72508	12085	5
6. Msasani	17.5	12,654	723.1	25760	1472	6.7	51293	2931	7
7. Kinondoni	3.1	6,754	2178.7	27879	8993	13.8	42387	13673	4
8. Mzimuni	1.5	11,361	7574.0	20153	13435	5.3	23985	15990	2
9. Kigogo	1.6	499	311.9	16343	10214	37.3	21222	13264	3
10.Mabibo	11.1	3,461	311.8	28187	2539	21.0	45963	4141	5
11.Manzese	3.5	3,352	957.7	28522	8149	21.5	54499	15571	7
12.Ubungo	63.2	15,261	241.5	23825	377	4.1	46980	743	7
13.Kibamba	97.7	2,649	27.1	8731	89	11.5	16711	171	7
14.Goba	44.3	3,539	79.9	12677	286	12.3	4753	107	-9
15.Kawe	22.4	9,355	417.6	17528	783	5.9	44085	1968	10
16.Kunduchi	53.6	6,326	118.0	11713	219	5.8	22743	424	7
17.Mbweni	24.0	763	31.8	1316	55	5.1	2159	90	5
18.Bunju	147.0	4,066	27.7	5032	34	2.0	9977	68	7
Sub-Total	505.3	129,822	256.9	364803	722	9.8	621399	1230	6

Table 6.7: *continued...*

Ward	Area (km2)	1967 Census	1967 Pop. Density/ km2	1978 census	1978 Pop. Density/ km2	1967-1978 growth) rate(%)	1988 Census	1988 Pop. Density /km2	1978-1988 Growth Rate (%)
ILALA DISTRICT									
1. Ukonga	42.2	5756	136	24,860	589	14	45203	1071	6
2. Pugu	22.3	826	37	2,011	90	8	6226	279	12
3. Msongola	71.5	2191	31	5,285	73	8	13351	187	10
4. Tabata	19.1	850	45	2,070	08	8	18465	967	25
5. Kinyerezi	28.0	1721	63	2,861	102	5	3048	109	1
6. Ilala	3.6	24545	6818	30,784	8,551	2	35048	9736	1
7. Mchikichini	0.6	13904	23173	14,319	23,865	0	15040	25067	2
8. Vingunguti	8.5	10006	1177	18,899	2,223	6	33690	3964	6
9. Kipawa	10.1	10559	045	16,277	1,612	4	36910	3655	9
10. Buguruni	2.4	9393	3914	32,679	13,616	12	48247	20103	4
11. Kariakoo	0.7	10632	15189	11,606	16,580	1	12569	17956	1
12. Jangwani	0.4	10892	27230	13,572	33,930	2	15320	38300	1
13. Gerezani	0.9	876	973	7689	8,543	22	7487	8319	0
14. Kisutu	0.6	7413	12355	7939	13,232	1	8358	13930	1
15. Mchafukoge	0.6	9275	15458	10907	18,178	2	8547	14245	-2
16. Upanga East	1.3	7625	5865	8441	6,493	1	9807	7544	2
17. Upanga West	1.0	5864	5864	10772	10,772	6	11020	11020	0
18. Kivukoni	1.7	4316	2539	5662	3,331	2.5	5372	3160	-1
Sub-Total	215.5	36644	634	26633	1052	4.7	33708	1549	4
TEMEKE DISTRICT									
1. Kigamboni	28.0	7967	284	17406	622	7.4	26078	931	4
2. Vijibweni	15.7	1444	92	1948	124	2.8	2557	163	3
3. Kibada	15.1	1694	112	2540	168	3.8	3003	199	2
4. Kisarawe	89.6	533	6	1276	14	8.3	2821	32	8
5. Somangira	96.5	1232	13	2999	31	8.4	6730	70	8
6. Kimbiji	272.5	1665	6	3327	12	6.5	6465	24	7
7. Mbagala	26.0	2238	86	11129	428	16	40866	1572	14
8. Chamazi	36.1	3467	96	4576	127	3	5452	151	2
9. Y-Vituka	17.1	1017	60	2477	145	8	13408	784	18
10. Charambe	36.7	1116	30	2719	74	8	18624	508	21
11. Toangoma	16.1	1479	92	4110	255	10	6652	413	5
12. Miburani	4.2	22022	5243	68473	16303	10.9	72892	17355	1
13. Temeke14	4.8	6655	1387	72844	15176	24.3	91144	18988	2
14. Mtoni	2.3	5024	2184	13124	5706	9	39417	17138	12
15. Keko	3.2	14943	4669.7	34762	10863	8.0	42868	13396	2
16. Kurasini	8.3	10597	1276.7	16375	1973	4.0	26776	3226	5
Sub-Total	672.2	83093	123.6	260085	387	10.9	405753	604	5
Grand Total	1393	349559	251	851521	611	8.4	1,360,860	977	5

Source: URT (1995)

Table 6.8. *Dar es Salaam City: Land Use by Wards - 1995*

WARD	RESIDENTIAL (ha.)					INDUSTRIAL (ha.)				INSTITUTIONAL			Agric	Open	Hazard
	Low	Medi-um	High	Unplan	Total	Light	Heavy	Port	Total	Gen	Military	Total			
KINONDONI DISTRICT															
1. Magomeni			85	22	107					5		5			28
2. Makurumla			27	144	171					2		2			157
3. Ndugumbi			67	13	80					3		3			27
4. Tandale			150	75	225	10			10	5		5			60
5. M'nyamala			294	178	472					10		10		38	80
6. Msasani	1,150	254	50	63	1,517	5			5	103		103		125	
7. Kinondoni		40	140	81	261					5		5		14	30
8. Mzimuni			92	25	117					2		2			31
9. Kigogo			25	25	50					2		2			108
10.Mabibo			200	313	513		74		74	38	5	43	124	213	143
11.Manzese			200	63	263	40			40	10		10			37
12.Ubungo			150	219	369	50	50		100	200		200	2,140	3,196	315
13.Kibamba				125	125								3,850	4,000	1,795
14.Goba				82	82					30	1,475	1,505	500	1,500	843
15.Kawe	104	108	188	41	441	70			70	95	400	495	821	300	113
16.Kunduchi	53	53	94	38	238	300	50		350	48		48	3,200	1,343	181
17.Mbweni										30		30	1,000	1,370	
18.Bunju				385	385								4,000	9,000	1,315
Sub-Total	1,307	455	1,762	1,892	5,416	475	174		649	588	1,880	2,468	15,63 5	21,099	5,263
ILALA DISTRICT															
1. Ukonga			70	184	254	50			50		367	367	2,500	257	792
2. Pugu				442	442	20			20	75		75	1693		
3. Msongola				381	381								3,200	3,056	513
4. Tabata	212	212	376	63	863	100			100	56		56	133	700	58
5. Kinyerezi				50	50								1,664	1,000	86

Table 6.8. *Continued......*

6. Ilala		34	61	28	123		4		4	36		36		17	180
7. Mchikichini		11			11	39			39	10		10			
8. Vingunguti				238	238	200	60		260	52		52	145		155
9. Kipawa		72	128	69	269	170	44		214	199		199	100	29	199
10. Buguruni		22	41	48	111	15			15	25		25			89
11. Kariakoo		57			57					13		13			
12. Jangwani		21		4	25					7		7			8
13. Gerezani		73			73	10			10	7		7			
14. Kisutu		29			29	2			2	16		16		13	
15. Mchafukoge		29			29	2			2	16		16		13	
16. Upanga East		78			78					26		26			26
17.Upanga West		55			55					19		19			26
18. Kivukoni		82			82			5	5	46		46		37	
Sub-Total	212	775	676	1,507	3,170	608	108	5	721	603	367	970	9,435	5,122	2,132
TEMEKE DISTRICT															
1. Kigamboni		35	65	86	186	50		10	60	43	226	269	1,000	1,151	134
2. Vijibweni			50	13	63	250		10	260	121		121	500	405	221
3. Kibada				25	25	10			10				500	938	37
4. Kisarawe													3,913	3,495	1,552
5. Somangira													4,137	3,842	1,671
6. Kimbiji													11,86 1	10,672	4,717
7. Mbagala	208	216	376	238	1,038	100	20		120	50	70	120	690	300	332
8. Chamazi				150	150								1,886	1,233	341
9. Yombo-Vituka		113	307	63	483	130	28		158	10		10		631	428
10. Charambe				188	188								1,978	1,132	372
11. Toangoma				375	375	90			90	30		30	818		297
12. Miburani			92	33	125	96			96	130		130		69	
13. Temeke 14			105	171	276	180	24		204						
14. Mtoni			15	58	73	40			40	52		52		8	57
15. Keko			106	85	191	54			54	24		24	30		21
16. Kurasini		93	159	131	383	220	30	110	360	26		26		61	
Sub-Total	208	457	1,275	1,616	3,556	1,220	102	130	1,452	486	296	782	27,31 3	23,937	10,180
GRAND TOTAL	1,727	1,687	3,713	5,015	12,14 2	2,303	384	135	2,822	1,677	2,543	4,220	52,38 3	50,158	17,575

Table 6.9: *Dar es Salaam Land Use 1978, 1992 By Land Typology*

Land Typology	Area (ha.)		Pop. 1992	Density/ha 2		Pop/ house	1992	Max	Vacant
	1978	1992		1992	Max				
Mixed Uses	525	485	59,300	122	155	11	5,391	6,834	21%
Planned: High	3,725	2,965	572,900	193	221	11	52,082	59,503	12%
Planned: Medium	Incl.	2,030	109,300	54	96	11	9,937	17,727	44%
Planned: Low	Incl.	2,295	72,300	32	60	11	6,537	12,518	47%
Unplanned: Fair Std	2,349	,135	42,900	38	85	11	3,900	8,770	56%
Unplanned: Low Std	Incl.	6,005	621,800	104	147	11	56,527	80,293	30%
Institutions	2,600	2,670	36,500	14	14	-	5,615	5,616	0%
Industrial	1,696	2,145	-	-	-	-	-	-	20%
TOTAL		19,730	1,515,000				140,026	191,261	
Planned		7,290	754,500						
Unplanned		7,140	664,470						
TOTAL		14,430	1,419,200						

So...ce: URT (1994b)

Table 6.10: *Dar es Salaam Land Development Projections 1992-2002 by Land Typology*

Land Typology	Area (ha.)	Pop. 1992	Vacant	Area (ha.)	Pop 2002	Vacant
Mixed Uses	485	59,300	21%	485	66,900	11%
Planned: High	2,965	572,900	12%	3,165	647,800	5%
Planned: Medium	2,030	109,300	44%	4,680	300,700	28%
Planned: Low	2,295	72,300	47%	2,295	98,500	28%
Unplanned: Fair Std	1,135	42,900	56%	1,135	784,400	32%
Unplanned: Low Std	6,005	621,800	30%	6,005	65,200	13%
Institutions	2,670	36,500	0%	2,670	36,500	0%
Industrial	2,145	--	20%	2,745	--	3%
TOTAL	19,730	1,515,000		23,180	2,000,000	

Source: URT (1994b)

The planned area to the north between Bagamoyo Road and the ocean is still largely undeveloped although the southern part of this area, especially in Kawe Ward has had recent residential development and occupation, a reflection of its close proximity to the developed areas of Mwenge and Msasani, and improved communications. Although the Morogoro Road corridor, stretching for about 15 km from Nelson Mandela intersection has a difficult terrain, it has had more intensive development of good quality residential accommodation. However, most of these houses are unplanned. The Tabata planned area to the west of Nelson Mandela Road has also been developed intensively, although the development has been assuming the character of unplanned settlement, ostensibly because of shortcomings in the land management and administrative arrangements.

Another extensive construction of housing has occurred to the east, along the old Pugu Road (now Nyerere Road) industrial area and south along Kilwa Road. As usual, most of this development has been unplanned. A new planned area has been opened at Yombo Vituka behind the ribbon of unplanned housing south of the Tazara Railway, but even here unplanned housing is increasing. (This is the settlement that has been selected by this study as a study area). In Mbagala ward a low and medium density planning scheme has been established at Mtoni Kijichi. Apart from Mtoni Kijichi, housing development has also begun at Kibonde Maji in the same ward.

In as far as industrial development is concerned, apart from the Chang'ombe, Pugu Road, Morogoro Road and the developing Mbezi and Kilwa Road industrial areas, a new industrial area has developed along Nelson Mandela Road, and further development is occurring at the Mikocheni industrial area along New Bagamoyo Road.

Compared with the projected densities of 125 people per residential ha. in the MMM Master Plan, the actual overall densities show an average of 150 people per residential ha. indicating a higher proportion of unplanned development as well as higher densities than in planned areas. It has already been pointed out that 98% of housing development in Tanzania is individually/ privately initiated, with the sector constructing about 90% of housing in urban areas. In Dar es Salaam, individual contribution to housing development is a bit lower, but still at 75% (URT, 1999a). According to Hoek-Smit (1990), about 50% of privately owned housing units in Dar es Salaam are occupied by more than one household, and about two thirds of the households are room renters.

Ngowi (1996) points out a number of limitations of current urban planning procedures in Tanzania as follows, namely:

- The physical plans, known as Town/City Master Plans, do not consider financial, economic, political, technological and other "non physical" realities which must be incorporated in realistic urban plans;
- Plans are formulated as if the local government and town/city councils can provide whatever funds are needed and will enact whatever laws and regulations are required to achieve the end result for many years to come;
- Town/city plans do not seem to have any linkages between long-range plans and a feasible sequences of shorter range operations and attainments;
- Town/city planning councils have sometimes presumed that they can avoid the most pressing, most difficult urban problems: poverty, unemployment, housing, sewage problems and so on. Consequently, urban master plans have been conceived and issued as inflexible printed publications, revised and republished only at long intervals, regardless of changing conditions, policies and events.

Land Delivery System in Dar es Salaam

As explained in Chapter Five, although officially under the old Land Law, land in Tanzania had no value, there had long been a thriving land market in the country, and the prices had been, and still are, very high particularly in Dar es Salaam. As was observed from Table 5.9, over 50% of land in urban areas of Tanzania is being purchased, with Dar es Salaam leading at 69.4%.

As reviewed earlier, and as also observed above from land use in Dar es Salaam, urban land is usually obtained formally or informally, and in fact, the informal sector provides much more land to land seekers than the formal sector. In Dar es Salaam, it is estimated that 75% of the city's population lives in unplanned areas (URT, 1999), where invariably, land is obtained through informal means. This proportion is the highest among all urban centres in Tanzania. It means that the official system of land allocation in Dar es Salaam has been outstripped by the acquisition of land through informal means like buying (Kironde, 1998). According to Hoek-Smit (1990), land in Dar es Salaam was obtained through the following ways:

• Occupied without anybody's permit	4%
• Occupied with the permit of a 10-cell leader	2%
• Occupied with the permit of a friend	6%
• Inherited	18%
• Bought vacant	49%
• Bought with a house	10%
• Allocated by the government	11%
Total	100%

The above findings suggest that by far the majority of landowners got the land through informal means.

In terms of housing, while the total number of houses in the unplanned areas of Dar es Salaam was about 50,000 housing units in 1974, the current number of houses in unplanned settlements is estimated at 200,000 (URT, 1999a). According to Campbell (1990), the absence of urban administration in Tanzania led to the deterioration in the level of basic services, and failed to ensure that settlements corresponded to the basic urban plan. Squatting therefore rose sharply. In Dar es Salaam, approximately 44% of the city's population were squatters by mid- 1970s, and by 1979, eleven persons lived in every squatter house compared to only about 8 persons per house in 1972, a rise in the occupancy rate by 40%.

INFRASTRUCTURE AND OTHER HOUSING RELATED SERVICES IN DAR ES SALAAM

As in most other urban centres, urban poverty is rampant in Dar es Salaam. According to a study carried out in 1996 (see URT, 1999b), 1,053,000 residents of Dar es Salaam, equivalent to 35% of the total city's population, were living below the poverty line. As usual, the manifestations of poverty in Dar es Salaam, apart from poor housing conditions and environment, include low literacy level, poor access roads, health problems, inadequate supply of clean and safe water, poor environmental sanitation and poor solid and liquid waste management.

Roads and Transportation System

Dar es Salaam urban areas have about 1,200 kilometres of roads, out of which 200 kilometres are arterial and collector roads, and the remaining 1,000 kilometres are access roads. Over 70% of all roads in the city are unpaved. As shown in Tables 6.11 and 6.12, the road condition in Dar es Salaam is poor.

Table 6.11: *Road Network Condition in Dar es Salaam*

Land Typology	Collector Roads (Km)				Access Roads (Km)			
	Good	Fair	Poor	Total	Good	Fair	Poor	Total
Mixed Uses	9.1	5.4	1.9	16.4	-	9.0 3	6.5	45.5
Planned: High	4.8	8.1	12.5	25.4	-	-	294.5	294.5
Planned: Medium	3.0	2.0	7.0	12.0	-	4.5	90.0	94.5
Planned: Low	11.5	-	18.9	30.4	6.5	6.5	118.0	131.0
Unplanned: Fair Std	-	-	-	0	-	-	88.5	88.5
Unplanned: Low Std	0.4	1.4	14.9	16.7	-	-	194.0	194.0
Institutions	-	0.8	3.0	3.8	2.0	13.0	52.5	67.5
Industrial	3.5	-	3.8	7.3	-	7.5	57.0	64.5
TOTAL	32.3	17.7	62.0	112	8.5	40.5	931.0	980.0
Arterials, MoW Trunk Roads	61.0	11.5	17.5	90.0				

Source: URT (1994b)

Table 6.12: *Types of Roads in Dar es Salaam*

Type of Roads	Trunk	Regional	Local	TOTAL
Paved Roads	35	52	251	338
Unpaved Roads	113	13	682	808
TOTAL	148	65	933	1146

Source: URT (1994b)

Apart from the poor state of the roads, there is also a shortage of access roads in the squatter areas, which account for up to 50% of the residential areas in the city. These poor settlements have only 22% of access roads (URT, 1994b). Budgetary constraints have been the major reason for failure of the central government and city fathers to construct and repair city roads. For example, during the financial year 1993/94, the City Engineer's approved development budget was only 10% of the requirement (URT, 1994b).

As cities like Dar es Salaam expand (usually horizontally), the distances that the poor urban dwellers must travel to work and to other places for income-generating activities also expands geometrically. As such poor access roads that hinder efficient and reliable transportation adversely affect urban people, particularly poor people living in poor settlements in the outskirts of the city. While there are acute transport problems within many residential areas, particularly in the poor and squatter settlements, there is severe traffic congestion in the few good city roads. As alluded to by Katima (1999), the severe traffic congestion currently experienced in Dar es Salaam will sooner than later cause health problems resulting from smog. Katima (1999) points out five reasons for the traffic congestion in Dar es Salaam. These are the absence of a coherent hierarchical road network; poor traffic management; chaotic development; on street parking on busy roads; ignorance of traffic rules and regulations, and lack of co-ordination among various public transport systems.

Public transport in Dar es Salaam constitutes mainly of buses, most of which are privately owned and known as *Daladala*. It is estimated that to date there are about 8,000 such private buses operating in Dar es Salaam, up from 2,700 that were there in 1996 (Mtaki, 1999). Minibuses carrying 25 passengers or less, and which constitute 63.5% of the sector, are more dangerous and chaotic. These minibuses commonly known as *vipanya* cause 23.6% of all fatal accidents in the city (Mtaki, 1999).

In a study conducted in 1997 (see Lugano, et al, 1999) on transportation problems in Dar es Salaam, seventeen (17) recommendations were aired by city transporters (bus and taxi owners) for improved transportation system. The most popular suggestions were however, the following seven:

1. The authorities should construct and maintain road infrastructure 27.70%
2. Traffic Police should institute strict supervision 14.86%
3. Traffic Police should be more professional 12.50%
4. Passenger transportation should be properly planned 7.09%
5. Driver licensing should be appropriate and strict 6.42%
6. Licensing authority should be flexible and efficient 5.74%
7. People should be educated on road use, 5.07%
8. Ten other recommendations, 20.62%

Prior to the recent liberalization of public transport in Dar es Salaam, there was a national parastatal company, UDA, created in 1974 to provide public transport in the city. But before long, UDA's fleet strength and thus its overall performance began to deteriorate. While it was able to carry 137 million passengers in 1983, this was achieved in the face of frequent breakdowns and constant overloading (Stren, 1990). From a fleet size of 374 buses of which an average of 257 were serviceable every day in 1975, UDA's fleet size fell to 205 in 1984, of which an average of only 131 were operational at any time. Quoting Kulaba (1986), Stren (1990) continued to testify that this shortfall was reflected in the fact that, during the 6 a.m. to 9 a.m. peak period, 22% of all waiting passengers on Dar es Salaam routes were left behind because of overcrowding on the buses.

One response to the shortfall in public transport facilities has been to permit the private sector to pick up some of the slack. However, the free market provision of public transport in Dar es Salaam has taken the city by storm and has therefore created a number of problems as a result of mainly, lack of proper co-ordination and management that has resulted in the current chaotic scenario of increased inconveniences and danger to other road users.

Health Problems

The groups that suffer more from certain health problems in Dar es Salaam, are the low-income earners and children under five. These people are usually found in squatters and poor settlements, and are confronted with the following problems:

- Lack of sufficient space and funds for construction of decent houses and toilets;
- Inadequate clean and safe water supply;
- Lack of access roads and streets;
- Poor solid and liquid waste management.

All the above problems contribute to the spread of communicable diseases especially feacal-borne diseases like cholera, dysentery, diarrhoea and typhoid. According to a recent report (URT, 1999b), some of these diseases are major causes of deaths in Dar Salaam (*see* Table 6.13).

Table 6.13. Leading Diseases in Dar es Salaam

1997			1998		
Disease	Cases	Deaths	Disease	Cases	Deaths
Malaria	275,689	145	Malaria	476,356	378
Diarrhoea	124,573	49	ARI	182,072	9
URTI	115,748	0	Diarrhoea	103,560	40
Skin diseases	62,115	0	Pneumonia	109,579	105
Anaemia	60,034	20	Intestinal Worms	45,035	0
Cholera	6,566	227	Skin diseases	47,595	0
Fungal infection	35,286	0	URTI	21,809	1
Worms	31,746	0	Cholera	4,668	138
Malnutrition	24,185	0	Clinical AIDS	876	144
Tuberculosis	9,047	50	Typhoid	2,499	0

Source: URT (1999b)

The Dar es Salaam Water Supply System

Dar es Salaam's water supply is characterized by an overall shortage of water and its uneven distribution in the city. For a long time the water supply system has been in a poor state, inadequate and unable to meet demand. Given the population of about 3,000,000 people, the current water demand of the city is estimated at 400,000 m^3/day (URT, 1996). However, the current water supply for the City is 273,000 m^3/day produced from three plants in the following ratios:

Upper Ruvu Plant - 82,000 m^3/day
Lower Ruvu Plant - 182,000 m^3/day
Mtoni Plant - 9,000 m^3/day

Following the recent drought and severe depletion of flows in river Ruvu, the Ministry of Water initiated a major drilling programme to augment the city's supply. Some old but high yield boreholes have been rehabilitated and more than 63 new boreholes drilled in various areas of the City. The overall estimated yield of these boreholes is around 20,500 m^3/day (URT, 1997c).

It is estimated that there are about 70,000 registered water connections in the city, out of which only 2,000 are metered, with only 40% of these functioning (URT, 1994a). As regards domestic connection, there are three types of water supply service levels in Dar es Salaam as follows:

- *House connection*: Within the house unit, a number of taps are available. Kitchen, toilet, bathroom etc all have water use equipment.
- *Yard connection*: Only one or two taps within the house premise are available. Usually taps are located in the yard at the back of the house, from which water is drawn and carried by buckets and containers into the house
- *No connection*: This type has no water connection within the house or house premise. Residents have to go to water kiosks or standpipes or to their neighbours to fetch water in buckets and other containers.

A study done by JICA in 1990 (see URT, 1994a) found that about 44% of Dar es Salaam's residents had no water connections within their premises and were therefore dependent on water kiosks, standpipes or buying water from private vendors (*see* Table 6.14). As seen earlier, a survey carried out in Dar es Salaam in 1986/87 (*see* Hardoy and Satterthwaite, 1989) of 660 households drawn from all income levels found that 47% had no piped water supply either inside or immediately outside their houses, while 32% had a shared piped-water supply. Of the households without piped water, 67% bought water from neighbours while 26% drew water from public water kiosks or standpipes and 7.1% bought water from water vendors.

Table 6.14: *Types of House Water Connections in Dar es Salaam*

Type of Connection	Connections		Population served	
	Number	%	Number	%
House connection	94,710	30%	428,851	32%
*High income	12,757	4%	69,663	5%
*Middle income	4,486	1%	24,467	2%
*Low income	77,467	25%	334,721	25%
Yard connection	74,150	24%	315,482	24%
No connection (kiosks/standpipe)	139,410	45%	590,695	44%
TOTAL	308,270	100%	1,335,028	100%

Source: URT (1994a)

A recent study of eight selected areas in Dar es Salaam (URT, 1997d) also confirmed the water situation as shown in Table 6.15.

In an effort to rehabilitate basic urban infrastructure including easing water problems in Dar es Salaam and other parts of the country, the government has been implementing various donor-funded projects. One such project is the Urban Sector Rehabilitation Project whose main objectives are sustainable economic development and urban poverty alleviation (see Swere, et al, 1999).

Table 6.15: *Water Sources in Dar es Salaam Selected Areas*

Water Source	Percentage of Households
Own tap	17.10%
Neighbour's tap	80.30%
Public tap	2.10%
Well	0.05%
River/rain water	0.40%

Source: URT (1997b)

The total cost of this project, which is to cover ten urban areas of Moshi, Arusha, Tanga, Morogoro, Tabora, Mwanza, Mbeya, Iringa, Dodoma and Dar es Salaam, is US $ 142 million, out of which US $ 10.8 million is for the Dar es Salaam Water Supply Improvements and Community Infrastructure. Another programme which, however, covers urban and rural areas outside Dar es Salaam, has been the Water and Environmental Sanitation (WES), whose goals were defined as establishing community based systems for management of water supplies and sanitary means of excreta disposal with the view of enhancing sustainability (URT/UNICEF, 1994).

WES is among the projects funded by the government of Tanzania in collaboration with UNICEF through 1992/96 country programme. The programme was launched against the background of the prevalence of water borne diseases such as malaria, diarrhoea and trachoma. The UNICEF/Tanzania country programme was devided into two parts: (a) national support and (b) community based support. In order to develop the community based system, WES implemented several community based activities such as the establishment of village water committees, the establishment of village water funds and the training of village artisans in rain water harvesting skills. In this endeavour, UNICEF support was directed towards three priority areas, namely: operational research and evaluation; national WES monitoring system and national co-ordination of WES development. In supporting these activities, UNICEF contribution rose steadly from US$ 1,265,000 in 1992 to US$ 1,537,000 in 1994

Solid Waste Management

In the late 1980s (see Hardoy and Satterthwaite, 1989), it was estimated that only a quarter of Dar es Salaam's refuse was being collected. Currently it is estimated that the daily rate of solid waste generation in Dar es Salaam is about 1,000 tonnes per day, out of which only 10% is being collected (URT, 1994b).

Katima (1999) also asserts that each person in Dar es Salaam is presently generating around 0.5 kilogrammes of solid waste per day. Other studies present more terrifying results. For example, Halla and Majani (1997) estimate that daily solid waste generation in the city is currently at 2,000 tonnes, of which only 11% is collected and dumped at a dump site at Vingunguti. The remainder is dumped along the streets and open spaces including cemeteries. Uronu (1999) also shows that garbage (solid waste) disposal in Dar es Salaam is done as follows:

- 46.6% is illegally disposed of;
- 14.7% is crudely disposed of;
- 22.2% is properly disposed of by public;
- 7.2% is recycled;
- 9.3% is properly collected and disposed of at official dumping sites.

Table 6.16 shows some solid waste generation and disposal statistics in Dar es Salaam.

Table 6.16: *Waste Generation and Disposal in Dar es Salaam, 1992*

Land Typology	Population 1992	Kg/c/ day	Generation tons/year)	Disposal		
				On-site	Industrial	Public
Mixed Uses	59,300	1.83	39,600	12,000	12,000	15,600
Planned: High	572,900	0.43	90,100	81,900	-	8,200
Planned: Medium	109,300	0.51	20,200	18,460	-	1,750
Planned: Low	72,300	0.63	16,500	14,850	-	1,650
Unplanned: Fair Std	42,900	0.49	7,700	6,900	-	800
Unplanned: Low Std	621,800	0.36	81,000	75,900	-	5,100
Institutions	36,500	0.78	23,700	19,290	1,890	1,800
Industrial	-	-	49,500	13,400	35,100	1,000
TOTAL	1,515,000		328,300	242,700	48,991	35,900
PERCENTAGE			100%	74%	15%	11%

Source: URT (1994b)

The solid waste management system in Dar es Salaam is under funded, facilities are poor and acquisition of suitable disposal sites has also been a problem. As Katima (1999) suggests, the collection methods used by waste management authorities are sometimes inappropriate, such as the use of open trucks to transport solid waste. The use of such poor disposal means results in even more littering and pollution of the local environment. Katima (1999) also asserts that Dar es Salaam city has inadequate waste bins and collection equipment. The private collectors also have no trained personnel and inadequate equipment.

Katima (1999) further points out that apart from poor waste transport system and management as well as lack of maintenance of vehicles and equipment, the public in some areas is not willing to co-operate with waste management system because they (the public) are either ignorant, are not involved in the planning of the waste management, or simply because they have no confidence in the scheme. As a result these people dump their waste in open spaces along roadsides and other places. The heaps of uncollected solid waste in open spaces in the city create bad smells and breeding grounds for disease-carrying insects and animals.

Wastewater and Sanitation

Dar es Salaam has inadequate sewerage and sewage treatment systems. Wastewater is therefore discharged directly into stabilization ponds, which seldom work properly, or in rivers and canals. Wastewater flowing into low-lying areas turns into stagnant pools, which become breeding grounds for vectors such as mosquitoes. In Dar es Salaam, the free flowing untreated sewage in most streets due to drainage blockages cause water pollution, which is exacerbated by the practice of dumping solid waste in waterways. This hinders water flow and degrades water quality. Many industries also dispose of their wastewater containing organic waste in rivers and other water bodies without proper treatment, causing harm to both humans and aquatic life.

Dar es Salaam is severely affected by lack of liquid waste treatment facilities and sanitation deficiencies due to high ground water tables, impermeable soils and increasing population, resulting into serious health and environmental hazards. Almost 80% of the city's population is served by on-site wastewater and excreta disposal (URT, 1994b; Kaseva, et al, 1999). Many septic tank systems, which are the predominant methods for on-site wastewater and excreta treatment and disposal, experience functional and operational problems. More than 50% of the population in areas such as Kijitonyama, Tabata, Mikocheni and Sinza use septic tanks. The problems experienced by these inhabitants include the need to frequently empty the septic tanks due to malfunctioning soak-away pits (Kaseva, et al, 1999). The result is flooding which in turn causes health hazards and damage to the environment.

As indicated earlier (see Hardoy and Satterthwaite, 1989), only 13% of the dirty water and sewerage produced in Dar es Salaam is regularly disposed of. Out of the 660 households drawn in the city, 89% had simple pit latrines, while only 4.5% had toilets connected to septic tanks or sewers. Most households had to share sanitary facilities causing a serious problem of overflowing latrines, especially during rainy seasons. A more recent study (URT, 1997d) confirms these figures. The study conducted in eight selected residential areas in Ilala and Temeke districts in Dar es Salaam indicates that 90.8% of all households surveyed used pit latrines (see Table 6.17).

Table 6.17: *Toilet Facilities in Selected Areas in Dar es Salaam*

Type of Toilet	Percentage of Households
Flush (exclusive)	5.90%
Flush (shared)	3.00%
Pit latrine	90.78%
"VIP" latrine	0.30%
None ("bush")	0.02%

Source: URT (1997d)

Another recent study (Halla and Majani, 1997) estimates that about 20% of Dar es Salaam residents have no proper sanitation facilities. The poor sanitation condition is exacerbated by the ageing sewers, which cause leakages through bursting. In areas with on-site sanitation facilities and where the water table is high, overflowing of pit latrines and septic tanks is persistent. Furthermore, inaccessibility in some densely built-up areas constrains pit emptying. Additional statistics given by Uronu (1999) on the Dar es Salaam sanitation profile are as follows:

- 83% of the population use pit latrines;
- 10% use septic tanks;
- 6% use conventional sewerage systems;
- 1% use other means.

The problem of sewerage system in Dar es Salaam was realized since the 1960s. The 1968 Dar es Salaam Master Plan proposed an extensive sewage coverage to discharge into the sea and river outfall. During this period, the only collection and disposal systems in existence were in the Central Business District and Ubungo. The latter was then under construction. The Plan proposed to abolish pit latrines replacing them with either communal septic tanks or connecting them to sewers. Apparently this wish could not be achieved due lack of sustainable implementation strategies including sourcing of funding.

Presently there are eleven (11) piped sewerage systems in Dar es Salaam as follows:

- One system serving the city centre, Kariakoo and Upanga which was constructed in 1948-52;
- Five systems provided and maintained by various institutions;

- One system serving Buguruni and neighborhoods, built in 1978;
- One system serving Regent Estate, built in 1975;
- One system serving Kijitonyama, constructed in 1972;
- One system serving Mikocheni, built in 1975-76; and
- One system serving Ubungo industrial area, built in 1968.

The above systems are small and inadequate. The largest one, which serves the city centre has 900 mm diameter outfall. Others have between 200 mm and 500 mm diameter outfalls. The city centre system has a sea outfall while the others discharge into oxidation ponds which discharge into natural waterways.

The 1979 Master Plan (Marshal Macklin Monaghan Ltd) recommended that sewage services must be flexible and be capable of being implemented in a phased manner. The basic philosophy behind this proposal was that on-site or septic tank/soak-away systems be considered as a first priority for all residential developments unless the environment dictates otherwise (URT 1997b). The then existing sewerage system had deteriorated and the level of service was not satisfactory. Overflows into streets and neighbourhoods, collapsed and malfunctioning treatment facilities were predominant. The Master Plan also recommended a major rehabilitation to get the systems into functional state. It was not until after 1982 that some rehabilitation was implemented under World Bank financing. The rehabilitation had been designed in the Dar es Salaam Sewerage and Sanitation Study (1982). Table 6.18 indicates the sanitary service provision in the city and proposed investment for improved sanitation by the year 2002 based on a 2,000,000 city population.

Table 6.18: *Dar es Salaam Sanitation Service Provision and Investment Proposal*

Land Typology	Year 1992				Year 2002				Secondary sewers and cesspit emptying	
	Population	On site	Septic	Sewers	Population	Onsite	Septic	Sewers	Cost $ 1000	O&M$ $1000
Mixed Uses	59,300	10%	10%	80%	66,900	0%	0%	100%	3,545	33
Planned: High	572,900	65%	31%	4%	647,800	70%	23%	7%	2,232	200
Planned: Medium	109,300	52%	35%	13%	300,700	65%	30%	5%	1,485	89
Planned: Low	72,300	20%	75%	5%	98,500	15%	75%	10%	769	32
Unplanned: Fair Std	42,900	80%	20%	0%	65,200	70%	30%	0%	127	18
Unplanned: Low Std	621,800	86%	14%	0%	784,400	90%	10%	0%	1,647	243
Institutions	36,500	3%	23%	74%	36,500	40%	40%	20%	1,051	42
Industrial	-	81%	7%	12%	-	60%	40%	12%	174	8
TOTAL	1,515,000				2,000,000				11,027	666

Source: URT (1994b)

7

CONCEPTUAL AND METHODOLOGICAL ISSUES

This chapter expounds on the conceptual and methodological framework introduced in chapter one, highlighting the research design, sampling design and methods of data collection.

THE DEVELOPMENT OF YOMBO VITUKA

The research for this book, undertaken in the months of August, September and October 1999, was conducted in Yombo Vituka Ward situated about 10 kilometres South-West of Dar es Salaam city centre in Temeke District, south of Tazara Railway Line.

Yombo Vituka was one of Dar es Salaam's rural wards until 1984 when it was encompassed and subjected to the bigger Dar es Salaam City Authority. At the time of the study, the ward had five administrative areas, namely Kilakala, Dovya, Vituka, Makangalawe and Buza. It is an old settlement which initially had scattered dwellings owned by native village inhabitants. Serious housing settlements started in the area in the late 1970s and early 1980s when invasion by squatters started. In 1982 the government started land surveying in selected portions of the area, particularly those areas which had not been heavily invaded by squatters. It is such piece-meal surveys and plans that resulted in Yombo Vituka having to-date both planned and unplanned (squatter) areas.

Apparently the initial aim and urgency of the government's opening of the new planned area behind this ribbon of unplanned housing was to relocate people who were being evicted from other planned industrial areas of Lumo-Chang'ombe and, later, "Malawi Cargo," Kurasini in the same district. Scores of people who were compensated and evicted from the said planned industrial areas and who were allocated new plots in Yombo Vituka moved and built their houses there. However, this study found that most of them simply sold the allocated sites in Yombo Vituka and moved elsewhere.

Fig. 7.1: *The author (right) inspecting a colonial identity card of Mzee Kinyogoli (left) of Yombo Vituka after the latter had narrated historical background of the study area since colonial era (Photo : September, 1999).*

Among the five mentioned areas, this research was conducted in three illustrative areas of Dovya, Vituka and Makangalawe. While Makangalawe is basically still an unplanned or squatter area, Dovya and Vituka have both planned and squatter settlements.

Household Population

According to respective area officials, at the time of this study, a household census was being finalized. According to the already gathered figures that were estimated to be almost 80% complete, the three areas had the following number of households:

Dovya	2,426
Vituka	1,642
Makangalawe	785
Total	4,853

No current population census had been undertaken of those households, but based on secondary data as evidenced in the previous chapters in this book, the average number of persons per household in similar Dar es Salaam settlement is between 8 and 10 persons. This means that the estimated population of the study area was 50,000 people.

Rationale for Selecting the Study Area

Yombo Vituka was selected as the study area for the following reasons:

1. The squatter or unplanned settlement of Yombo Vituka is contagious to the planned area that is rapidly developing in the same area. This was regarded as opportune and convenient because one of the objectives of this study is to compare and contrast the housing poverty aspects in formal and informal settlements in order to derive some tentative conclusions on land delivery system in urban areas and its consequential effect on motivation for improved housing and related services.
2. Yombo Vituka, like other new housing settlements in the city, presents real, non-illusory challenges and opportunities to stakeholders in housing-related poverty alleviation schemes and programmes. This is unlike the old, highly proliferated and densely populated squatter settlements, which though are obviously more congested with more poverty-stricken urban population, present little opportunity for improved environments due to the already decayed and "irreparable" infrastructure and services. As a matter of fact, it is the conviction that such old and densely populated squatter settlements like Manzese, Mwananyamala, Kurasini Shimo la Udongo, Buguruni and Vingunguti should not be subjects of improvement plans which is the essence of this study, but should, in the long-term perspective, be subject to slum

clearance and redevelopment because they consist of insanitary houses deemed unfit for human habitation. This latter concept, we believe, has a different hue and texture and requires another study altogether.

Conceptual Framework Revisited

Literature and research on housing in Tanzania, like in many developing countries, have hitherto concentrated on sociological surveys of housing development including public housing programmes, slums and squatter upgrading and sites-and-services schemes through factual reporting of statistical categories to indicate the general housing conditions. Very little research has gone to the extent of analyzing the causal relationships between housing and socio-economic aspects like income, poverty, health, the environment and general economic development.

It is apparent that housing problems, although widely realized, have been perceived simply as welfare problems, which can only be solved though transfer of physical or financial resources to those who lack adequate housing. Furthermore, most literature and research on housing have not hitherto considered improved housing conditions as means of reducing poverty, claiming that poverty reduction is achievable only through increasing the real income of poor individuals or households. This research attempts to argue, through empirical analysis, that adequate housing is not simply a welfare problem, but a socio-economic issue. Proper housing promotes not only security and welfare of a community, but also health, wealth and other social aspirations of poor people. Housing, it is also argued, directly and indirectly contributes to, or affects real incomes of poor households. The question is: who are the stakeholders in the provision and improvement of adequate and decent housing and what are their perceptions towards this noble task?

RESEARCH DESIGN

Research Design and Formulation

The research problem in this study has already been stated as lack of properly and empirically derived linkage between poor housing conditions and poverty, poor perception of the role of improved housing and its environment in alleviating poverty and lack of appreciation of the potential and desire of the poor people in improving their housing and environments so as to ameliorate their poor conditions. The research questions were therefore stated as: How have the poor and unhealthy housing and environmental conditions compounded poverty situation in poor urban settlements, and what are the potentials and pre-requisites for individual households and private sector in housing provision, improvement and environmental regeneration in urban areas?

In the light of the above research problem and research questions, as well as several research hypotheses highlighted earlier, it is important to be very careful in formulating a research design that could enable the collection and analysis of data in a way that would combine relevance to the research objectives with economy in the procedure. The aim is to come up with a conceptual structure that enables the research to be conducted efficiently and economically given the prevalent financial limitations.

Sampling Design and Sample Size

The first step was to draw a definite plan for obtaining a sample from the desired population. As seen above, the three areas in the study ward, i.e. Yombo Dovya, Buza and Makangalawe, have about 5,000 households. This was therefore the finite universe to be studied. In choosing the sample size, the parameters of interest in the research and time and budgetary constraints were considered. Having done the initial survey of the study area, it was decided that in every vicinity, neighbourhood or "street" of about 15 households with more or less similar housing structures and surroundings, one household should be randomly selected for the study. In this way, out of the estimated population of 5,000 households as given above, a random sample of 300 households was selected for the study. Assuming that the procedure to be applied had a small sampling error, this sample size was considered representative, reliable and flexible. The initial plan was to interview 150 households in squatter areas; and 150 in planned areas.

Primary Data Collection Methods

For the purposes of statistical analysis and hypotheses testing, only primary data was used in this study. Secondary data collected was used only to form the theoretical framework during the initial stages of literature review. However in presenting research results and interpretations from primary data analysis, secondary data might be referred to in order to draw some relevant and supportive conclusions. The study for this book involved sample surveys in which data collection was through observation, questionnaires and interviews.

Observation Method

Researchers were required to observe general housing conditions, surroundings and other housing related services, and systematically record results. The aim was to enable the determination of physical conditions of the houses and therefore assess whether a house was in good or poor condition. Although available evidence suggests that assessment of house condition is difficult because housing condition is largely a qualitative variable in respect of house structure (see Willis, 1990), a logical assessment of housing condition in such a survey can be reliably done by observing and collecting categorical data on whether the house is built of mud and wattle walls, thatched by grass or coconut leaves, has cracks in the walls or the walls are not fully plastered, lacks roof ceiling, has poor and rough courtyard surface, and the presence of gutter. Data on external house features such as the condition and quality of outside surface and presence or absence of rubbish lying around could also be collected in such a survey. These were some of the data used in our study of Yombo Vituka settlements. The housing condition as assessed through such random observation was later modeled to see whether statistical results could support such random assessment.

Questionnaire and Interview Methods

Questionnaire and interview methods were used concurrently. A well prepared and focused questionnaire intended to capture all salient information needed to test all the four hypotheses was used. Given the literacy background of the inhabitants in these poor settlements, the questionnaire was to be administered by researchers (interviewers) conducting structured interviews with the intended respondents by reading through the questionnaire, elaborating the exact meaning or requirement of each question and objectively filling in the answers from the respondents. However, where a respondent was considered literate and knowledgeable enough to fill in the questionnaire unguided, such people were given the questionnaires and accorded ample time (but not exceeding two days) to fill in the forms which were later collected after carefully examining them to ensure that they were appropriately filled in and that all questions which could be answered without prejudice were indeed answered. In case of incomplete answers to such self-administered questionnaires, further direct interviews were conducted to obtain complete and reliable responses.

Questionare Design

A household survey questionnaire was designed with the aim of capturing pertinent information and data relevant to the study and which could suffice to test all the four hypotheses. Although most of the questions in the questionnaire were basically in the form of multi-choice and closed questions in the form of "Yes" or "No" answers, there were few open-ended questions.

Part one of the questionnaire was on general information on the study area, location and identity of each house. Part two was on household particulars that included the name of the head of the household, his/her sex, age, marital status, dependants, and number of rooms in the house. Part three had questions related to tenure, such as whether the house was owner-occupied or rented out, rent paid if any, other payments such as electricity and water. If the house was owner-occupied, whether it was self-constructed or purchased or inherited, and rent receivable if it was partly rented out. How land or site was acquired and the length of stay in the house was also asked.

In part four of the questionnaire, housing condition was assessed by asking questions such as age of the house and observing the conditions and materials used for roofing and walling as well as the condition of the surroundings including toilets and heaps of garbage around the house, if any. Whether the house was architecturally planned and availability of access road were also observed and asked. Part five of the questionnaire dwelt on the employment and income variables of heads of the households and other family members. Sources of income and amount earned by the household were inquired. Expenditure pattern of each household was also inquired in this part.

In part six, the availability of housing-related services within and around the relevant households was assessed. These services include water supply, sewerage systems, garbage disposal and sanitation. Whether or not the services, if any, were provided freely or bought also featured. Furthermore, the respondents were asked about their level of satisfaction with services provision by the local and central government, and whether they considered poor land delivery system and lack of access to credit as affecting their desire to improve housing and related services. The impact of poor or unhealthy and inadequate housing conditions/environment on income generating capacity, children's health and school attendance/performance and social and mental satisfaction was also queried. Finally, willingness and ability of households to pay/contribute towards improved housing and services was also asked.

In part seven of the questionnaire, questions related to in-house income generation capacities and contribution were asked, while the last part assessed the presence and impact, if any, of community based organizations (CBOs) and non-governmental organizations (NGOs).

Field Work Planning and Problems

In an effort to solicit closer relations and maximum support of householders, one of the research assistants was identified from the same area, and together with two other assistants, were first exposed to a one-day review of the questionnaire under the guidance of the principal researcher. The group also spent another two days undertaking casual surveys of the study area and met the area leaders to explain the objectives of the survey and solicit the leaders support and co-operation in explaining to the intended respondents the aim of the study and allay any fears as to the real purpose of the study.

The initial questionnaire review and random pilot survey proved very useful in improving the questionnaire, omitting and adding some relevant information, and smoothening the actual running of the survey later during the main survey. Although the response during the main survey was encouraging, there were problems related to the non-availability of some of the heads of the households at the arranged time. Where the intended householder could not be interviewed during the first visit, either due to absence of the head of the household or the need to have enough preparatory time, an appointment, usually for the next day, was fixed. However, despite such agreed upon appointments, some earmarked respondents could not be found at home even after three or four visits. A total of 26 earmarked respondents could not be interviewed after visiting their houses many times without getting them at home. 11 people, however, bluntly stated that they were not interested.

Another problem was with the respondents who were not ready to instantly answer the questions verbally and requested that the questionnaires be left with them so that they would fill them at their own time and convenience. Out of 38 questionnaires left in this way, 12 could not be received back until the end of the fieldwork. Due to these problems, out of 150 questionnaires earmarked for the squatter areas, 107 (71.3%) were filled in, while out of 150 questionnaires for the planned areas, 144 (96.0%) were filled in.

Of course, there was also the problem of some respondents declining to answer certain questions, particularly those related to their income. Even where income was stated, one could easily note that some people were not giving true figures, since there was irony, for example where the stated total expenditure of a household was higher than the stated total income from all sources of the particular household. In such cases the stated "total income" was ignored, and the stated total expenditure taken as the total income.

8

DATA PRESENTATION AND ANALYSIS

In this chapter, we present and analyze data collected during the survey mainly using percentages, while in the next three chapters we shall test our stated hypotheses by applying statistical models to analyze and interpret results from these data.

VISUAL HOUSING CONDITIONS

Researchers in this study were required to visually observe physical conditions of houses surveyed using pre-determined criteria and variables and record whether a house was in poor or good condition. The variables and rationale agreed upon were as indicated in Table 8.1.

Table 8.1: *Variables and Rationale for Visual Housing Conditions*

Variable	Rationale
1. Wattle and/or mud house	Mud houses constructed purely from laterite clay without any cement additive are likely to deteriorate, generate cracks and possibly crumble easier and earlier.
2. Grass or coconut leaves-thatched house	Houses roofed by grass or coconut leaves are more susceptible to damage by rain, winds and fire than those roofed by corrugated iron sheets, asbestos or tiles.
3. House with no ceiling	Houses without ceiling do not provide protection against heat, falling objects, disease vectors and do not promote decent, quite and private living atmosphere. They do not also provide long-life housing.
4. Walls not fully plastered	House walls not fully plastered easily allow cracks that become breeding grounds for bugs that live in cracks and crevices of walls and could transmit diseases such as "chagas."

Table 8.1: *continued*

5. Dirty surroundings and uncollected garbage	Housing environment with dirty surroundings including uncollected garbage, dirty and poorly built and maintained toilets serve as food and breeding grounds for disease vectors.

It was agreed that houses which, according to visual observation, met all or most of the above five conditions should be regarded as poor housing.

Subject to a later statistical modeling and analysis and based on the above criteria, it was visually observed that 72.9% of the houses in squatter settlements of the study area were in poor conditions, and 32.6% in planned (formal) settlements were in poor condition (see Table 8.2), obviously indicating that houses in squatter (informal) areas are in poorer condition than those in formal or planned areas (*see* also figure 8.1).

Table 8.2: *Visual Housing Conditions*

	Planned Areas		Squatters		Total	
	No.	%	No.	%	No.	%
Houses in poor condition	47	32.6	78	72.9	125	49.8
Houses in good condition	97	67.4	29	27.1	126	50.2
Total	144	100.0	107	100.0	251	100.0

Source: Field Survey, 1999

Figure 8.1: *Some poor housing units in unplanned settlements of Yombo Vituka* (photo: September 1999

PERSONAL CHARACTERISTICS OF THE RESPONDENTS

Sex of Heads of Households

Out of 144 heads of households interviewed in planned areas, 88.2% were men, while 11.8% were women. The corresponding percentages in unplanned areas were 90.7% and 9.3.% respectively (see Table 8.3), indicating that the type of settlement had only little influence on male or female-headed household structure.

Table 8.3: *Sex of Heads of Households*

	Planned Settlements		Unplanned Settlements		Total	
	No.	%	No.	%	No.	%
Male-Headed households	127	88.2	97	90.7	224	89.2
Female-headed households	17	11.8	10	9.3	27	10.8
Total	144	100.0	107	100.0	251	100.0

Source: Field Survey, 1999

Age of Household Heads

Although 14 respondents could not state nor guess their ages or even age range, safe guesses were made by interviewers so that age ranges for all 251 respondents were recorded as shown at Table 8.4. In both planned settlements and squatters, most heads of households were of the age between 30 and 50 years (55.6% in planned areas and 56.1% in unplanned areas). Furthermore, the percentage for each age group did not substantially differ for both tenure groups implying no or little relationship between age of householders and the type of settlement they lived in.

Table 8.4: *Age of Household Heads*

Age Range	Planned Settlements		Unplanned Settlements		Total	
	No.	%	No.	%	No.	%
30 years	17	11.8	14	13.1	31	12.4
30-50 years	80	55.6	60	56.1	140	55.8
50 years and above	47	32.6	33	30.8	80	31.8
Total	144	100.0	107	100.0	251	100.0

Source: Field Survey, 1999

Respondents' Marital Status

Out of 144 respondents from planned settlements, 113 (78.5%) household heads were married, while 13 (9%) were single and 18 (12.5%) were divorcees or widowers. The corresponding numbers for unplanned settlements were 89 (83.2%), 4 (3.7%) and 14 (13.1%) respectively. Again like with the age, marital status seemed to have little impact on the type of settlement one lived in (see Table 8.5).

Table 8.5: *Marital Status of Heads of Households*

	Planned Settlements		Unplanned Settlements		Total	
	No.	%	No.	%	No.	%
Married	113	78.5	89	83.2	202	80.5
Single	13	9.0	4	3.7	17	6.8
Divorced/Widower	18	12.5	14	13.1	32	12.7
Total	144	100.0	107	100.0	251	100.0

Source: Field Survey, 1999

HOUSEHOLD CHARACTERISTICS

Occupancy particulars as observed and responded to by interviewees were recorded as can be observed from Table 8.6. Based on these data, further analysis was done to determine household occupancy, rooms per household and room occupancy as indicated in Tables 8.7, 8.8 and 8.9 respectively.

Table 8.6: *Occupancy Characteristics*

	One-room houses		2- room houses		3- room houses		4+ room houses	
	P*	U*	P*	U*	P*	U*	P*	U*
1 person	1	-	-	-	-	-	-	-
2 persons	1	-	2	1	-	-	-	-
3 persons	7	4	16	3	2	-	-	-
4 persons	2	4	18	7	3	-	-	-
5 persons	1	3	24	18	10	-	-	-
6 persons	-	-	5	17	11	4	1	-
7 persons	-	-	9	18	6	7	-	-
8 persons	-	-	4	2	7	5	-	-
9 persons	-	-	1	-	4	6	1	1
10 persons	-	-	-	1	5	-	-	1
11 persons	-	-	-	1	2	1	-	2
12 persons	-	-	-	-	1	-	-	1
Total	12	11	79	68	51	23	2	5

Source: Field Survey, 1999

Household Occupancy

As seen from Table 8.7, 63.9% of all households surveyed in planned areas had five or more people living in one household, while the corresponding figure for unplanned settlements was 82.2%, indicating that overcrowding was more severe in squatter areas.

Table 8.7: *Household Occupancy*

Persons per House	Planned Settlements		Unplanned Settlements		Total	
	No.	%	No.	%	No.	%
Single person	1	0.7	-	-	1	0.4
2 persons	3	2.1	1	0.9	4	1.6
3 persons	25	17.3	7	6.6	32	12.7
4 persons	23	16.0	11	10.3	34	13.6
5 persons	35	24.3	21	19.6	56	22.3
over 5 persons	57	39.6	67	62.6	124	49.4
Total	144	100.0	107	100.0	251	100.0

Source: Field Survey, 1999

Rooms per Household

Regarding the number of rooms for each household, it was found that in both planned and squatter settlements, most households had 2 or 3 rooms, accounting for 90.3% in planned areas and 85.1% in unplanned areas. However, in unplanned settlements 73.9% of households had only one or two rooms compared with 63.2% for planned areas (see Table 8.8).

Table 8.8: *Rooms per Household*

Rooms per Household	Planned Settlements		Unplanned Settlements		Total	
	No.	%	No.	%	No.	%
1 room	12	8.3	11	10.3	23	9.2
2 rooms	79	54.9	68	63.6	147	58.6
3 rooms	51	35.4	23	21.5	74	29.4
4 rooms	2	1.4	5	4.7	7	2.8
Total	144	100.0	107	100.0	251	100.0

Source: Field Survey, 1999

Room Occupancy

Again assuming that more than two persons per room constitutes overcrowding, there was an obvious overcrowding in unplanned (squatter) settlements compared to planned areas. While in planned areas 50% of all households surveyed had more than two people on average living in one room, in squatter settlements 78.5% of all households surveyed had more than two people living in one room as shown at Table 8.9.

Table 8.9: *Room Occupancy*

Persons per Room	Planned Areas		Unplanned Areas		Total	
	No.	%	No.	%	No.	%
One person	8	5.6	1	0.9	9	3.6
2 person	64	44.4	22	20.6	86	34.3
3 person	52	36.1	54	50.5	106	42.2
4 person	18	12.5	25	23.3	43	17.1
5 person	2	1.4	5	4.7	7	2.8
Total	144	100.0	107	100.0	251	100.0

Source: Field Survey, 1999

House Tenure

In the planned settlements, it was found that 125 (86.8%) of respondents had owner occupied houses, while 19 (13.2%) were renters. In the squatter areas, the respective figures were 89 (83.2%) and 18 (16.8%).

Of the 125 owner-occupiers in planned areas, 107 (74.3%) constructed or purchased their houses using their own savings, ten people (6.9%) constructed or purchased their houses from compensation money given to them by the government after being evicted elsewhere, while 8 people (5.6%) had inherited those houses from their parents/relatives.

Table 8.10: *House Tenure*

	Owner Occupied								Renting		Grand Total	
	Constructed/ Purchased from own Savings		Constructed/ Purchased from compensation		Inherited		Total owner occupied					
	No.	%	No	%	No	%	No	%	No	%	No.	%
Planned Settlement	107	74.3	10	6.9	8	5.6	125	86.8	19	13.2	144	100.0
Unplanned Settlements	80	74.8	-	-	9	8.4	89	83.2	18	16.8	107	100.0
Total	187	74.5	10	4.0	17	6.8	214	85.3	37	14.7	251	100.0

Source: Field Survey, 1999

In the unplanned areas, 80 people (74.8%) constructed/purchased their houses from their own savings, while 9 people (8.4%) had inherited the houses.

Land Tenure

Of course the government now formally allocates all plots in the planned settlements. However, as shown at Table 8.11, prior to the surveys done by the government in these areas, there were 16 plots which had been allocated to the present owners by ward/village authorities, 6 plots had just been invaded by current owners who now hold rights of occupancy, and 4 plots were sub-divided by original owners/ villagers and given to the present owners. In the present squatter settlements, 67 out of 107 houses (62.6%) were informally allocated to the people by ward/area authorities, 26 (24.3%) were invaded and 14 (13.1%) were subdivided.

Table 8.11: *Land Tenure*

	Allocated by Government		Allocated by Ward Area Authorities		Invaded		Sub-divided		Total	
	No	%	No	%	No	%	No	%	No	%
Planned Areas	144	100	(16)*	-	(6)*	-	(4)*	-	144	100
Squatter Areas	-	-	67	62.6	26	24.3	14	13.1	107	100
TOTAL	144	57.4	67	26.7	26	10.3	14	5.6	251	100

Source: Field Survey, 1999

HOUSING CONDITIONS AND SERVICES

Roofing Conditions

In assessing housing conditions, the roofing material and its condition was considered as an important variable. All houses surveyed in both planned and unplanned settlements were roofed using either tiles, corrugated iron sheets/ asbestos or grass/coconut leaves (see Table 8.12). All six houses with tile roofs surveyed were in planned areas. There was no single tile-roof house in all surveyed households in squatter areas. There was also no single house with grass roof in planned areas surveyed, while in unplanned areas, 3 houses were found with roofs thatched by grass (coconut leaves). However, the majority of the houses (95.8% in planned areas and 97.2% in unplanned areas) were roofed by corrugated iron sheets or asbestos in a few instances.

Table 8.12: *Roofing Conditions*

	Tiles		Corrugated iron sheets/asbestos		Grass		Total	
	No.	%	No.	%	No.	%	No.	%
Planned Areas	6	4.2	138	95.8	-	-	144	100.0
Unplanned Areas	-	-	104	97.2	3	2.8	107	100.0
Total	6	2.4	242	96.4	3	1.2	251	100.0

Walls and Ceiling Conditions

Other housing conditions observed in this study were whether the houses had ceilings and whether the walls had been fully plastered (and painted) or not. Out of 144 units surveyed in planned areas, 101 (70.1%) had ceilings, while 90 units (62.5%) were fully plastered. The corresponding figures for unplanned areas were only 40.2% and 33.6%, indicating that houses were in poorer conditions in squatter settlements (see Table 8.13).

Table 8.13: *Walls and Ceiling Conditions*

	Planned Areas				Unplanned Areas				Total			
	YES		NO		YES		NO		YES		NO	
	No.	%	No.	%	No	%	No	%	No.	%	No	%
Ceiling	101	70.1	43	29.9	43	40.2	64	59.8	144	57.4	107	42.6
Fully-plastered walls	90	62.5	54	37.5	36	33.6	71	67.4	126	50.2	125	49.8

Source: Field Survey, 1999

Architectural Drawings

Respondents were also asked whether their houses were built basing on architecturally planned drawings or not. It was assumed that houses built without proper drawings were not in good architectural conditions. As can be observed from Table 8.14, out of 144 housing units surveyed in planned areas, 125 (86.8%) were architecturally planned, while only 20.6% in squatter areas had architectural drawings.

Table 8.14: *Architectural Drawings*

	YES		NO		TOTAL	
	No.	%	No.	%	No.	%
Planned Areas	125	86.8	19	13.2	144	100.0
Unplanned Areas	22	20.6	85	79.4	107	100.0
TOTAL	147	58.6	104	41.4	251	100.0

Source: Field Survey, 1999

Water Services

All Yombo Vituka areas surveyed had no piped-water services. Although it was reported that there were water pipes that were laid in the area some years back, presently no piped water reaches the place, and in fact, most of those pipes were vandalized and removed illegally.

As seen from Table 8.15, 6.9% of households surveyed in planned areas use shallow wells alone as their main source of water, 10.4% use private water vendors only, while 79.9% use both private vendors and shallow wells. 2.8% use own private wells constructed within their compounds. As in planned areas, most households surveyed in unplanned areas were using shallow wells and private water vendors. However, only one household (compared to 4 in planned areas) had a private well within the compound. Figure 8.2 shows an example of unsafe water source.

Table 8.15: *Water Services*

	Planned Settlements		Unplanned Settlements		Total	
	No.	%	No.	%	No.	%
1. Piped water	-	-	-	-	-	-
2. Shallow wells only	10	6.9	27	25.2	37	14.7
3. Private water vendors only	15	10.4	38	35.5	53	21.1
4. Private vendors and shallow wells	115	79.9	41	38.3	156	62.1
5. Own private wells	4	2.8	1	1.0	5	2.0

Source: Field Survey, 1999

Fig. 8.2: *Natural drains or canals like this one are used not only as wastewater, garbage and human waste disposal outlets, but also sometimes, as sources of drinking water at Yombo Vituka (Photo: September, 1999).*

Sanitation

In both planned and unplanned households surveyed, inhabitants were using only two types of sanitation, namely pit latrines and septic tanks. There was no conventional sewerage sanitation system in the area. In the planned areas, 24.3% of those interviewed used pit latrines, while 75.7% had septic tanks. In the squatter areas, the situation was worse since 75.7% used pit latrines (most of which were in pathetic conditions as shown by figure 8.3), while only 24.3% had septic tanks (see Table 8.16).

Table 8.16: *Sanitation*

	Planned Settlements		Unplanned Settlements		Total	
	No.	%	No.	%	No.	%
Pit Latrine	35	24.3	81	75.7	116	46.2
Septic Tank	109	75.7	26	24.3	135	53.8
TOTAL	144	100.0	107	100.0	251	100.0

Source: Field Survey, 1999

Fig. 8.3: *A typical unhygienic, unsafe and unsecure pit latrine in Yombo Vituka's unplanned area (Photo: September, 1999).*

INCOME AND EXPENDITURE PATTERNS

As mentioned earlier, most respondents did not give the true income of their households. This is confirmed by the fact that the stated total income was in most cases much lower than the total expenditure stated as per household expenditure patterns. In such cases, the expenditure pattern stated was taken as the more reliable data and total expenditure was taken to be the true income of the household.

On the above basis, twenty income groups were recorded as shown at Table 8.17. Out of 144 respondents from planned areas, 9 people could not give their income particulars, while 12 in unplanned areas also refused to give data on their income and expenditure. The income analysis was therefore based on a total of 135 and 95 respondents from planned and unplanned settlements respectively. As seen in Table 8.17, the majority of households in both planned and unplanned settlements had a monthly income of between T.shs. 150,000.00 and T.shs.190,000.00 accounting for 50.4% in planned areas, and 52.6% in unplanned areas.

Table 8.17: *Income/Expenditure Distribution*

Income Range T.shs	Midpoint incomeT.Shs.	Planned Areas		Unplanned Areas	
		No.	%	No.	%
50,001-60,000	55,000	1	0.7	2	2.1
60,001-70,000	65,000	-	-	1	1.1
70,001-80,000	75,000	3	2.2	3	3.1
80,001-90,000	85,000	4	3.0	2	2.1
90,001-100,000	95,000	5	3.7	3	3.1
100,001-110,000	105,000	6	4.4	3	3.1
110,001-120,000	115,000	4	3.0	3	3.1
120,001-130,000	125,000	4	3.0	4	4.2
130,001-140,000	135,000	7	5.2	5	5.3
140,001-150,000	145,000	8	5.9	8	8.4
150,001-160,000	155,000	14	10.4	13	13.7
160,001-170,000	165,000	19	14.1	18	18.9
170,001-180,000	175,000	23	17.0	12	12.6
180,001-190,000	185,000	12	8.9	7	7.4
190,001-200,000	195,000	9	6.7	5	5.3
200,001-210,000	205,000	6	4.4	2	2.1
210,001-220,000	215,000	4	3.0	1	1.1
220,001-230,000	225,000	3	2.2	1	1.1
230,001-240,000	235,000	2	1.07	1	1.1
240,001-250,000	245,000	1	0.7	1	1.1
TOTAL		135	100.0	95	100.0

Source: Field Survey, 1999

Table 8.18 and 18.9 show the pattern of household expenditure (and thus income) among the respondents from planned and unplanned areas respectively. Some interviewees who responded on their expenditure patterns either did not respond on some expenditure items or stated that those items did not apply to them. Out of 135 respondents from planned areas and 95 from squatter areas, 11.6% and 7.7% respectively did not respond to the rent expenditure because they were occupying own houses. 77 (57%) and 36 (37.9%) of the respondents from planned areas and unplanned areas respectively did not respond to the expenditure on charcoal/kerosene, since most of them were either using electricity for lighting and cooking or did not wish to reveal the fact that they were using charcoal or kerosene. 106 people (78.5%) and 74 people (77.9%) respectively did not respond to the expenditure on entertainment and recreation, obviously because they had meagre incomes to afford such luxuries. Similarly, only 31 respondents (23%) and 18 respondents (18.9%) respectively stated that they could afford some savings, and even among them, 80.6% and 83.3% respectively could manage to save not more than T.shs. 10,000.00 per month. This proves the hypothesis that savings ratios are a function of income and are nominally small in the low-income groups.

Table 8.18 and 18.19 also show that it is only on food where the expenditure is well spread out over the income spectrum and where 70.1% and 65.2% of the respondents respectively used above T.shs. 20,000.00 per month. Although transport/fuel and education expenditures are also well spread out, only 19.4% and 37.7% for planned areas and 7.3% and 33% for unplanned areas respectively spend over T.shs. 20,000 per month for each of these two items. As for house rent, 73.7% and 77.8% of all respondents in planned and unplanned areas respectively use not more than T.shs. 20,000.00 per month.

Given data in Tables 8.18 and 8.19, and using arithmetic mean to measure average expenditure pattern of households interviewed, the average income of households in these two types of settlements is T.shs. 163,277.00 and 150,676 respectively as shown at Table 8.20.

Table 8.18: *Household Expenditure Patterns per Month (Planned Settlements)*

T.shs	1,000 to 10,000		11,000 to 20,000		21,000 to30,000		31,000 to40,000		41,000 to50,000		51,000 to60,000		61,000 to 70,000		71,000 to 80,000		More than 80,000		Total Respondents	
	No	%	No	%	No	%	No	%	No	%	No	%	No	%	No	%	No	%	No	%
Food	9	7	31	23	78	58	10	7	4	3.0	1	0.7	1	0.7	1	0.7	-	-	135	100.0
Clothing	48	36	50	37	21	16	10	7	4	3.0	2	1.5	-	-	-	-	-	-	135	100.0
Rent	8	42	6	32	5	26	-	-	-	-	-	-	-	-	-	-	-	-	19	100.0
Medical	89	66	32	24	10	7	3	2	1	0.8	-	-	-	-	-	-	-	-	135	100.0
Charcoal/ Kerosene	45	78	5	9	3	5	5	9	-	-	-	-	-	-	-	-	-	-	58	100.0
Transport/ Fuel	86	69	16	13	6	5	10	8	4	3.0	1	0.8	1	0.8	1	0.8	-	-	125	100.0
Education	11	9	70	55	36	28	6	5	4	3.1	2	1.5	-	-	1	0.8	-	-	130	100.0
Utilities (Water, electric. ect	61	47	52	40	12	9	4	3.1	2	1.5	-	-	-	-	-	-	-	-	131	100.0
Entertain-ment & Recreation	7	24.1	18	62.1	2	6.9	2	6.9	-	-	-	-	-	-	-	-	-	-	29	100.0
Drinks & Tobacco	78	85.7	10	11.0	2	2.2	1	1.1	-	-	-	-	-	-	-	-	-	-	91	100.0
Savings	25	80.6	4	12.9	2	6.5	-	-	-	-	-	-	-	-	-	-	-	-	31	100.0
Others	7	63.6	2	18.2	1	9.1	1	9.1	-	-	-	-	-	-	-	-	-	-	11	100.0

Source: Field Survey, 1999

Table 8.19: *Household Expenditure Patterns per Month (Planned Settlements)*

T.shs	1,000 to 10,000		11,000 to 20,000		21,000 to30,000		31,000 to40,000		41,000 to50,000		51,000 to60,000		61,000 to 70,000		71,000 to 80,000		More than 80,000		Total Respondents	
	No	%	No	%	No	%	No	%	No	%	No	%	No	%	No	%	No	%	No	%
Food	11	11.6	22	23.2	49	51.6	9	9.5	2	2.1	1	1.0	1	1.0	-	-	-	-	95	100.0
Clothing	31	32.6	50	52.6	12	12.6	1	1.0	1	1.0	-	-	-	-	-	-	-	-	95	100.0
Rent	8	44.5	6	33.3	4	22.2	-	-	-	-	-	-	-	-	-	-	-	-	18	100.0
Medical	77	81.0	13	13.7	2	2.1	2	2.1	1	1.0	-	-	-	-	-	-	-	-	95	100.0
Charcoal /Kerosene	36	61.0	21	35.6	2	3.4	-	-	-	-	-	-	-	-	-	-	-	-	59	100.0
Transport/ Fuel	45	54.9	31	37.8	5	6.1	-	-	1	1.2	-	-	-	-	-	-	-	-	82	100.0
Education	15	16.5	46	50.5	22	24.2	5	5.5	1	1.1	-	-	1	1.1	1	1.1	-	-	91	100.0
Utilities (Water, electricity ect]	41	44.1	50	53.7	1	1.1	1	1.1	-	-	-	-	-	-	-	-	-	-	93	100.0
Entertainment & Recreation	9	42.9	7	33.3	3	14.3	2	9.5	-	-	-	-	-	-	-	-	-	-	21	100.0
Drinks& Tobacco	48	77.4	12	19.4	2	3.2	-	-	-	-	-	-	-	-	-	-	-	-	62	100.0
Savings	15	83.3	3	16.7	-	-	-	-	-	-	-	-	-	-	-	-	-	-	18	100.0
Others	4	57.1	2	28.6	1	14.3	-	-	-	-	-	-	-	-	-	-	-	-	7	100.0

Source: Field Survey, 1999

Table 8.20: *Average Households Expenditure Pattern*

	Planned Areas		Unplanned Areas	
	T.Shs.	%	T.Shs	%
Food	24,093	14.8	22,974	15.2
Clothing	16,463	10.1	14,026	09.3
Rent	13,921	08.5	13,278	08.8
Medical	10,315	06.3	8,342	05.5
Charcoal/Kerosene	9,983	06.1	9,737	06.4
Transport/Fuel	12,860	07.9	10,988	07.3
Education	20,346	12.4	18,907	12.6
Utilities	12,828	07.9	11,414	07.6
Entertainment etc	15,155	09.3	14,548	09.7
Drinks and Tobacco	7,368	04.5	8,081	05.4
Savings	8,081	04.9	7,167	04.8
Others	11,864	07.3	11,214	07.4
Total	163,277	100.0	150,676	100.0

Source: Field Survey, 1999

9

REGRESSION ANALYSIS AND HOUSING CONDITIONS

INTRODUCTION TO REGRESSION ANALYSIS

In this chapter, we intend to test our hypothesis number 1 that poor housing conditions are consequential and are combined effects of not only the low income of households, but also other manifestations of poverty like overcrowding, lack of safe and adequate water supply, poor sanitation and sewerage system and other housing characteristics and attributes. We shall apply regression analysis in this endeavour. Regression analysis is a commonly used technique for exploring relationships between variables. Suppose that we are interested in the relationship between a variable Y and a set of variables X_2, ... X_k , and that a total of n observations on each of these variables is available. We will adopt the following notation: The *n* observed values of the variable Y will be written as Y_t, where *t* runs from 1 to *n*. Y_1 (Y_t, with t = 1) is the first observed Y value; Y_n (Y_t, with *t* = n) is the *n*'th and final observed Y value. Similarly, X_{2t}, with *t* = 1,2,., *n*, denotes *n* observations on the variable X_2, X_{3t}, with *t* = 1, 2,.., *n*, denotes *n* observations on the variable X_3,...., X_{kt}, t = 1, 2 ..., *n*, denotes *n* observations on the variable X_k. Y is called the explained (or dependent) variable, and X_2, X_3,..., X_k are called explanatory (or independent) variables. As the terminology suggests, the emphasis is on using X_2, X_3,..., X_k to explain Y.

There are many forms of regression analysis but a basic distinction can be made between regressions that use continuous data and those using discrete data. The classical regression model is, however, based on a continuous dependent (response or endogenous) variable (Y) which, as seen above, is dependent upon a number of independent predictor or exogenous) variables (X_1, X_2, X_3,...X_k). Such a model implies cause and effect; a given change in X_1 will cause Y to change by a specific amount; but it does not prove cause and effect.

Simple linear relationships use one variable model in which the relationship between the dependent variable (Y) and the independent variable (X) can be written as a linear equation

$Y = a + bx$

Where, for example,

Y = household expenditure (say, food)

X = household income

a = true Y intercept for the population

b = true slope for the population

Figure 9.1 shows a number of observations between the food expenditure of a household and household income. The equation, which represents the data is: $Y = 0.25 + 0.5x$

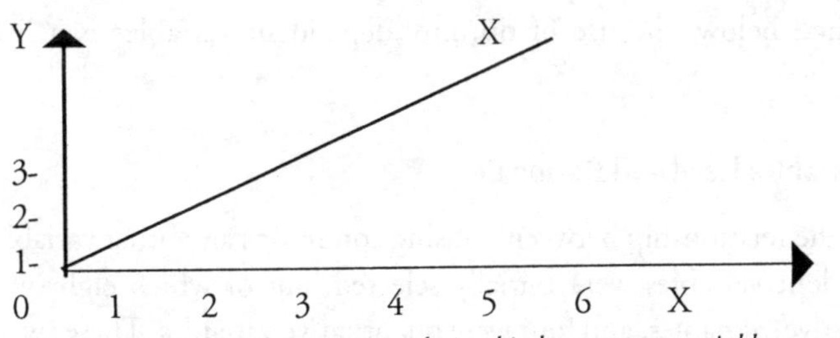

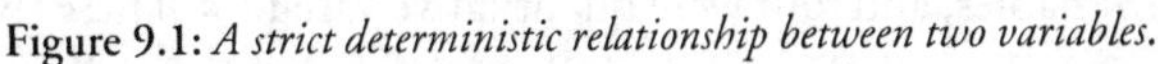

Figure 9.1: *A strict deterministic relationship between two variables.*

If a prediction of food expenditure is required when income = 6, and if 6 is substituted into the equation in place of X, and the equation solved, the value of Y is 3.25. The slope of the line (b) indicates how responsive Y is to a change in X.

In multiple regression models, several explanatory variables can be used to predict the value of a dependent variable. In fact, they can be used to sort out the separate effects of several explanatory variables. Multiple regression is usually in the following form:

$Y = a + b_1X_1 + b_2 X_2 + b_3X_3$ t...... $+ b_kX_k + u$

Where Y = dependent variable

$X_1, X_2, X_3 \ldots X_k$ = independent variables

a = Y intercept

b_1= slope of Y with variable X_1 holding variables $X_2, X_3, \ldots, X_k$ constant

b_2= slope of Y with variable X_2 holding variable $X_1, X_3, \ldots, X_k$ constant

b_3= slope of Y with variable X_3 holding variable $X_1, X_2, X_4, \ldots, X_k$ constant

u = random error in Y

Multiple Regression for Determination of Housing Conditions

Our first hypothesis in this study involves testing the causal relationship between housing conditions and other explanatory variables that together can be termed as manifestation of housing poverty.

The Use of Dummy Variable Models

In regression analysis, the explained (or dependent) variable and explanatory (or independent) variables are normally assumed to be quantitative. However, there are situations whereby categorical or qualitative variables, usually called dummy variables, need to be considered as part of the model development process. The use of dummy variables permits the researcher to consider qualitative (dependent and/or independent) variables as part of the regression models. However, as shall be explained below, the use of dummy dependent variables is a little complicated.

Explanatory Variables Used and Rationale

In determining the relationship between housing conditions and other variables, twelve independent variables were initially selected, out of which eight were dummy (qualitative) variables, and four were quantitative variables. These twelve explanatory variables were hypothesized to be influencing housing conditions in the study area of Yombo Vituka. These explanatory variables together with the rationale behind each are as follows:

1. *Household Income (INCOME)*

Household income obviously affects housing conditions in that households with low income cannot afford to improve their housing structures and provide basic services and amenities.

2. *Household Occupancy (PERSONS)*

It was considered that a household with a large number of occupancy may adversely affect housing condition. Conversely, where the household's total income is low (where many occupants are not income earners), the household cannot afford to save much for improvement of housing and services. On the other hand, a large number of income earners in a household can physically and materially contribute in housing improvements.

3. *Number of bedrooms (BEDROOMS)*

Number of bedrooms in a house was considered to have the same effect as occupancy rate explained above, since the number of people in a house depended, to a large extent, on the number of bedrooms.

4. *Male-headed households (MALEHEAD) - dummy variable*

It was assumed that, while female-headed households have less ability to improve their housing conditions, male-headed households could be in a position to afford improvements thereby putting their housing in a good condition. In part this is because apart fom other formal employment, men are able to engage in other income generating activities outside their homes, unlike women who have extra family and household responsibilities such as child rearing and caring which hinders their participation in income generating activities.

5. *Age of household heads (AGE)*

It was hypothesized that young household heads had no or a very small number of dependants or house occupants who could contribute to degradation and spoiling of environments and general conditions of the house. Having a small family also meant that extra income could be saved for housing improvements.

6. *Households with both spouses (SPOUSE) - dummy variable*

Household heads who are single, divorced or widowers have no helping hand in ideas and material support in housing improvements. It was therefore hypothesized that households with two (both) spouses might have houses that were in a better condition compared to households with single headed households or single parents.

7. *Rented houses (RENTAL) - dummy variable*

Since renters are not owners, invariably they have no urge to improve the houses they rent. It was therefore assumed that such houses would be in poorer conditions compared to owner-occupied houses.

8. *Houses with no ceilings (CEILING) - dummy variable*

Houses without ceiling do not provide protection against heat, falling objects, disease vectors and do not promote a decent, quite and private living atmosphere. They do not also provide long-life housing. As such these were considered to be in poor condition.

9. *Walls not fully plastered (WALLS) - dummy variable*

House walls not fully plastered easily allow cracks that become breeding grounds for bugs that live in cracks and could transmit diseases such as "chagas." Such houses were therefore also considered to be in poor condition.

10. *Houses without architectural drawings (ARCHITEC) - dummy variable*

Houses that were built not according to any architectural plans or drawings were considered to be in poor conditions because they were likely in poor structures that could be susceptible to crumbling or cracks and short life.

11. *Safe and adequate water supply (WATER) - dummy variable*

Households without safe and adequate water supply face the danger of water-borne diseases as amply narrated in the literature review part of this book. Such households were therefore considered to be in poor housing conditions. Since there was literally no piped water service in Yombo Vituka, only those households with own private wells were considered to be in good condition - on the basis of this criterion.

12. *Septic tank latrines (SEPTIC)- dummy variable*

In surveying sanitation systems in the study area, it was found that there were only two systems, i.e pit latrines and septic tanks. There was no conventional sewerage system at all. That being the case, households with septic tank system were considered to be in good condition while those with only pit latrines were considered to be in poor conditions.

Dummy Dependent Variables

The simplest procedure in analysing regression models, even where the dependent or explained variable is a dummy variable, is to use the usual least squares method, which utilizes the linear probability model. In our present case, where the dependent variable (Y) or house condition is a qualitative variable, housing condition would have only two categories (good or poor). In this case, only one dummy variable is used to represent the two categories. The particular dummy variable Y would be defined as:

$Y = 0$ if the housing condition is poor
$Y = 1$ if the housing condition is good

However, housing conditions cannot simply take one of the two discrete values, 0 or 1. Rather, these points simply denote the interval within which the "true" conditions of the houses fall. A house condition may take any value between 0 and 1. Such in-between values are not observable. This being the case, we need another regression model as follows:

$$Y^* = a + b_1X_1 + b_2X_2 + b_3X_3 + \ldots + b_k X_k + u$$

Where, Y* is not observed. This is commonly called "latent" variable. So, what we observe is a dummy variable Y_i

$Y_i = 1$ if $Y^* > 0$
$Y_i = 0$ if otherwise

This is the idea behind *logit* and *probit* models (see Maddala, 1989), which we shall examine a little later on.

Linear Probability Model

For simplicity's sake and comparison purposes, we begin our regression analysis of housing conditions by utilizing linear probability models, for the meantime, ignoring the assumptions regarding the specification of the error term in the linear model. We first assume that housing condition is a dichotomous variable that takes on only two values: poor and good. Later on, we shall use the Logit model to remove shortcomings of linear models as described above.

Significance of the Relationship Between Housing Conditions and the Twelve Explanatory Variables.

Data relating to observations of 144 households in planned areas and 107 households in unplanned settlements were recorded separately for the housing conditions as visually observed and assessed (dependent variable) and the twelve independent variables explained above. It was intended to test separately the significance of the relationship between housing conditions and those explanatory variables for planned and unplanned settlements, first, by using linear models. Since in one variable (household income) there were only 135 and 95 respondents in planned and unplanned settlements respectively, those who could not respond to this particular question were completely omitted in the model even if they responded in others. The numbers of observations used in this model were therefore 135 and 95 for planned and unplanned areas respectively.

A linear regression model was then fitted to the set of respective data so as to determine whether there is a significant relationship between the dependent variable (housing condition) and the set of explanatory variables. Since there are more than one explanatory variable, the null and alternative hypotheses were set up as follows:

$H_0: X_1 = X_2 = 0$ (There is no linear relationship between the dependent variable - housing condition - and the explanatory variables)
$H_1: X_1 \neq Y_2 \neq 0$ (At least one regression coefficient is not equal to zero)

Utilizing an *F*-test and applying the MINITAB statistical computer package, the above null hypothesis was tested.

THE INFLUENCE OF HOUSING CONDITIONS IN PLANNED SETTLEMENTS

Testing for Significance of Relationship

Using the MINITAB computer package, the regression model for our data produced an output as shown at table 9.1. The output at table 9.1 gives, first, the regression equation for our model with Y being housing conditions (HOUSCOND). From statistical knowledge we know that F-test is used when testing the ratio of two variances. When testing for the significance of the regression coefficients, the measure of random error is called the error variance, so that the F- test is the ratio of the variance due to the regression divided by error variance. Thus:

$$F_{p,n-p-1} = \frac{MSR}{MSE}$$

Where,

p = the number of explanatory variable in the regression model
MSR = Regression Variance
MSE = Error Variance

Table 9.1: *Regression Analysis: Planned Settlements* The regression equation is:

HOUSCOND = 0.0737 -0.000001 INCOME + 0.0085 PERSONS - 0.0103 BEDROOMS - 0.0373 MALEHEAD + 0.00148 AGE + 0.0033 2SPOUSE - 0.0165 RENTAL + 0.527 CEILING + 0.320 WALLS - 0.0272 ARCHITEC + 0.0416 WATER + 0.287 SEPTIC

Predictor	Coef	Stdev	t-ratio	p
Constant	0.07368	0.06282	1.17	0.243
INCOME	-0.00000131	0.00000050	-2.61	0.010
PERSONS	0.00852	0.01168	0.73	0.467
BEDROOMS	-0.01030	0.03130	-0.33	0.743
MALEHEAD	-0.03732	0.03397	-1.10	0.274
AGE	0.001477	0.001470	1.01	0.317
2SPOUSE	0.00331	0.02930	0.11	0.910
RENTAL	-0.01654	0.03832	-0.43	0.667

Table 9.1: *continued...*

Predictor	Coef	Stdev	t-ratio	p
Constant	0.07368	0.06282	1.17	0.243
CEILING	0.52725	0.04485	11.76	0.000
WALLS	0.31971	0.04336	7.37	0.000
ARCHITEC	-0.02721	0.04138	-0.66	0.512
WATER	0.04160	0.07260	0.57	0.568
SEPTIC	0.28695	0.04441	6.46	0.000

s = 0.1188 R-sq = 94.2% R-sq(adj) = 93.6%

Analysis of Variance

SOURCE	DF	SS	MS	F	P
Regression	12	27.9369	2.3281	164.91	0.000
Error	122	1.7223	0.0141		
Total	134	29.6593			

SOURCE	DF	SEQ SS
INCOME	1	4.6139
PERSONS	1	0.1821
BEDROOMS	1	0.0028
MALEHEAD	1	0.0769
AGE	1	0.1982
2SPOUSE	1	0.2712
RENTAL	1	0.1073
CEILING	1	20.5874
WALLS	1	1.2926
ARCHITEC	1	0.0023
WATER	1	0.0128
SEPTIC	1	0.5894

Unusual Observations

Observations	Income	Houscond	Fit	Stdev.Fit	Residual	Std.Resid
6	155000	0.0000	0.3825	0.0513	-03825	-3.578
7	248000	1.0000	1.0048	0.0677	-0.9948	-.005x
16	166800	1.0000	0.7620	0.0473	0.2380	2.18r
18	128000	0.0000	0.4357	0.0500	-0.4357	-4.04r
23	234200	1.0000	0.9089	0.0733	0.0911	0.97x
26	91800	0.0000	0.4996	0.0492	-0.4996	-4.62r
36	167000	1.0000	0.7558	0.0465	0.2442	2.23r
39	192000	1.0000	0.6928	0.0454	0.3072	2.80r
50	204000	1.0000	1.0425	0.0642	-0.0425	-0.42x
53	166500	0.0000	0.4045	0.0522	-0.4045	-3.79r
58	98000	1.0000	0.7928	0.0597	0.2072	2.02r

Table 9.1: *continued*

Observa tions	Income	Houscond	Fit	Stdev.Fit	Residual	Std.Resid
68	168200	1.0000	0.7140	0.0417	0.2860	2.57r
72	105000	1.0000	0.7616	0.0559	0.2384	2.27r
88	238100	1.0000	1.0439	0.0693	-0.0439	-0.46x
119	106000	0.0000	-0.0221	0..652	0.0221	0.22x

Key

r denotes an observation with a large st. resid.
x denotes an observation whose X value gives it large influence.
Source: MINITAB Output

For data of the study areas of planned settlements, the ANOVA table is also displayed in the computer output in table 9.1

If a level of significance of 0.05 is chosen, we determine (from any F-distribution table) that the critical value on the F-distribution with 12 and 122 degree of freedom is 1.75 as depicted in figure 9.2.

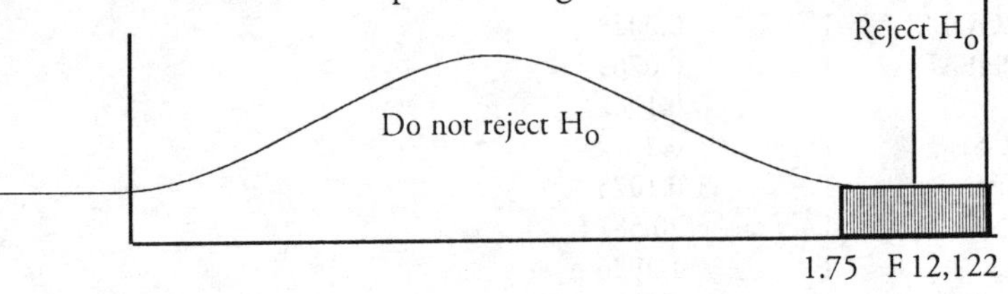

Fig. 9.2. *Testing the significance of a set of regression coefficients at the 0.05 level of significance with 12 and 122 degrees of freedom.*

As can be observed from the ANOVA section in the computer output in table 9.1,

$$F_{12,\,122} = \frac{MSR}{MSE} = \frac{2.3281}{0.0141} = 164.92$$

Since 164.92 > 1.75, we can reject Ho and conclude that at least one of the explanatory variables (among the twelve) is influential on housing condition.

Measuring Association in the Multiple Linear Regression Model for Housing Conditions

Computer output at table 9.1 was also computed and produced the coefficient of determination, R^2 (R-squared). In our regression, since there are more than one explanatory variable, R^2 represents the proportion of the variation in housing condition that is explained by the set of twelve explanatory variables.

In our model (see also table 9.1), $R^2 = \frac{SSR}{SST} = \frac{27.9369}{29.6593} = 0.942$

This can be interpreted to mean that 94.2% of the variation in the housing conditions in Yombo Vituka planned settlements can be explained by the variation in the twelve explanatory variables. To reflect the effect of both the number of explanatory variables in the model and the sample size, an adjusted R^2 is usually used and calculated thus:

$$R^2 \text{ adj.} = 1 - [(1-R^2)\frac{n-1}{n-p-1}]$$

In our case, and as can be seen from table 9.1:

$$R^2 \text{ adj.} = 1 - [(1-R^2)\frac{135-1}{135-12-1}]$$

$$= 1 - [(1-0.942)134/122]$$

$$= 0.936$$

Hence our multiple regression models can explain 93.6% of the variation in housing conditions after adjusting for the number of predictors and sample size.

Correlation Matrix for Housing Conditions

In order to further study the relationship among the variables, it may be useful to examine the correlation between each pair of variables included in the model. Again, applying MINITAB statistical computer package, a correlation matrix that indicated the coefficient of correlation between each pair of variables in Yombo Vituka planned areas was produced as shown in Table 9.2.

From Table 9.2, it is apparent that there is a strong positive association between dependent variables (HOUSCOND) and CEILING, WALLS and SEPTIC. Otherwise between independent variables themselves, there is a strong association between INCOME and PERSONS; INCOME and BEDROOMS; INCOME and ARCHITEC; PERSONS and BEDROOMS; PERSONS and AGE; BEDROOMS and AGE; BEDROOMS and RENTAL; CEILING and WALLS; CEILING and SEPTIC; and WALLS and SEPTIC. Otherwise all other remaining relationships are weak positive relationships except MALEHEAD and WATER as well as 2SPOUSE and WATER, which have weak negative correlation. In fact there is virtually no correlation between any other variable and MALEHEAD except 2SPOUSE, RENTAL and CEILING. There is also virtually no association between 2SPOUSE and ARCHITEC; 2SPOUSE and SEPTIC; RENTAL and WATER; ARCHITEC and SEPTIC; and WATER and SEPTIC.

Table 9.2: *Pearson Correlations for Planned Settlements*

	Houscond	Income	Persons	Bedrooms	Malehead	Age	2spouse	Rental
Income	0.394							
Persons	0.185	0.624						
Bedrooms	0.204	0.609	0.795					
Malehead	0.087	0.091	0.050	0.066				
Age	0.192	0.462	0.745	0.631	0.048			
2Spouse	0.146	0.154	0.347	0.311	0.236	0.375		
Rental	0.128	0.395	0.384	0.552	0.115	0.386	0.336	
Ceiling	0.933	0.363	0.156	0.204	0.113	0.191	0.186	0.157
Walls	0.892	0.435	0.130	0.153	0.187	0.133	0.119	0.168
Architect	0.425	0.615	0.356	0.319	0.058	0.311	0.097	0.280
Water	0.122	0.332	0.291	0.120	-0.071	0.143	-0.112	0.071
Septic	0.802	0.591	0.327	0.342	0.011	0.213	0.068	0.125

	Ceiling	Walls	Architec	Water
Walls	0.833			
Architec	0.414	0.458		
Water	0.113	0.136	0.069	
Septic	0.706	0.715	0.499	0.097

Source: MINITAB output

Determining the Contribution of Each Explanatory Variable

Usually the aim in developing multiple regression models is to utilize only those explanatory variables that are useful in predicting the value of, or which influence, the dependent variable. If an explanatory variable is not useful in this prediction or influence, then it could as well be deleted from the multiple regression model and a model with fewer explanatory variables utilized instead. There are at least two methods of determining the contribution of an explanatory variable, namely the partial F-test criterion and the standard error of regression coefficient. Let us briefly explain the latter method.

The contribution of each variable to the regression sum of squares can easily be available from output of a computer package. In our MINITAB package, such contribution (SEQ SS) is also shown in Table 9.1. Now, in order to determine whether a particular explanatory variable significantly improves a model after all other explanatory variables have been included, the contribution of each variable to the regression sum of squares given in Table 9.1. is divided by MSE. Thus for our planned settlements, we obtain the following results for the 12 explanatory variables.

Table 9.3: *Contribution of Explanatory Variables (Planned Settlements)*

Explanatory Variable	Contribution
INCOME	327.23
PERSONS	12.91
BEDROOMS	0.20
MALEHEAD	5.45
AGE	14.06
2SPOUSE	19.23
RENTAL	7.61
CEILING	1,460.10
WALLS	91.67
ARCHITEC	0.16
WATER	0.91
SEPTIC	41.80

The null and alternative hypothesis to test for the contribution of each of the above variables to the model would be:

H_0 : variable Xi does not significantly improve the model once the other eleven variables have been included.

H_1: variable Xi significantly improves the model once the other eleven variables are included.

Since there are now 11 and 122 degrees of freedom respectively, if a 0.05 level of significance is selected, we again observe from the F distribution table that the critical value of F is 1.79. Looking at the results from the contribution of each explanatory variables as given in Table 9.3 above, it can be seen that all explanatory variables except three (number of bedrooms, architectural drawings and water supply) have values greater than 1.79. Our decision is therefore to reject Ho in the remaining nine explanatory variables but we cannot reject Ho in those three variables (BEDROOMS, ARCHITEC and WATER). In other words, the other nine variables contributed by significantly improving our model. Therefore our model should only include those remaining nine variables.

The MINITAB package can again easily give output for the nine "significant" explanatory variables.

The Problem of Multi-colinearity

In multiple regression analysis, even after removing some explanatory variables that do not significantly contribute to the regression model, researchers are still usually faced with the problem of multicolinearity of the explanatory variables. This condition refers to situations in which some of the explanatory variables are highly correlated with each other. In such cases it becomes difficult to separate the effects of such variables on the dependent variable.

Regression models with fever explanatory variables are inherently easier to interpret, because they are less likely to be affected by the problem of multicolinearity. This being the case, we can attempt, in our model of twelve variables, to determine the explanatory variables that might be deleted from the complete model. One of the widely used "search" procedures is called stepwise regression, which attempts to find the "best" regression model without examining all possible regressions.

The MINITAB computer package, for example, has a very useful command that identifies the best group of explanatory variables to use in the model. The command, STEPWISE, uses the stepwise regression procedure to arrive at this most useful subset. This regression is an iterative process with three district forms. The basic method calculates the F statistic for each variable in the model. The variable with the smallest *F*-value below a certain boundary level is removed from the model and the process starts again without the omitted variable. If no variable is removed, the programme will try to add a variable not in the model and the variable with the largest *F*-value is added to the model.

In our model of 135 observations in planned settlements, if a level of significance of 0.05 is selected, the critical value of F for each explanatory variable (1 and 133 degrees of freedom) is 3.84. Using the STEPWISE command, four explanatory variables (MALEHEAD, 2SPOUSE, RENTAL and WATER) with respective *F*-values of 1.02, 2.91, 2.20 and 1.99, which are each less than 3.84 are automatically omitted from the model. Although the remaining eight explanatory variables have F-value exceeding 3.84 each, only CEILING (896.52), WALLS (520.18) and SEPTIC (239.07) are eventually accepted in the model (see table 9.4).

In other words, in planned areas of Yombo Vituka, it is the presence or absence of roof ceiling, houses without or with well-plastered walls and the types of latrines (septic tank type and pit latrines) that best explain housing conditions in the areas.

Table 9.4: *Stepwise Regression*

F-to-Enter: 4.00 F-to-Remove: 4.00
Response is HOUSCOND on 8 predictors, with N = 135

Step	1	2	3	4
Constant	-2.22E-08	-2.71E-08	-6.98E-025	.746E-02
CEILING	0.958	0.636	0.558	0.539
T-Ratio	29.94	13.46	12.86	12.68
WALLS		0.364	0.279	0.293
T-Ratio		8.17	6.74	7.26
SEPTIC			0.233	0.290
T-Ratio			6.30	7.18
INCOME				-0.00000
T-Ratio				-3.07
S	0.170	0.139	0.122	0.118
R-Sq	87.08	91.42	93.41	93.86

Source: MINITAB Output

TESTING FOR INFLUENCES OF HOUSING CONDITIONS IN UNPLANNED SETTLEMENTS

The analysis and modeling as done for planned settlements was carried out for data on unplanned settlements in the study area. MINITAB REGRESS command produced an output as seen in Table 9.5. Again, if a level of significance of 0.05 is chosen, we determine that the critical value on the F distribution with 12 and 82 degrees of freedom is 1.89 as depicted in Figure 9.3.

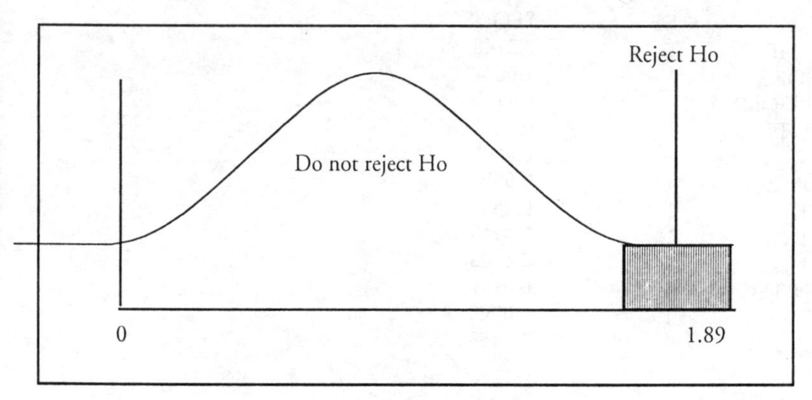

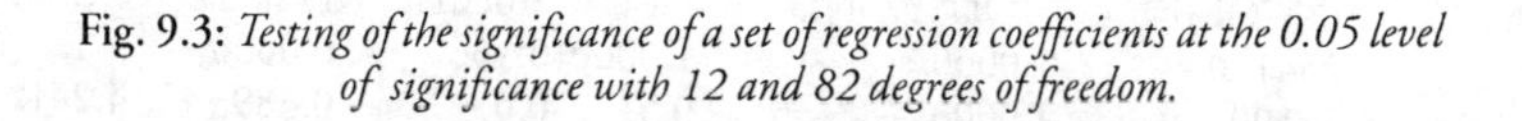
Fig. 9.3: *Testing of the significance of a set of regression coefficients at the 0.05 level of significance with 12 and 82 degrees of freedom.*

Table 9.5. Regression Analysis: Unplanned Settlements

The regression equation is:

HOUSCOND = 0.329 -0.000003 INCOME + 0.0053 PERSONS + 0.0185 BEDROOMS - 0.0780 MALEHEAD + 0.00008 AGE + 0.0438 2SPOUSE + 0.0495 RENTAL + 0.0578 CEILING + 0.269 WALLS + 0.0192 ARCHITEC + 0.129 WATER + 0.725 SEPTIC

Predictor	Coef	Stdev	t-ratio	p
Constant	0.32934	0.08527	3.86	0.000
INCOME	-0.00000286	0.00000081	-3.52	0.001
PERSONS	0.00530	0.01636	0.32	0.747
BEDROOMS	0.01850	0.04011	0.46	0.646
MALEHEAD	-0.07804	0.04917	-1.59	0.116
AGE	0.000078	0.002009	0.04	0.969
2SPOUSE	0.04378	0.04656	0.94	0.350
RENTAL	0.04947	0.04914	1.01	0.317
CEILING	0.05781	0.05762	1.00	0.319
WALLS	0.26897	0.07572	3.55	0.001
ARCHITEC	0.01925	0.05130	0.38	0.709
WATER	0.1293	0.1514	0.85	0.395
SEPTIC	0.72452	0.06072	11.93	0.000

s = 0.1363 R-sq = 91.7% R-sq(adj) = 90.5%

Analysis of Variance

SOURCE	DF	SS	MS	F	p
Regression	12	16.8976	1.4081	75.79	0.000
Error	82	1.5235	0.0186		
Total	94	18.4211			

SOURCE	DF	SEQ SS
INCOME	1	0.2748
PERSONS	1	1.0032
BEDROOMS	1	0.1129
MALEHEAD	1	0.2887
AGE	1	0.0605
2SPOUSE	1	0.5595
RENTAL	1	0.3582
CEILING	1	7.9749
WALLS	1	3.4508
ARCHITEC	1	0.0947
WATER	1	0.0740
SEPTIC	1	2.6453

Unusual Observations

Obs.	INCOME	HOUSCOND	Fit	Stdev.Fit	Residual	St.Residual
4	234100	1.0000	1.0000	0.1363	0.0000	* X
6	56100	1.0000	0.5107	0.0727	0.4893	4.24R

Table 9.5: *continued...*

Obs.	INCOME	HOUSCOND	Fit	Stdev.Fit	Residual	St.Residual
18	117800	1.0000	0.4436	0.0807	0.5564	5.06R
21	163900	0.0000	0.2751	0.0631	-0.2751	-2.28R
33	182300	0.0000	0.2737	0.0591	-0.2737	-2.23R
56	73800	0.0000	0.5222	0.0697	0.4778	4.08R
66	176300	0.0000	0.2895	0.0546	-0.2895	-2.32R
85	178500	0.0000	0.2602	0.0637	-0.2602	-2.16R

R denotes an obs. with a large st. resid.
X denotes an obs. whose X value gives it large influence.
Source: MINITAB Data Output

Since $F_{12,82} = 75.79$, which is greater than 1.89, we can again reject Ho and conclude that at least one of the explanatory variables among the twelve is influential on housing conditions.

Using adjusted R^2 it can be observed that 90.5% of the variations in housing conditions can be explained by our regression model after adjusting for a number of predictors and sample size. Correlation matrix for dependent and explanatory variables for unplanned settlements (see Table 9.6) suggests that there is a strong positive association between dependent variable (HOUSCOND) and CEILING, WALLS, ARCHITEC and SEPTIC. Otherwise between independent variables themselves, there is a strong positive association between INCOME and PERSONS; INCOME and BEDROOMS; INCOME and AGE; INCOME and RENTAL; PERSONS and BEDROOMS; PERSONS and AGE; PERSONS and RENTAL; BEDROOMS and AGE; AGE and RENTAL; CEILING and WALLS; CEILING and ARCHITEC, CEILING and SEPTIC; WALLS and ARCHITEC; WALLS and SEPTIC; and ARCHITEC and SEPTIC. Otherwise most other relationships are weak positive and negative relationships. In fact there is virtually no correlation between any other variable and MALEHEAD, 2SPOUSE and RENTAL respectively. There is also hardly any correlation between HOUSCOND and PERSONS, BEDROOMS, AGE and 2SPOUSE.

Table 9.6: *Pearson Correlations for Unplanned Settlements*

	Houscond	Income	Persons	Bedrooms	Malehead	Age	2spouse	Rental
INCOME	0.122							
PERSONS	-0.039	0.807						
BEDROOMS	0.050	0.768	0.834					
MALEHEAD	-0.133	-0.056	-0.060	-0.103				
AGE	0.018	0.663	0.783	0.707	-0.000			
2SPOUSE	-0.069	0.424	0.291	0.344	-0.140	0.136		
RENTAL	-0.114	0.519	0.532	0.465	-0.050	0.531	0.345	

Table 9.6: *continues...*

	Houscond	Income	Persons	Bedrooms	Malehead	Age	2spouse	Rental
CEILING	0.732	0.298	0.148	0.234	-0.103	0.260	0.000	-0.034
WALLS	0.859	0.221	0.081	0.165	-0.082	0.189	-0.068	-0.047
ARCHITEC	0.630	0.342	0.139	0.206	-0.009	0.213	0.082	0.025
WATER	0.173	0.224	0.272	0.115	0.033	0.152	0.045	0.046
SEPTIC	0.919	0.267	0.037	0.112	-0.078	0.043	-0.036	-0.086

	CEILING	WALLS	ARCHITEC	WATER
WALLS	0.852			
ARCHITEC	0.580	0.687		
WATER	0.126	0.148	0.200	
SEPTIC	0.672	0.789	0.635	0.188

Source: MINITAB Data Output

If the contribution of each variable to the regression sum of squares is divided by MSE, the following results are obtained for our unplanned settlement model.

Table 9.7: *Contribution of Explanatory Variables (Unplanned Settlements)*

Explanatory Variable	Contribution
INCOME	14.77
PERSONS	53.94
BEDROOMS	0.17
MALEHEAD	6.07
AGE	15.52
2SPOUSE	30.08
RENTAL	19.26
CEILING	428.76
WALLS	185.53
ARCHITEC	5.00
WATER	3.98
SEPTIC	142.22

Since there are now 11 and 82 degrees of freedom respectively, if a 0.05 level of significance is selected, we observe that the critical value of F is 1.93. Looking at the results from the contribution of each explanatory variables as given at Table 9.7 above, it can be seen that all explanatory variables except BEDROOMS have values exceeding 1.93. Our decision is therefore to reject Ho in all the eleven variables. In other words, the eleven variables contributed by significantly improving our model.

However using STEPWISE regression, we see that, while F value, for 1 and 93 degrees of freedom, is 3.96, only CEILING, WALLS, ARCHITEC and

SEPTIC have F values greater than 3.96 at 107.31, 261.05, 61.06 and 502.53 respectively. However, STEPWISE regression goes on to omit CEILING and ARCHITEC, so that the only "fit" explanatory variables which best explain housing conditions in unplanned settlements in Yombo Vituka are SEPTIC and WALLS, that is, sanitation system and (poor) walls.

THE USE OF LOGIT MODEL FOR DUMMY DEPENDENT VARIABLE

The conclusions derived above stem from the use of linear probability models with the dependent variable being a dummy variable. As noted earlier, when we have a dummy dependent variable, linear probability models usually violate the assumptions regarding the specifications of the error term in the model. Moreover, such linear models do not constrain predictions within 0-1 limit as required by dichotomous (dummy) dependent variable principle. In order to get more reliable results in such cases, we need to apply logit or probit models.

The probit and logit models are almost similar except that they differ in the specification of the distribution of the error term, *u*. The logit model, for example, will constrain all predictions within 0-1 limit. The logit model transforms the values of the attribute X to a probability which lies in the range 0-1, and the model is based on the cumulative logistic probability function as follows:

$$P_i = F(a + bX) = 1/[1 + e^{-(a + bX_i)}]$$

Where,

P_i = probability of the house being in good condition
X_i = attributes of the house and household
e = natural logarithm

Logit Model and Housing Conditions in Planned Settlements

The results of the logit regression of housing conditions in planned areas are presented in Table 9.8. and 9.9. Table 9.8 shows the influence of variables, through the logit regression coefficients, in determining house condition. As seen from Table 9.8, the three most significant variables determining house condition in planned areas are absence or presence of ceiling roofs, well-plastered walls, and sanitation (septic-type of latrines). Others are household income, and houses built according to architectural drawings. Male-headed or female-headed households and water do not seem to have any effect on housing condition. Water supply does not also affect housing condition, ostensibly since the problem of water in Yombo Vituka is a common phenomenon to all households.

Table 9.9 presents the allocation of individual houses on the basis of worse (poor) or better (good) condition classifications. In the planned areas, 44 houses were actually in worse condition and 91 were in better condition than average. Our logit model, however, predicted 40 and 95 respectively in these categories. Thus, this model, trying to capture the outcomes of individual decisions, performed much better than random, achieving a 97.05% overall correct classification of houses.

Table 9.8: *Probability of "better" housing conditions: Logit Function (Planned Settlements).*

Dependent variable: house condition (HOUSECON)
Number of Observations: 135
Number of poor condition: 44
Number of good condition: 91

Variable	Coeff	Std error	Sig.	R
INCOME	0.00000	0.00000	0.0000	0.3339
PERSONS	0.03796	0.05920	0.0318	0.1237
BEDROOMS	-0.04495	0.15465	0.0177	0.1459
MALEHEAD	-0.16326	0.16035	0.3105	0.0000
AGE	-0.01138	0.00789	0.0258	0.1320
SPOUSE	-0.00721	0.14703	0.0889	0.0724
RENTAL	0.01887	0.18832	0.1382	0.0340
CEILING	0.09725	0.22921	0.0000	0.8234
WALLS	0.20046	0.21584	0.0000	0.7868
ARCHITEC	-0.67243	0.20023	0.0000	0.3620
WATER	-0.24523	0.36916	0.1580	0.0000
SEPTIC	0.15026	0.22407	0.0000	0.7051

Source: SPSS Logit Model Data Output

Table 9.9: *Predicted Values Compared to Actual (Observed) Values*

		Poor	Good	Total	% Correct
Observed Values	Poor	40	4	44	90.91%
	Good	0	91	91	100.0%
	Total	40	95	135	97.04%

Source: SPSS Logit Model Data Output

Logit Model and Housing Conditions in Unplanned Settlements

Table 9.10 shows the influence of variables, through the logit regression coefficients, in determining housing conditions in the Yombo Vituka unplanned settlements. As can be observed, the four significant variables determining housing conditions in unplanned areas are absence or presence of ceilings under house roofs, well-plastered walls, architectural drawings of houses and septic latrines.

Table 9.11 presents allocation of individual houses on the basis of worse (poor) or better (good) conditions classification in the unplanned settlements. It shows that 70 houses were actually in worse conditions and 25 were in better conditions than average. However, our logit model predicated 73 and 22 respectively in these categories. Thus, this model performed much better prediction than the random, achieving 96.85% overall correct classification of houses.

Table 9.10: *Probability of "better" housing condition: logit function* - Unplanned settlements

Dependent variable: house condition (HOUSECON)
Number of observations: 95
Number of poor condition: 70
Number of good condition: 25
Variable Regression

	Coeff.	Std Error	Signif.	R
INCOME	0.00000	0.00000	0.2339	0.0000
PERSONS	-0.03025	0.09247	0.7017	0.0000
BEDROOMS	0.17135	0.22233	0.6231	0.0000
MALEHEAD	-0.01871	0.27179	0.1943	0.0000
AGE	-0.00336	0.01139	0.8614	0.0000
SPOUSE	-0.09665	0.24667	0.5012	0.0000
RENTAL	-0.00164	0.27124	0.2652	0.0000
CEILING	0.01768	0.25084	0.0000	0.6682
WALLS			0.0000	0.7883
ARCHITECT	-0.27952	0.26235	0.0000	0.5706
WATER	0.17549	0.80345	0.0925	0.0871
SEPTIC	0.47965	0.29399	0.0000	0.8449

Source: SPSS Logit Model Data Output

Table 9.11: *Predictive Values Compared to Actual (Observed)*

Predicted Value					
		Poor	Good	Total	Percent Correct
Observed Values	Poor	70	0	70	100.00
	Good	3	22	25	88.00
	Total	73	22	95	96.84

Source: SPSS Logit Model Data Output

In summary, we can see from the above results that housing conditions in the study area are generally poor (particularly in unplanned settlements) and that the major influences on such conditions are poor sanitation systems, poor structurally designed houses, and overcrowding.

10

INCOME GENERATING CAPACITY AND CONTINGENT VALUATION MODELS

In this chapter, we shall test hypotheses 2 and 3 of income generating capacity of housing, and willingness and ability of householders to pay for both housing and non-housing goods and services.

INCOME GENERATING CAPACITY

According to Wegelin and Borgman (1995), housing is a major form of asset creation and savings. To low income families, housing is a shelter, commodity and investment. A home is a workshop, storehouse and a source of inputs. It has a large income generating capacity. In analyzing the income generating capacity of residents of the study area within their housing and neighbourhoods, and to test hypothesis 2, it was found that many residents were also using the houses or their compounds for income generating ventures as shown at Table 10.1.

Table 10.1: *Households' Other Income Generating Activities*

Activity	Planned Areas		Unplanned Areas		Total	
	No	%	No	%	No	%
1. Partly rented houses:						
- for residential	7	4.9	3	2.8	10	4.0
- for business	8	5.5	12	11.2	20	7.9
2. Own business extensions	31	21.5	28	26.2	59	23.5
3. Poultry	5	3.5	3	2.8	8	3.2
4. Cattle rearing	4	2.8	2	1.9	6	2.4
5. Gardening	8	5.5	4	3.7	12	4.8
6. Piggery	3	2.1	-	-	3	1.2
7. Not applicable	78	54.2	55	51.4	133	53.0
Total	144	100.0	107	100.0	251	100.0

Source: Field Survey, 1999

Table 10.1 shows that 45.8% of households interviewed in planned settlements also used their houses or compounds for other income generating activities; while the percentage for squatter areas was 48.6%. What the interviewers observed was that most of those households who were not using their houses for other income generating activities had space problem, rather than capital problem. Unfortunately many respondents were not truthful enough in answering questions related to income, including income generated from other activities within the compound of their households. It seemed that many respondents only provided income figures related to formal employment or activities, and could not, or refused to reveal income from other informal activities, which, as per Table 10.1, must have been accounting for a sizeable households' income. As evidenced earlier (see Chapter Seven), this could be proved by the fact that household income revealed was, in most cases (181 out of 251 respondents, or 72%), less than the stated total expenditure pattern revealed by the same respondents. Casual inquiries into the cause of such differences revealed that it was due to income generated from other activities performed either within the households as shown above, or other informal activities outside the households. This proves our hypothesis that households (especially spacious/adequate housing) could be a major source of income generating activities for poverty alleviation in the households concerned.

Table 10.2: *Effects of Poor Housing Conditions/Environments*

	Planned Areas				Unplanned Areas				Total			
	YES		NO		YES		NO		YES		NO	
	No.	%	No.	%	No.	%	No	%	No	%	No	%
Poor/inadequate housing conditions affect:												
• Income generating capacity	95	66	49	34	89	83	18	17	184	73	67	27
• Children'sschool attendance/ performance	78	54	66	46	78	73	29	27	156	62	95	38
• Children's health?	85	59	59	41	71	66	36	34	156	62	95	38
• Social and mental satisfaction, and thus, productivity	79	55	65	45	75	70	32	25	154	61	97	39

Source: Field Survey, 1999

As evidenced from Table 10.2, 66% of the people interviewed from planned settlements and 83% from unplanned settlements said that their poor housing conditions and environments (especially lack of adequate housing space) affected their capacity to generate additional income in-house. In other words, if one had good and adequate housing, he would be able to generate more income through in-house activities. This proves the hypothesis that adequate housing is a source of income and could therefore be used to alleviate poverty.

Table 10.2 suggests that poor housing conditions also affected children's health and education and family's social and mental satisfaction for the majority of households in both planned and unplanned settlements.

CONTINGENT VALUATION AND WILLINGNESS TO PAY FOR IMPROVED HOUSING

Measuring Welfare or Utility

When one is analyzing economic welfare of a unit, the decision is normally anchored on two opposing considerations: maximization of the unit's welfare on the one hand, and its limited resources and other constraints on the other. In our present study, the unit is a household in planned or unplanned poor settlement. It should also be appreciated that welfare or utility is difficult to define or measure, but for our purpose, utility or welfare of a household is assumed to derive from the consumption of housing and non-housing goods and services. Empirical statement of this theoretical framework is therefore that it is the consumption of a bundle of housing and non-housing goods and services that contributes to welfare or utility of a household. The willingness to pay by households for improved housing services is also dependent on the utility or welfare theory.

The remainder of this chapter expounds on this theory and, using filed data, analyzes willingness to pay for better (improved) housing and associated services by households using the contingent valuation method, thus testing our third hypothesis that there is willingness to pay for improved housing services by poor households in urban settlements.

Utility Theory and Willingness to Pay

For better understanding of this utility and maximization theory, let us first examine an illustrative example in line with the work by Hui (1999). Suppose a household faces quantity constraints on its housing consumption, denoted by a vector $z' = (z'_1, z'_2, \ldots, z'k)$; but is unconstrained in its non-housing consumption, denoted by a vector $x = (x_1, x_2, \ldots, x_k)$. The household's utility function is written as:

$u = [x, z']$

The budget constraint is denoted by:

$Y = p_x + P_z',$

Where $P > 0$ is the vector of prices (in our case) of poor housing in poor urban settlements. The household's total income is Y. The budget constraint represents that total expenditure cannot exceed total income. Furthermore, the household faces the quantity constraints $z = z'$, where $z > 0$ is a vector of imposed quantities.

Researchers on housing economics have shown that given quantity constraints, under-consumption exists among poor households. In the case of under-consumption, households are compelled to consume less of z' than they would choose if unconstrained. It is assumed that a feasible x exists, and that the direct utility function is approximately differentiable or smooth. Based on the above equations on utility function and budget constraint, the quantity constrained indirect utility function associated with this maximization problem can be written as:

$$u\,[x, z] = \max\,[u(x, z)p_x + P_z = Y]$$
$$= u\,[x(p, Y - Pz, z), z]$$
$$= V\,(p, Y - P_z, z)$$

Where, $x(p,Y-P_z, z)$ is the demand equation for non-housing consumption, x. The amount of each non-housing item depends on income and the amount of housing consumption. This indirect utility function shows the maximum welfare level, V, that can be realized with income Y, when prices are p and P; and quantities are x and z. The more useful tool for welfare analyses in relation to quantity-constrained situation is the following:

$$e = \mathrm{Min}_x\,[\,px + P_2z\,U\,(x, z) > = U'\,]$$
$$= e\,(p, P, z, U')$$

Where, U' is a specified utility level, say initial or final level. This function denotes the minimum level of expenditure for any given price, values of the quantity constraints and level of utility. Suppose we compare two situations, whose only difference between them is a change in the quantity constraints from z^o to z^1, a higher standard. Before the quantity change, the expenditure function reads:

$$e^o = e\,(p, P, z^o, U^o)$$

But after the quantity change, the expenditure function reads:

$$e^1 = e\,(p, P, z^1\,U^o)$$

For both equations above, the welfare of the household is held constant at the initial level. It has been evidenced that the best approach is to calculate this amount as the change in the area under a compensated z between z^o and z^1. If the household's utility is fixed at the initial level, the difference between the expenditure functions with a change in quantity constraints from z^o to z^1, after improved (better) housing is provided, can be written as:

$$e^1 - e^o = e\,(p, P, z^1, U^o) - (p, P, z^o, U^o)$$
$$= f\,(p, z^o, z^1) \text{ at } U^o, \text{ from which we can simplify by taking off x:}$$
$$= f\,[(Y\text{-}Pz), z^o, z^1] \text{ at } U^o$$
$$= f\,(Y, r^o, z^o, z^1) \text{ at } U^o$$

Where, r^o (= Pz) is the existing rent or house price.

With the increase in housing consumption, $(e^1\text{-}e^o)$ is the amount of money household is willing to pay in view of the reduction of non-housing consumption, subject to budget constraints. The marginal willingness to pay (WTP) which is $(e^1\text{-}e^o)$, is the maximum amount a household is willing to pay for improved housing leaving the household equally well-off in both situations of before and after the change.

The notion of willingness to pay must therefore be introduced when considering the effects on welfare and the revenue generating potential of local governments and other stakeholders of fixing charges for improved housing services. In practice, however, many other factors influence the demand for housing. For example, the size of household needs to be taken into account. If all such intervening variables are denoted by h $(h_1, h_2, \ldots, h_k)$, we can express the WTP for higher level of housing services as:

$$WTP = f\,(z^1, z^o, r^o, Y; h)$$

Where WTP is willingness to pay for better housing in aggregate terms (including related services).

Contingent Valuation Method

One of the approaches in making reliable estimates of households' willingness to pay is simply to ask an individual how much he or she would be willing to pay for improved housing services, for instance. This survey approach is termed the contingent valuation method because the researcher within the context of a hypothetical market poses the questions. One of the advantages of contingent valuation method is that it can be used in situations in which a good or service is not currently available to a particular group of households (like lack of piped-water in Yombo Vituka settlements). However, quoting Cummings et al (1986), Whittington et al (1990) states that contingent valuation surveys have been conventionally considered as unreliable because of the pervasive feeling that interrogated responses by individuals to hypothetical propositions must be, at best, inferior to "hard" market data, or, at worst, off-the-cuff attitudinal indications which might be expected to reflect efforts by individuals to manipulate the survey to their selfish ends.

Research Design

In our current study of Yombo Vituka, the research design was developed to test whether contingent valuation could be used to estimate better or improved housing and related services demand relationships suggested by consumer demand or economic theory and thus if we could reliably estimate individual households' willingness to pay for improved housing services. Economic theory suggests that an individual's demand for a good or service is a function of the price of the good or service, prices of substitute and complementary goods, the individual's income and the individual's tastes, usually measured by the individual's socio-economic characteristics.

From the surveys and research tests conducted of Yombo Vituka, it is clear that housing structures and other related services such as adequate and safe water supply, sanitation systems, access roads and solid waste disposal systems are in poor state. The aim of this contingent valuation was therefore to test households' willingness to pay for improved housing services if local authorities with the support of other private agencies were to provide such services, and if they could even provide housing loans to improve the housing structures and spaces.

Maximum willingness to pay for housing services will vary from household to household and should be a function of all of the variables in the demand function except the price of the required services themselves. In our case, the households' WTP bids should thus be positively related to household income (HINCOME), the costs of obtaining the current levels of water services (HWATER). These are cost of buying water from water vendors, shallow walls and the "cost" or health risks from currently using unsafe water. Other costs which are positively related to WTP bids are costs and risks of current poor sanitation services (SANITAN), poor access roads (ACCESS), lack of solid waste disposal system (WASTE) and the cost and risks of staying in the current housing structures (HCOND). However the WTP bids could be negatively correlated with the individuals' perception of the quality of the present housing conditions and services. It could be hypothesized that WTP bids for old people (AGES) would be lower than those of younger households since the former consider their remaining life shorter to warrant huge commitments in housing improvements. Bids of householders with a large number of occupants (HPERSONS) could also be hypothesized to be higher than of those with fewer occupants. Male-headed (HMALE) householders could also be assumed to be willing to pay more for housing services, in general, than women-headed households, although for water services, particularly, WTP bids of women respondents would be higher than those of men because women carry most of the water (see, for example, Whittington et al, 1990). WTP bids of renters (HRENTAL) would also be expected to be lower than of owner-occupiers since they (renters) are basically temporary occupants. In carrying out the contingent valuation survey by interviewing heads of households in the selected sample population, the following assumptions were made (see also Hui, 1999):

1. The householder's decisions are predominantly determined by his desire to "consume" housing services, and paying for improved housing services is simply the method of achieving this objective i.e. an increasing demand for housing (at the level of individual person or household).
2. The improvements of housing services being offered in this study is viewed by each household as real and possible.
3. The decision by the household on the WTP is characterized by the utility function U = U (z, x), where x is a composite non-housing commodity, and $z = (z_1,\ldots, z_n)$ a vector of housing attributes, or characteristics and qualities. Under the hypothetical situation of improved housing, each household is free from the existing supply constraint, and can demand extra amounts of given attributes, maximizing its utility subject to budget constraints.
4. The respondent (head of household) who answers the WTP bids is making decisions on behalf of the family over housing matters, and there is a household consensus among each member of the household, providing the same level of utility. The head of household is also in a position of knowing how much the household would be paying for the improved housing services as offered, and which housing attributes the household prefers.
5. Householders in the study area nowadays are generally more affluent than in the past and have higher expectations and aspirations towards better housing. Meanwhile, each household has its own preferences among different housing attributes.
6. It is assumed that there are no biases, which are normally typical in contingent valuation surveys (see Whittington *et al*, 1990), i.e. strategic bias, starting

point bias and hypothetical bias. In other words, it is assumed that respondents answer WTP bids truthfully without strategic bias; the starting point or initial price indicated in the questionnaire is not interpreted as a clue as to the "correct" bid; and that there is no hypothetical bias i.e. respondents correctly understand and perceive the characteristics of the housing services being described and take the questions very seriously.

Empirical Data and Analysis

Before WTP was asked, the study first inquired about the satisfaction with the present housing condition and services in general (housing structure, water services, sanitation, sewerage, access roads etc.).

Empirical evidence was first collected of satisfaction and willingness to pay for better (improved) housing conditions and services among households in both planned and unplanned settlements in the study area using uni-variate analysis; and then the relationship between willingness to pay and independent variables was tested using multivariate analysis as hypothesized earlier. In this latter analysis, we attempt to investigate specifically the extent to which variations in willingness to pay the amount in question for improved housing services can be related to various factors embodied in variables of household characteristics and the financial ability of the households. We look at the housing services (HOUSERV) in its totality, which is to be improved in both planned and unplanned settlements.

Satisfaction With Housing Services

Given the poor conditions of housing structures and other related services like lack of adequate and safe water supply, poor sanitation conditions, poor access roads, poor drainage systems and solid waste management in both planned and unplanned settlements of Yombo Vituka, it can be safely assumed that residents are not satisfied with the present conditions of their housing and related services. Nonetheless, they were asked about their satisfaction with housing conditions and services, and responses were as shown at Table 10.3.

As can be observed from Table 10.3, the mean of level of satisfaction with housing conditions/services in planned areas was 2.54, which can be interpreted to be between unsatisfactory (2) and just adequate (3). The variability that exists in the data, measured by standard deviation for data in planned areas is just 0.84, indicating that the average value, or mean, well depicts the data.In the squatter settlements, the level of satisfaction is 1.91, which is just below unsatisfactory level (2).

Table 10.3: *Satisfaction With Housing Conditions/Services*

Level of Satisfaction	Narration	Planned Areas		Unplanned Areas		Total	
		NO	%	NO.	%	NO.	%
1	Very Unsatisfactory	15	10.4	24	22.4	39	15.5
2	Unsatisfactory	64	44.5	71	66.4	135	53.8
3	Just Adequate	49	34.0	10	9.3	59	23.5
4	Satisfactory	15	10.4	2	1.9	17	6.8
5	Very Satisfactory	1	0.7	-	-	1	0.4
	Total	144	100.0	107	100.0	251	100.0
	Observations	144		107		251	
	Mean	2.54		1.91		2.23	
	Standard Deviation	0.84		0.62		0.65	

Source: Field Survey, 1999.

This proves that people living in unplanned areas are more unsatisfied with their housing conditions/services than those living in planned areas. Again the standard deviation is small at 0.62. If the whole sample for both planned and planned settlements of Yombo Vituka is considered, the level of satisfaction is 2.23 which is just above unsatisfactory level, and the standard deviation is 0.65.

Willingness to Pay for Improved Housing

To measure willingness to pay for improved housing services, the respondents were told that:

1. For improving their housing structures and space (including erecting better but affordable housing units in place of the present poor housing structures) it was possible for some agencies and local communities to arrange the

establishment of housing credit loans. Given that possibility, it was important to know whether interested and affected residents could be willing and able to repay such loans.

2. For improved housing related services (water, sanitation, drainage, access roads, health care etc), local government with the support of donor and other NGOs could provide such services at some contributory terms i.e. local residents to pay part of the cost of these services. Residents' willingness to pay for such costs was therefore also required to be known.

The first step was to inquire whether the households were willing to pay more than what they are currently incurring for housing -related services if these services could be improved. A majority of respondents answered "yes". In fact between 105 and 119 people out of 144 (72.9% - 82.6%) and between 70 and 81 out of 107 (65.4% - 75.7%) in planned areas and unplanned areas respectively answered in the affirmative, that they would be willing to pay more if housing-related services were improved depending on the extent of services (see Levels I - III below), including repaying housing loan by installments if these were reasonable.

They were then asked how much they would be willing and able to pay if the levels of services to be improved were as follows:

Level I: Provision of piped-water, drainage system and better access roads
Level II: Provision of the above (level I) plus sewage and sewerage systems and health care centres.
Level III: Provision of all the above (levels I and II) plus surveyed and serviced plots (for unplanned settlements) and provision of housing loans.

The responses were as shown at Table 10.4.

The results from Table 10.4 show that each household in planned areas was willing to pay an average of T.shs. 13,837 more for level I (if water supply, drainage system and access roads were to be improved). The corresponding figure for unplanned settlements was T.shs. 9,953. The standard deviations for these means are large at T.shs. 10,784 and T.shs. 9,991 respectively, indicating that the actual willingness to pay for various households are widely dispersed about their mean (see Sanders, 1995).

If improvements of housing services were to include also sewage and sewerage systems and better health care centres (level II), the WTP of households in planned areas and unplanned areas increased to a mean of T.shs. 14,215 and T.shs. 10,393 respectively. In case housing loans were also to be provided and un-surveyed plots were also to be surveyed (Level III), the mean WTP increased to Tshs. 15,656 and Tshs. 12,481 for residents in planned and unplanned areas respectively. In other words, for level III, WTP of residents in planned areas increased by only 10.1% compared to level II, while WTP of those living in squatter settlements increased by 20.1%, proving the hypothesis that squatter residents were more concerned with their poor housing structures and insecure land tenure.

Table 10.4: *Willingness to Pay for Improved Housing Services*

T.shs. per month	Level I				Level II				Level III			
	Planned Areas		Unplanned Areas		Planned Areas		Unplanned Areas		Planned Areas		Unplanned Areas	
	No	%	No	%	No	%	No	%	No	%	No	%
0 / No response	39	27	37	35	30	21	33	31	25	17	26	24
1,000-10,000	21	15	33	31	28	19	38	36	33	23	30	37
11,000-20,000	50	35	15	14	49	34	12	11	45	31	15	14
21,000-30,000	21	15	16	15	27	19	17	16	23	16	15	14
31,000-50,000	11	8	6	6	8	6	7	7	15	10	11	10
51,000-70,000	2	1	-	-	2	1	-	-	3	2	1	1
Total	144	100	107	100	144	100	107	100	144	100	107	100
Observation	144		107		144		107		144		107	
Mean	13,837		9,953		14,215		10,393		15,656		12,481	
Std Deviation	10,784		9,991		10,397		10,392		12,097		12,101	

Source: Field Survey, 1999

Probit Model of Contingent Valuation Bids

As can be observed from Table 10.4, standard deviations for WTP for all levels of service were large in both planned settlements and squatters. This shows that WTP bids were widely dispersed about their means. In order to understand the cause of such wide dispersion, variations in the bids for improved housing services were modeled as a function of the variables that were considered to be affecting willingness to pay. As explained earlier, independent variables thought to be affecting WTP, and which were included in our model were: household income, safe and adequate water supply (dummy), sanitation system (dummy), access roads (dummy), waste disposal system (dummy), housing condition (dummy), age of head of household, number of persons per household, male headed household (dummy) and renter-householders (dummy).

As for the dependent variable (WTP), this was not considered to be a continuous variable as it seems, because in the real sense, the most reliable data generated from this bidding game were the set of yes/no responses to questions about specific, discrete prices like between T.shs. 11,000 to T.shs. 20,000, or between T.shs. 21,000 and T.shs. 30,000. This being the case, the observed dependent variable obtained from such questions could not be the maximum amount the household would be willing to pay, but rather, an interval within which the "true" willingness to pay falls. Linear regression cannot therefore be an appropriate procedure for dealing with such an ordinal dependent variable because the assumptions regarding the specification of the error term in the linear model will be violated (see Maddala, 1989). Therefore an ordered probit model was used to explain the variations in our WTP bidding game.

In this model, let Wh be the maximum willingness to pay for improved housing services of household "h". Based on consumer demand theory, Wh can be hypothesized as a function of the attributes of the new and existing housing conditions, services and other households' socio-economic characteristics. Thus,

$$W_h = a + X_h b + e_h$$

Where X_h is a vector of the household's characteristics and other attributes (independent variables); a and b are parameters of the model and e_h is a random term with a standard normal distribution. Since W_h is not observable from this bidding game, the above equation cannot be estimated. However, from the interview responses, the ranges within which W_h will fall are known. Let $R_1 \ldots$, R_m be the "m" prices which divided the range of WTP space into m + 1 categories, and let y_h be a categorical variable such that:

$$Y_h = 0 \text{ if } W_h < R_1,$$
$$= 1 \text{ if } R_1 < W_h < R_2$$
$$= M\text{-}1 \text{ if } W_h > R_m$$

If we let i = 1,....., M + 1, from the earlier equation, we have:

$$Y_h = 1 \text{ if } R_i - 1 < a + X_h b + e_h < R_i$$
$$\text{or } Ri - 1 - a < X_h b + e_h < R_i - a$$
$$\text{or } (Ri - 1 - a - X_h b)/sd < e_h/sd$$
$$< (Ri - a - X_h b)/sd,$$

Where sd is the standard deviation of e_h. Assuming e_h follows a standard normal distribution, then,

$$P (Y_h = i) = P (R_i\text{-}1 < W_h < R_i)$$
$$= P (ui - 1 - Xhb < eh < Ui - 1 - X_h b)$$
$$= F (ui - X_h b) - F (ui - 1 - X_h b),$$

Where $u_i = R_i - a$ and F(.) is the cumulative standard normal density function. The last equation above is the ordered probit model used to explain the variations in WTP bids.

As seen above, the mean WTP for planned and unplanned areas for level III (see Table 10.3) were Tshs. 15,656 and Tshs. 12,481 respectively. For our probit model of planned settlements, we therefore assume that,

$$WTP = 0 \text{ if } Y < 15,656$$
$$= 1 \text{ if } Y \geq 15,656$$

And for unplanned settlements,

$$WTP = 0 \text{ if } Y < 12,481$$
$$= 1 \text{ if} \geq 12,481$$

Responses for WTP were as shown in Table 10.5 below

Table. 10.5. *Willingness to Pay for Level III*

Willingness to Pay	Planned Areas		Unplanned Areas		Total	
	No	%	No	%	No.	%
Tshs.0–15,656/ No responses (0)	78	54.2	71	66.4	149	59.4
Tshs. 15,656 and more (1)	66	45.8	36	34.6	102	40.6
Total	144	100.0	107	100.0	251	100.0

Source: Field Survey, 1999

The results of the estimations or WTP for level III using probit model are presented in Table 10.6 and Table 10.7 for planned areas and unplanned areas respectively.

Table 10.6: *Willingness to Pay Bids for Improved Housing* (Planned Settlements)

- Dependent Variable: WTP (The Probability that a household's willingness to pay for better housing falls within a specified interval)
- Independent variables:

	Regression Coeff	Std Error
HINCOME	0.00000	0.0000
HWATER	0.35905	0.45442
SANT	0.13623	0.38259
HCOND	0.11417	0.29253
AGES	0.01108	0.01198
HPERSON	0.02491	0.07208
HMALE	0.04422	0.25045
HRENTA	0.07769	0.26093

Chi Square = 80.406
Degrees of freedom =126
P = 0.999

Source: SPSS Probit Analysis Data Output

Table 10.7: *Willingness to Pay Bids for Improved Housing* (Unplanned Settlement)

- Dependent Variable: WTP (The Probability that a household's willingness to pay for better housing falls within a specified interval).
- Independent variables:

	Regression Coefficient	Std Error
Hincome	0.00000	0.00000
Hwater	0.15949	0.86971
Sanitation	0.09023	0.68307
Hcond	0.05254	0.63570
Ages	0.00360	0.01150
Hperson	0.00004	0.08440
Hmale	0.18150	0.32606
Hrental	0.10625	0.29973

Chi Square = 87.249
Degrees of freedom = 86
P = 0.442

Source: SPSS Probit Analysis Data Output.

From table 10.6 and 10.7 the chi-square statistics for planned and unplanned areas illustrate that the overall models are highly significant. In the planned settlements, households with water and sanitation problems tend to bid more.

Households with more persons [HPERSON] also tend to be more willing to pay for improved housing conditions, as shown by the direction of the coefficients of the independent variable. In unplanned settlements, male-headed households and households with sanitation problems tended to be more willing to pay for improved housing conditions.

In summary, it can therefore be concluded that WTP bids are not just random numbers but are systematically related to the variables suggested by economic theory. This suggests that it is possible to do a contingent valuation survey, using WTP bids, among a very poor, illiterate population and obtain reasonable, consistent answers.

POOR PEOPLE'S INVOLVEMENT

The last part of the questionnaire required the respondents to state any other comments they might have which had relevance to the study. Most of the respondents stated that they had nothing more to comment, but 49 respondents (32 from planned settlements and 17 from unplanned settlements) gave varying, interesting but somehow interrelated comments. On the face of it, these comments could simply pass as irrelevant, unimportant or just casual comments, but analyzed deeply, the comments could be the major cornerstone of problems associated with poverty within the poor communities.

Although not given in so many words, these comments could be summarized as follows:

- "Alleviation of poverty without considering and deeply analyzing the concerns of poor people will always be a futile ambition."
- "The government officials ignore our involvement in our development plans and programmes."
- "The bureaucrats just sit in luxurious offices up there and prepare plans and programmes for the poor people without even knowing them earnestly."
- "Are you really doing this study for our benefit or just for your education and career purposes?'
- "How can somebody living in a two-storey villa at Msasani Peninsula seriously deal with housing problems of poor people in Yombo Vituka?"
- "We, the poor are considered too poor, even in our heads and commitment, to plan and execute programmes affecting our development! This is absurd and quite untrue."
- "Rich people can never pretend to be wholeheartedly committed to alleviating poverty of the poor people."

- "A large proportion of donor assistance earmarked for poverty alleviation in poor communities end up in pockets and welfare of rich or well-to-do politicians and planners."
- "You, educated people and politicians, are underrating the will and ability of poor people in planning and undertaking our own development programmes"
- "Power to plan, manage and effect development programmes and schemes which has been devolved by the central government to city commission or municipalities need to be further devolved down to us poor people and our community organizations. As it is, there is very little difference and impact between city commission's ways of doing things, and those which used to be applied by the central government".

What poor people are saying, as represented by sentiments of Yombo Vituka's poor households, is that rich people cannot wholeheartedly be concerned with poor people's plights. They are more concerned with enriching themselves even further in total disregard of the poor people. The apparent moves by the rich people, bureaucrats, professionals, researchers and rich donors to assist the poor, are mostly illusory and for their own benefits rather than poor people's welfare. That is why, as also alluded to by Chambers (1997), more people than ever before are wealthy beyond any reasonable need for a good life, and more are poor and vulnerable below any conceivable definition of decency.

Poor people tend to think, rightly so, that rich people cannot properly and definitely analyze and reflect upon the poverty situations of poor people, and plan and implement strategies to alleviate poverty amidst the poor. It is the poor people themselves who can do all these in a much more realistic and concerned way. Yet the over class holds power, and bears the main responsibility for what is to be done or not done for the poor. It is the politicians, the bureaucrats, the researchers and the donors who decide what anti-poverty programmes should be enunciated and implemented. More often than not, these programmes do no effectively alleviate poverty amongst the poor either because the affected people were not directly involved in the planning and implementation resulting in misdirection of efforts and resources, or the involved over class deliberately diverted the resources for their own benefits. For instance, donors and creditors who proclaim their commitment to anti-poverty programmes nevertheless require poor debtor countries to pursue policies which benefit the donors but which further weaken and impoverish the poorest (Chambers, 1997).

In the local front, politicians and bureaucrats impose anti-poverty policies and programmes on the affected people which finally either fail or stagnate to the detriment of the poor, but without affecting those upper policy makers, or at worse, further enriching them collectively or individually. The conclusion from the above findings and analysis is that poor people, in their communities, have more ability, commitment and reason to plan and implement poverty alleviation programmes in their areas than any third party not directly affected. The policy makers and donors need just to support such ability and commitment, but should never sideline the affected people in the endeavour to plan and implement these programmes, if they have to succeed.

11

EFFECTS OF INCOME LEVELS AND INSECURE LAND TENURE ON HOUSING IMPROVEMENTS

HOUSING CONDITIONS IN PLANNED AND UNPLANNED SETTLEMENTS

As per hypothesis number 4, this chapter seeks to test whether low income and/or insecure land tenure hinder or de-motivate people from improving their housing structures and housing conditions. Although both the planned and unplanned areas of Yombo Vituka basically comprise of poor settlements, there is an obvious difference between housing conditions in unplanned (squatter) areas compared to planned areas as also evidenced in the preceding chapter. In planned areas, the housing conditions, though poor by general standards, are at least bearable in contrast to those in squatter areas, which are mostly in pathetic conditions.

One of the following three statements should be the key to this glaring difference in housing conditions in the two land typologies:

1. The incomes of households in unplanned settlements are significantly lower than those of the people living in planned areas;
2. The insecure land tenure is discouraging or de-motivating people living in squatter areas from improving their housing conditions;
3. This condition is a result of both the above two reasons.

INSECURE LAND TENURE

People with households in squatter settlements were asked whether insecure land tenure was affecting their desire to improve their housing structures and environments. As can be observed from Table 11.1, out of 107 respondents from unplanned settlements, 92 (86%) replied that insecure land tenure was discouraging them from improving their housing structures and housing conditions. In other words, they were unsure of their future occupation of those plots and were therefore wary of making any expensive improvements that could any time be demolished when the government decides to survey those areas. The low level of their income and lack of credit facilities of course exacerbated this.

Table 11.1: *Insecure Land Tenure and Lack of Funds/Credit*

	Planned Settlements				Unplanned Settlements				Total			
	YES		NO		YES		NO		YES		NO	
	No	%	No	%	No	%	No	%	No	%	No	%
1. Insecure Land tenure discourages improvement	-	-	-	-	92	86	15	14	92	86	15	14
2. Lack of funds/credit inhibits improvement	103	72	41	29	85	79	22	21	188	75	63	25

Source: Field Survey, 1999

LOW LEVELS OF INCOME

Residents in both planned and unplanned areas also indicated that their low levels of income and lack of credit facilities contributed to their failure to improve their housing conditions. As noted from Table 11.1, 72% of respondents in planned areas and 79% in unplanned areas blamed their low income and lack of credit lines for their failure to improve their housing conditions.

Lack of credit obviously hinders these poor people from significantly improving their housing structures and services around them. However, is it really true that people in squatter settlements have significantly lower incomes as to be unable to improve their housing, at least up to the standard of those houses in planned poor settlements, or is the problem that of insecure land tenure?

QUANTITATIVE DIFFERENCE BETWEEN VARIABLES

In order to test whether the levels of income of households in squatter settlements were significantly lower than those of people in planned areas, it was decided to test whether there existed any difference between the average income (mean) of people in planned settlements and unplanned settlements. The test to be performed shall therefore be two-tailed since we want to know whether the two population means are merely different.

APPROXIMATING MEAN, VARIANCE AND STANDARD DEVIATION OF HOUSEHOLD INCOMES

So as to give a summary of incomes of households surveyed in both planned and unplanned settlements, it was necessary to group the data into frequency distributions as seen in Table 8.17. Using confidence interval estimation, we can then estimate the means and standard deviations of household incomes. Using statistical computer packages this task can be easily performed. But even in the absence of such computer packages, statistical analysis and manipulations can be done as shown in tables 11.2. and 11.3.

Table 11.2: *Estimating Mean and Standard Deviation of Households' Incomes in Planned Settlements*

Midpoint income (T.shs. (000) M_1	Frequency f_1	m_1f_1	$m_1 - \overline{x_1}$	$(m_1 - \overline{x_1})^2$	$(m_1 - \overline{x_1})^2 f_1$
55	01	55	(55-159.81)	10,985.1361	10,985.1361
65	00	0	(65-159.81)	8,988.9361	0
75	03	225	(75-159.81)	7,192,7361	21,493.3983
85	04	340	(85-159.81)	5,596,5361	22,311.3344
95	05	475	(95-159.81)	4,200.3361	20,936.8705
105	06	630	(105-159.81)	3,004.1361	17,970,0066
115	04	460	(115-159.81)	2,007.9361	7,986,9344
125	04	500	(125-159.81)	1,211.7361	4,812,1344
135	07	945	(135-159.81)	615.5361	4,283.9427
145	08	1,160	(145-159.81)	219.3361	1,739.8788
155	14	2,170	(155-159.81)	23.1361	319.0954
165	19	3,135	(165-159.81)	26.9361	516.9759
175	23	4,025	(175-159.81)	230.73361	5,322.1203
185	12	2,220	(185-159.81)	634.5361	7,639.6232
195	09	1,755	(195-159-81)	1,238.3361	11,180.2149
205	06	1,230	(205-15981)	2,042.1361	12,298.0066
215	04	860	(215-159.81)	3,045.9361	12,238.9344
225	03	675	(225-159.81)	4,249.7361	12,814.3983
235	02	470	(235-159.81)	5,653.5361	11,382.2622
245	01	245	(245-159.81)	7,257.3361	7,257.3361
	135	21,575			193,488.6035

Source: Field Survey, 1999

$$\text{Mean } (\overline{x_1}) = \sum m_1 \frac{f_1}{n1}$$

$$= \frac{21575}{135} = 159.81 \text{ or Tshs. } 159{,}810$$

$$\text{Standard Deviation of sample } (s_1) = \sqrt{\sum (m_1 - \overline{x}_1)^2 \frac{f_1}{n_1 - 1}}$$

$$= \sqrt{\frac{193488.6035}{135-1}}$$

$$= \sqrt{\frac{193488.6035}{134}}$$

= 37.9992

= say, Tshs. 38,000

Table11.3: *Estimating Mean and Standard Deviation of Households' Incomes in Squatter Settlements*

Mid point Income (T.shs.'000)	Frequency				
M_2	f_2	$m_2 f_2$	$m_2 - \overline{x_2}$	$(m_2 - \overline{x_2})^2$	$(m_2 - \overline{x_2})^2 f_2$
55	2	110	(55-153)	9,604	19,110
65	1	65	(65-153)	7,744	7,774
75	3	225	(75-153)	6,084	18,252
85	2	170	(85-153)	4,624	9,248
95	3	285	(95-153)	3,364	10,092
105	3	315	(105-153)	2,304	6,912
115	3	345	(115-153)	1,444	4,332
125	4	500	(125-153)	784	3,136
135	5	675	(135-153)	324	1,620
145	8	1,160	(145-153)	64	512
155	13	2,015	(155-153)	04	52
165	18	2,970	(165-153)	144	2,592
175	12	2,100	(175-153)	484	5,808
185	7	1,295	(185-153)	1,024	7,168
195	5	975	(195-153)	1,764	8,820
205	2	410	(205-153)	2,704	5,408
215	1	215	(215-153)	3,844	3,844
225	1	225	(225-153)	5,184	5,184
235	1	235	(235-153)	6,724	6,724
245	1	245	(245-153)	8,464	8,464
	95	14,535			135,022

Source: Field Survey, 1999

Mean $(\overline{x_2}) = \sum m_2 \frac{f_2}{n_2}$

$= \frac{14535}{95}$

= 153 i.e. Ths. 153,000.

Standard Deviation of a sample (s_2) = $\sqrt{\sum (m_2 - \overline{x_2})^2 \frac{f_2}{n_2 - 1}}$

$$= \sqrt{\frac{135022}{95-1}}$$

$$= \sqrt{\frac{135022}{94}}$$

= 37.899

= say, Ths. 37,899

DETERMINATION OF THE DIFFERENCE BETWEEN THE POPULATION MEANS

The statistic used to determine the difference between the population means is based upon the difference between the sample means . Because of the central limit theorem, the statistic will follow the normal distribution since there are large enough sample sizes. The test statistic is therefore,

$$z = \frac{(\bar{x}_1 - \bar{x}_2) - (u_1 - u_2)}{\sqrt{\frac{\sigma_1^2}{n_1} + \frac{\sigma_2^2}{n_2}}}$$

Where u = population mean
σ^2 = population variance

Since we do not know the standard deviation of either planned area population or squatter area population, $((\delta_1, \delta_2)$, we have to assume that each population is normally distributed and that the population variances are equal $(\delta_1 2 + \delta_2 2)$. That being the case, a *t*-test with $n_1 + n_2 - 2$ degrees of freedom can be used to determine whether there is any difference between the means of the two populations. In this regard, and using a two-tailed test, the null and alternative hypotheses will be:

$H_o = u_1 = u_2$ or $u_1 - u_2 = 0$
$H_1 = u_1 \neq u_2$ or $u_1 - u_2 \neq 0$

This is shown in figure 11.1 below.

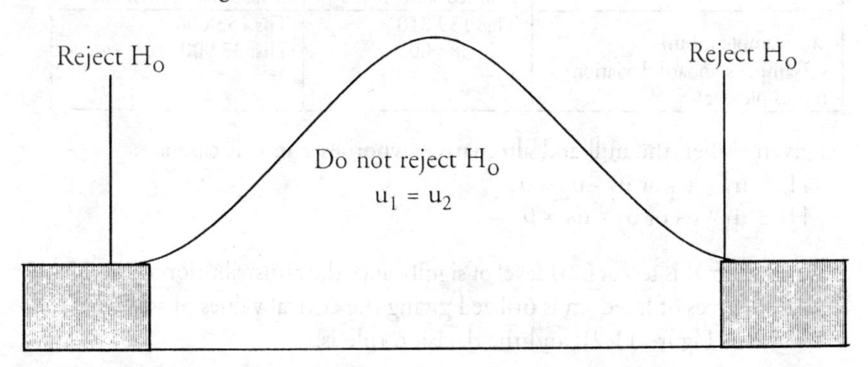

Figure 11.1: *Rejection regions for the two tailed test for the difference between two means*

As given above, we have assumed equal variances in the two populations. The variances of the two samples (s_1^2, s_2^2) can therefore be pooled together to form one estimate$(s_p^2)$of the "common" population variance. The test statistic will be:

$$t_{n+n_2-2} = \frac{(\overline{x_1} - \overline{x_2}) - (u_1 - u_2)}{\sqrt{s_p^2 (\frac{1}{n_1} + \frac{1}{n_2})}}$$

Where,

s^2_p = pooled variance of the two groups

$$= \frac{(n_1 -_1)s_1^2 + (n_2 -_1)s_2^2}{n_1 + n_2 - 2}$$

$\bar{x}_1$ = sample mean for population 1 (planned settlements)
s_1^2 = sample variance in population 1
n_1 = sample size for population 1 (planned settlements)
$\bar{x}_2$ = sample mean in population 2 (unplanned settlements)
s_2^2 = sample variance in population 2
n_2 = sample size for population 2

In this study we want to know whether there is any difference between the average income of people living in planned settlements and those living in unplanned settlements. The results can be summarized as follows:

	Planned settlements	Unplanned settlements
$\overline{x}$ (sample mean)	Ths. 159,810	Ths.153,000
s (sample standard deviation)	Ths. 38,000	Ths. 37,900
n (sample size)	135	95

As given earlier, the null and alternative hypotheses in this case are:
$H_o: u_1 = u_2$ or $u_1 - u_2 = 0$
$H_1: u_1 {}^1 u_2$ or $u_1 - u_2 \neq 0$

If we conduct this test at 0.01 level of significance the *t*-distribution with 135+92-2 =228 degrees of freedom is utilized giving the critical values of +2.5758 and -2.5758 (see Figure 11.2), and the decision rule is:

Reject H_o if $t_{228} > + 2.5758$
Or, if $t_{228} < - 2.5758$

Otherwise we cannot reject H_o

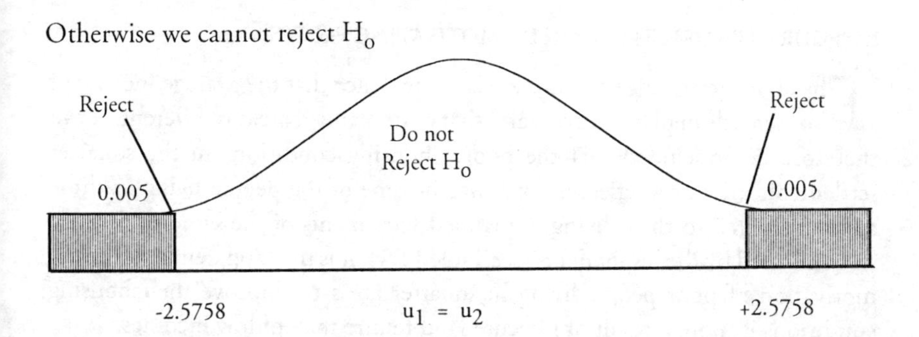

Figure. 11.2: *Two-tailed test of hypothesis for the difference between the means at the 0.01 level of significance.*

For the above data, we have:

$$t_{228} = \frac{\overline{x_1} - \overline{x_2}}{\sqrt{s_p^2(\frac{1}{n_1} + \frac{1}{n_2})}}$$

$$= \frac{s_p^2 = (n_1 - 1)s_1^2 + (n_2 - 1)s_2^2}{n_1 + n_2 - 2}$$

$$= \frac{134(38^2) + 94(37.9^2)}{135 + 95 - 2}$$

$$= \frac{193496 + 135023}{228}$$

$$= 1440.9$$

$$= \frac{159 - 153}{1440.9(\frac{1}{135} + \frac{1}{95})}$$

$$= \frac{6.81}{5.0786}$$

$$= 1.3409$$

Since -2.5758< 1.3409 < +2.5758, we can not reject H_o.

INSECURE TENURE: THE MAIN DE-MOTIVATING FACTOR

The above tests suggest that there is no evidence that the average income of households in planned areas and that of unplanned areas is different. It can therefore be concluded that the poorer housing conditions in the squatter settlements are not a reflection of lower income of the people living in those areas compared to those living in planned settlements of the same study area. As confirmed by the respondents (see Table 11.1), it is thus apparent that the de-motivation of poor people living in squatter areas to improve their housing conditions is more a result of insecure land tenure than of low incomes.

12

POLICY RECOMMENDATIONS AND CONCLUSIONS

INTRODUCTION

In developing countries, poverty has usually been associated with the rural areas. Indeed, empirical evidence suggests that poverty is more rampant in rural areas. However, the unprecedented urbanization, particularly in developing countries like Tanzania, coupled with the effects of world recession, has resulted in a significant increase in the magnitude of urban poverty. It is in view of such rapid urban growth which manifests in high levels of urban poverty, shortage of adequate shelter and other essential services and poor environmental conditions, that it was found necessary to undertake this publication on urban poverty.

Specifically this book was written on the premise that there is a serious problem in the structural frameworks and conceptualization on the part of the government of Tanzania, like most governments in developing countries and other stakeholders about the whole question of provision and improvement of housing and living conditions of the urban poor. It seems that no proper and empirically derived linkage had been made between poor housing conditions and poverty. The role of improved housing and its environment in alleviating poverty had also not been well perceived. Worse still, the true players and their roles in this task seemed to have not been properly identified by most researchers and policy makers. In other words, there are gaps between conceptual, contextual and empirical understanding of housing poverty in our country. This book sought to fill this gap.

The approach taken was first to review the available literature on urban housing development and improvement policies in developing countries generally and Tanzania in particular, highlighting their impact, if any, on alleviating housing poverty. Empirical analyses were then carried to show the causal relationship between housing and other manifestations of poverty with the aim of showing that improving housing conditions is, in fact, improving the living conditions, and thus, reducing poverty among the urban poor. The willingness and ability of the urban poor to pay for improved housing and related services was also positively tested.

SUMMARY OF RESEARCH FINDINGS

The findings of the research on which this book is based have been grouped under two distinct headings: general findings related to urban housing poverty and specific findings from the survey data and analyses.

General Findings

1. Evidence suggests that the rate of urban poverty is increasing rapidly, particularly in urban slum and squatter settlements that face social and economic exclusion, limited access to basic social infrastructure and services, with very poor housing, which reduce further their capacity for productive activities. This implies that urban poverty is accentuated by housing poverty.
2. Housing poverty is directly associated with general income poverty since housing is a productive asset. Decent and adequate housing can supplement households' income, thereby significantly contributing towards income poverty alleviation. It was also found that although investment in housing and related services does not directly add to household's income, it is an important contributor to the income.
3. It was evidenced that about one billion people in the world live in absolute poverty without adequate food, clothing and shelter with more than 90% of these living in the South and one-third of them being urban dwellers in developing countries. About 600 million people in urban areas of Africa, Asia and Latin America live in poor and unhealthy homes and neighbourhoods because of the very poor housing and living conditions and lack of adequate provision for safe, sufficient water supply, sanitation, drainage, removal of garbage and health care. In Tanzania, slightly over 50% of all Tanzanians are poor with about 40% regarded as absolutely (hard-core) poor. In urban areas, it is estimated that 30% of all urbanites in Tanzania are poor, and live in very poor housing conditions and they lack basic social amenities.
4. Housing policy is inextricably linked to social and economic policy of any country. To improve housing conditions is to improve social and economic wellbeing of the inhabitants. Adequate housing promotes security, health, wealth and welfare of the people and is a pre-requisite for national socio-economic development.

5. Despite the above fact, it was found that there is a misconception in many developing countries, including Tanzania, that housing problem is entirely a welfare problem whose only solution is to transfer physical or financial resources to people who lack adequate shelter. Policy advice and research work on poverty eradication in Tanzania have also hitherto underplayed the problem of poor urban housing conditions.
6. Many governments in developing countries, including Tanzania, have involved themselves in the construction and financing of housing and amenities in urban settlements. However, these efforts have disappointingly proved to be inconsequential in bridging the gap between the demand and supply of housing, let alone improvement of existing housing stock and other urban services.
7. There is now a realization that the goal of adequate shelter for all in the developing countries requires concerted efforts of central and local governments, community-based organizations (CBOs), building industry, financial institutions, donor community, non-government organizations (NGOs) and, not least, the people who need shelter.
8. There has been inadequate involvement of the affected people in the planning and implementation of housing and environmental regeneration programmes in developing countries including Tanzania.

Specific Findings From Survey Data and Analysis

1. Urban people living in squatter (unplanned) settlements are much poorer in terms of housing structures and housing related services than those living in planned areas, even within the same vicinity.
2. Overcrowding is more severe in squatter settlements than in planned settlements.
3. Households in unplanned settlements have fewer rooms compared to those in planned areas.
4. Safe and adequate water and sanitation services in poor urban settlements are very poor.
5. Although households do not reveal their true income from all sources, it is apparent that informal income generation activities earn them a substantial income. This is proved by the estimated expenditure pattern of households. Whereas the minimum wage in Tanzania is about T.shs. 50,000 (about US $ 60) per month, the total household expenditure of such minimum wage earner is not less than T.shs. 100,000 (about US $ 125).
6. Savings ratios are indeed functions of income and are nominally small in the low-income groups.
7. Food in a poor household is the largest expenditure item and which is well spread out over the income spectrum of households.

8. There is a direct relationship between poor housing conditions and poor environmental and social services situations of the households. Thus, poor sanitation system, inadequate supply of safe water, uncollected garbage and other solid waste, overcrowding, and poor access roads, all combine with low incomes to compound the housing poverty facing poor urban people.
9. Housing is a productive asset, because it is not only a shelter, but is also a commodity and investment all in one. Adequate housing can be a source of income generation and a means of improving households' general living conditions. This can be achieved by utilizing the household spaces for other income generating activities.
10. There is both willingness and ability on the part of poor households to pay for improved housing conditions and services if there is a genuine conviction that such services shall alleviate their housing poverty.
11. Although low income is a contributor towards the failure of poor urban people living in squatter settlements to improve their housing conditions, the major de-motivating factor for these people to improve their housing conditions and services is their insecure land tenure.

POLICY RECOMMENDATIONS AND IMPLICATIONS

The general and specific research findings as elucidated above give rise to a number of significant recommendations. Their possible policy implications are outlined below.

The Urbanization Problem

Control of Rural-Urban Migration

a) Evidence from this study has revealed that Tanzania is among few African countries with the highest urbanization rates. With an estimated urbanization rate of 9% per annum, it is expected that half of Tanzania's population will be living in the urban areas by year 2020. It is therefore recommended that the government should formulate strategies to control rural-urban migration. Since it has been realized that the major reasons for rapid urbanization are the shift of jobs from agriculture to industry and service, and concentration of economic opportunities in urban areas, strategies to be formulated by the government must be directed towards prioritizing agricultural sector by ensuring the application of new agricultural technologies, training of more agriculturists, providing incentives to farmers, encouraging co-operative or large scale farming and promoting private/foreign investment in agriculture. Currently agriculture in Tanzania has not attracted much private or foreign investment. According to the Tanzania Investment Centre, out of total investment of T.shs. 3,256 billion in 1,025 projects approved by the Centre from September 1990 to March, 1998, only 85 projects with total investment of T.shs. 77 billion, or 2.3%, were related to agriculture and livestock development.

b) The government should also try to reduce disparities in economic and social opportunities between urban and rural areas by, again, redirecting more resources to the provision of social and economic services and infrastructure in rural areas. Yet another strategy would be to fight unemployment and urban loitering.

Housing Delivery

a) The problem of urbanization in Tanzania is mostly translated in a mismatch between housing supply and demand. There is thus a very great demand for housing in urban Tanzania. It is estimated that currently supply of housing in Tanzania is only 20% of the demand. Furthermore, most urban people live in sub-standard housing, characterized by overcrowding and poor sanitation that is also accompanied by malnutrition and other health hazards.
It is recommended that recommendations put forth by the newly formulated National Human Settlements Development Policy regarding provision of more housing in urban areas are actually implemented. In this regard the government should not involve itself directly in the provision of housing. Rather, it should only facilitate and encourage private investment in housing. The government should lay down a conducive financial and legal framework for private investment in housing involving individuals, community based organizations, local governments and other partners like the HABITAT and Shelter Afrique.

b) A review of the literature indicates that investment in housing in developing countries, including Tanzania, has been low mainly because of the past single - handedness and unrealistic policies of the governments in housing provision and the weak or informal housing market. In Tanzania, programmes and policies that were initiated by the government towards housing investment and development worked incoherently for lack of a clear and comprehensive housing policy. The current National Human Settlements Development Policy should reflect and address, in more workable terms, the shortcomings of past housing policies. Such measures and strategies should include:

- Providing and encouraging higher investment in housing so that the contribution of housing investment to GDP is raised from the current level of around 5%.

- Marco-economic policies should prominently reflect the role of private investment in housing provision and improvement.
- Development of financial sources, particularly credit and mortgage facilities.
- The government should provide political and legislative support to private housing development efforts, including minimizing bureaucracy in land allocation and granting of building permits.
- Developing of strong housing markets by facilitating and synchronizing demand and supply of housing. This is crucial because given the current low income levels of most households in Tanzania, the legal rights and complexities in the registration and ownership of land and title deeds, and lack of housing finance, effective housing demand is far below actual demand.

c) Since legal systems as they relate to land and property/housing ownership have been deleterious to housing sector development in Tanzania, and since the newly enacted Land Act of 1999 still seems to have some flaws, it is recommended that necessary amendments to the new Law be made to enable it clearly spell and enforce land tenure provisions that will encourage private investors in housing development. Turning of houses into reliable collateral for long-term mortgage loans and enforcement of foreclosures should be made more effective and unambiguous in the new Act. Furthermore, the current bureaucratic system in the surveying and registration process of land and title deeds should be effectively reduced by the Act.

d) Cognizant of the low income levels of most Tanzanians, it is recommended that property developers, such as the National Housing Corporation, housing societies and CBOs should put more emphasis on the construction of low-cost affordable houses. Consideration should also be put on semi-finished [core] houses, which are sold and left to be finished by buyers at their own pace as their income flow would allow.

Housing Finance

a) The development of sustainable housing finance system in the country is a joint responsibility of the government and the private sector. It is therefore recommended that the contribution of the government in this regard should be made in a manner consistent with market principles and economic efficiency for the promotion of long-term growth, development and viability of the housing finance system.

b) It is recommended that the government should support and encourage the establishment of housing finance institutions by private groups and, if such groups do not emerge, the government should establish the institution itself. The institutions should be allowed to compete effectively for savings and respond to market demand for housing loans.

c) It is recommended that although a specialized primary housing finance institution is desirable, other commercial banks should also be encouraged and motivated to undertake mortgage lending for housing.

d) Housing finance institutions and other housing credit facilities should be allowed the flexibility to develop products and services to the various borrowing needs of its customers such as basing on income strata. This should of course consider also the long-term profitability of the institutions.

e) It is recommended that the government should nurture the development of micro-finance and community based credit institutions for poor households by providing adequate regulatory frameworks.

Urban Environment, Infrastructure and Social Services

1. It is appreciated that a growing proportion of Tanzanians will soon live in urban centres, which are increasingly subject to environmental decline, among other adversities. It is therefore recommended that environmental planning and management should be strategically done to ensure that urban settlements are livable and sustainable.
2. It is realized that Tanzania's urban centres greatly lack adequate infrastructural services as a result of lack of capital, inappropriate high standards and technology, inadequate maintenance of existing facilities, poor cost recovery for both capital and maintenance requirements, lack of trained manpower to run the infrastructural services. It is therefore recommended that:
   - Planning for, and implementation of, urban infrastructure provision and maintenance should be a multi-sectoral issue involving the central government, local governments, community and donor groups, and all the people affected. The latter are crucial since, as empirically evidenced in this study, poor urban households are able and willing to participate and pay for improved infrastructure services.
   - Investment in infrastructure should be in response to well analyzed effective demand, and should be consistent with available financial resources so as to provide immediate benefits.
   - Realistic approach to infrastructure provision should be sought which apply appropriate technologies to provide affordable services, particularly to low income households.
   - Full cost recovery should be the basis for pricing of infrastructure services to ensure that apart from selected cross subsidy strategies the services are

sufficiently priced to serve as a dis-incentive to waste and over consumption.

- The role of the central government and even local authorities in the implementation of infrastructure provision should be restricted to planning and tendering procedures, so that the responsibility for construction is left to the private sector.

3. Both analytical and empirical evidence from this study suggests that the poor urban people face the problem of limited access to services such as water supply, sanitation [including solid waste management], drainage, access roads, public transport, street lighting and traffic management. It is therefore recommended that:

   - Design and service standards of urban services [hence capital costs] should not be set at levels unaffordable by the local governments and their residents because this limits expansion of such services to the poor household.
   - Urban infrastructure and services should be designed to allow for incremental upgrading as the incomes and affordability of poor households to pay for such service increase.
   - Subsidies from central government for urban infrastructure and services should be prioritized and actually directed towards poorer urban settlements because experience indicates that such subsidies to poor people in Tanzania, like in other developing countries, even if well intended, often do not reach the poor, but are pre-empted or "gentrified" by middle and higher income groups already served by the system.

4. The empirical results from this study of willingness to pay for improved urban services of poor households strongly suggest that contingent valuation surveys are a feasible method for estimating individuals' willingness to pay for improved housing related services like water, improved sanitation system, garbage collection and even repayment of housing loans. It is therefore recommended that the government and other agencies concerned with the provision and improvement of housing and other related services should consider applying such contingent valuation methods when considering cost sharing or cost recovery service provision schemes in poor settlements.

Urban Land Policies and Procedures

1. Empirical evidence in this study suggest that lack of access to land is a major bottleneck preventing the urban poor to participate meaningfully in the urban economy to alleviate their poverty. Access to land is highly restricted as a result of antiquated land legislation, unambiguous and expensive institutional framework, costly land registration process and unnecessarily high standards associated with land development. It is therefore recommended as follows:

- The central and local governments should make the land market work efficiently and effectively by regularizing land tenure and simplifying the registration process, particularly to improve access of the poor urbanites to serviced land.
- Devolution of powers from the central government to local governments as regards land allocation issues is encouraged so that local authorities can reform and co-ordinate land management, in order to overcome the current scattered responsibilities for land management and delivery in the country.

Urban Management and Planning

1. It is realized that local governments are nearer to the people, and therefore, know better their problems and capacity. It is therefore recommended that the central government should strengthen these local governments by bolstering their capacity to plan, manage and finance programmes for improving housing and the environments of low-income urban people, including mobilizing people's efforts in participatory activities to improve the living places. This can be done by:
    - Dividing powers between the central government and the local governments, and allocation of resources in major areas of land management, housing and housing finance, infrastructure and services.
    - Improving the capacity and efficiency of local governments in all aspects of urban management, urban finance mobilization and effective planning.
    - On their part, local governments should consider the development of private sector infrastructural service delivery systems by laying down a regulatory framework that encourages the expansion of the role of the private sector, including NGOs, in the provision and improvement of urban housing and infrastructure on cost recovery basis.
2. Local governments need to encourage and facilitate establishment and accessibility of local credit facilities that meet the demands of low-income groups to reduce the burden of the poor to depend on expensive formal and informal credit. As evidenced by empirical results in this study, given affordable credit terms, poor people are willing and able to repay housing improvements loans.
3. As empirically evidenced in this study, it is strongly recommended that poor household should be fully involved in the planning and implementation of programs and schemes for alleviating their poverty, because they have better knowledge of their problems and have better commitment to their poverty alleviation drives. Any attempt to exclude them in the planning and

implementation of such programs will only end in futility. As a Swahili saying runs, "A child's pain is better understood by the mother."

CONCLUSION AND AREAS FOR FURTHER RESEARCH

This research has provided an adequate theoretical and empirical analysis of causal relationship between housing and environmental poverty and other conventional manifestations of poverty like low incomes, health hazards, illiteracy, inadequate supply of safe water, insanitation, poor solid waste management and poor access roads. Global experience of the magnitude and severity of poor housing and environmental conditions facing millions of urban dwellers was deeply reviewed. Further, empirical evidence was collected and analyzed to test various hypotheses which relate poor housing conditions and environments to general poverty manifestations. Nevertheless, the study was too general. It would now be appropriate to narrow down further study to specific issues.

It will be recalled that there are five themes which have been initially identified by REPOA for research. These are: Implications of public policies on poverty alleviation; social and cultural factors influencing poverty; the use of technology in alleviating poverty; environmental issues on poverty alleviation, and gender and poverty alleviation. It is unfortunate that hitherto research work on these topics has not adequately linked poverty and housing conditions of the poor. Since our current work is a more generalized linkage, it would be important to further study specific and narrow areas which link each of the selected five topics to the question of housing conditions and environments of the poor. Such specific areas for further study could be as follows:

- In analysing public policies on poverty eradication since independence, it is not enough to concentrate on the analysis of policies which are related directly to income generation and distribution. While indeed policies such as economic recovery programmes were also geared towards improvement and revitalization of infrastructure and social services, and although housing provision is one of social services, it would be important to specifically study and make explicit reference to low-cost housing policies as means for eradicating poverty among the (urban) poor.
- There is a very close linkage between environment, housing and poverty. In analysing the relationship between poverty and environment, it would be interesting to study how the rapid urbanization has caused environmentally unsafe squatter and slum settlements, which exacerbate poverty among the poor urban. The sufferings of the poor from environmental disasters caused by, or taking place in, unplanned or poorly planned housing settlements need to be in the agenda when linkage between poverty and environment is made.

- Technology is a fundamental requirement for the successful advancement of civilization. Technology can be treated as a substitute indicator for development since the two are highly correlated. The importance of technology in improving housing standards and housing related infrastructural services in the poor households' communities should be one of the agenda items for research on poverty alleviation.
- Women play a major role in ensuring safer housing conditions in any household. Healthy housing and their environment therefore depend, to a large extent, on how women (whether in male-headed households or, and particularly, in female-headed households) participate in the improvement of housing and living conditions. As an area for further research on gender issues and poverty alleviation, it would be important to study issues such as the contribution of women physically, and through ideas, in the planning and maintaining of housing requirements for the households. What can women, for example, do to mobilize self-help efforts among neighbourhood women for the improvement of their housing environments? The issue of women and housing conditions is crucially and particularly important in women-headed households. It should be realized that women-headed households form a rising proportion of households. It is estimated that one-fifth of all households in the world are women-headed households (HABITAT, 1996b).
- In discussing the socio-cultural factors influencing poverty in Tanzania, one needs to cover the social and cultural factors that influence housing standards and various ethnic living cultures and habits, extended families etc. Such factors may contribute to overcrowding and the urge (or lack of it) for improving or extending housing accommodation.

BIBLIOGRAPHY

African Housing Fund (1994)
Three Years Plan 1995 - 1997.

Aina, Tade Akin (1990)
"Petty Landlords and Poor Tenants in a Low-Income Settlement in Metropolitan Lagos, Nigeria," in Amis, P. and Lloyd, P. (eds): *Housing Africa's Urban Poor*, International African Institute, Manchester University Press.

Aitken, E, et al (1990)
"The SCORE System: The Early Start Scheme in the Tayside, Grampian and Fife regions", *Research Report* (No. 14) to Scottish Homes.

Alder, G. (1995)
"Tackling Poverty in Nairobi Informal Settlements: Developing an Institutional Strategy, Urban Poverty II: From Understanding to Action." *Environment and Urbanization*, Vol, 7, No.2 October,

Alile, Hayford I, (1994)
Keynote Address to the Symposium on "Secondary Mortgage Markets in Africa", Abuja, Nigeria, May.

Amis, Philip (1990)
"Key Themes in Contemporary African Urbanization," in Amis, P and Lloyd, P (Eds.): *Housing Africa's Urban Poor*, International African Institute, Manchester University Press.

Amoa-Mensah, K., (1997)
"Strategies Developed and Applied locally Towards Increased Construction Efficiency to Achieve Enhanced Housing Delivery in Ghana." Paper presented at the Regional Seminar on 'Maintaining Sustainable Mortgage Finance Schemes in Africa: Lessons and Perspectives for Developing Countries,' Accra, Ghana December.

Anzorena, Jorge, et al (1998)
"Reducing Urban Poverty: Some Lessons from Experience: Beyond the Rural-Urban Divide," *Environment and Urbanization*, Vol.10, No.1, April 1998: 172-185.

Arrossi, S; Bombarolo, F; Hardoy, J., Mitlin. D; Coscio, L, and Satterthwaite, D (1994)
Funding Community Initiatives: Written by IIED for UNDP, Earthscan Publications, London.

Asiama, S. O. (1990)
"Land for Housing the Urban Poor in Africa - Some Policy Options," in Amis, P. and Lloyds, P. (eds): *Housing Africa's Urban Poor*, International African Institute, Manchester University Press.

Atkinson, R., and Kintrea, K., (1998)
"Reconnecting Excluded Communities: The Neighbourhood Impacts of Owner Occupation," *Research Report* (No. 61) to Scottish Homes.

AUHFI (1987)
"The Mangochi (Malawi) Recommendations on Shelter and Urban Development," Paper presented at a workshop organized by the African Union of Building Societies and Housing Finance Institutions, March, 1987.

-- (1995)
Informal Lending Organizations in Africa. Proceedings of a Workshop held in Nairobi, Kenya, June, 1995.

Ayogu, Melvin D., (1994)
"Establishing Secondary Mortgage Markets: Halfway to Affordable Housing", Symposium on Secondary Mortgage Markets in Africa, Abuja, May 1994.

Bagachwa, M. S. D., (1994)
"Changing Perceptions of Poverty and the Emerging Research Issues," in Bagachwa (ed.): *Poverty Alleviation in Tanzania: Recent Research Issues*, Dar es Salaam University Press and REPOA.
-- (1995)
"A Study of Formal Financial Institutions in Tanzania", ESRF - World Bank Seminar on Financial Integration and Development in Sub-Saharan Africa, Vol. 2, September, 1995.
Bangu, N. T. A., (1996)
"Appropriate Farming Technologies for Alleviation of Poverty in the Rural Sector in Tanzania," Paper presented at a workshop on Poverty Alleviation in Tanzania, 25th -27th March.
Berenson, M. L. and Levine, D.M., (1992)
Basic Business Statistics - Concepts and Applications, Prentice Hall, Englewood Cliffs, New Jersey, Fifth Edition.
Bhattacharya, K. P., (1990)
"Housing in India - Observations on the Government's Intervention Policies," in Shidlo, G. (ed.): *Housing Policy in Developing Countries*, Routledge, Chapman and Hall Inc.
Bryant - Tokalau, J. J. (1995)
"The Myth Exploded: Urban Poverty in the Pacific," *Urban Poverty II: From Understanding to Action - Environment and Urbanization*, Vol. 7, No.2, Oct, 1995.
Buchan, L., (1999)
"Water Purification - A Home Industry" Paper presented at the AWEC Conference on Water Supply and Sanitation Services in the next Millennium, Arusha, Tanzania, November.
Button, K. J. and Pearce, D. W., (1989)
Improving the Urban Environment: How to Adjust National and Local Government Policy for Sustainable Urban Growth. Pergamon Press, Vol. 32 part 3 1989: 141.
Campbell, John (1990)
World Bank Urban Shelter Projects in East Africa: Matching Needs With Appropriate Responses?, in Amis, P. and Lloyd, P. (eds): *Housing Africa's Urban Poor,* International African Institute, Manchester University Press.
Carley, Michael (1995)
"A Community Participation Strategy in Urban Regeneration," Working Paper for Scottish Homes.
Carlson, Eric (1980)
"Human Needs Related to Dwellings," Paper presented at a conference on "Towards A National Housing Policy," organized by the Building Research Unit (BRU) and Centre for Housing Studies at AICC, Arusha, March.
Chambers, Robert (1997)
Whose Reality Counts? - Putting the First Last. International Technology Publications.
Chamwali,A. A. (1996)
"Women's Status and Poverty in Zanzibar" Paper presented at a Workshop on Poverty Alleviation in Tanzania, 25th-27th March.
Chan, Cecilia (1994)
"Responses of Low-Income Communities to Environmental Challenges in Hong Kong," in Williams and Main (eds): *Environment and Housing in Third World Cities*, John Wiley & Sons.
Chandra, Prasanna (1995)
Projects: Planning, Analysis, Selection, Implementation and Review, Tata McGraw-Hill Publishing Company Limited, fourth edition.

Chungu, A, and Mandara, G.R.R. (1994): "The use of Technology in Alleviating Poverty in Tanzania", in Bagachwa (ed): Poverty Alleviation in Tanzania: Recent Research Issues, University of Dar es Salaam and REPOA.

Clapham, D., Kemp, P. and Smith, S. J. (1990)
Housing and Social Policy, Macmillan Education Ltd.

Cooksey, B. (1994)
"Who's Poor in Tanzania? A Review of Recent Poverty Research," in Bagachwa (ed.): *Poverty Alleviation in Tanzania: Recent Research Issues,* Dar es Salaam University Press and REPOA.

Cooksey, B. and Lokuji, A (1995)
Some Practical Research Guidelines, *REPOA Special Paper* No.12.

Connolly, P. (1990)
"Housing and the State in Mexico," in Shidlo, G (ed): *Housing Policy in Developing Countries*, Routledge, Chapman and Hall inc.

Devco Ireland (1994)
"Urban Sector Engineering Project: Short-Term Consulting Services for the Institutional Strengthening Programme - Draft Report on Dar es Salaam Stage 2 Study (TASK 3)"

Devconsult International Ltd. (1995)
"Report on the Re-Introduction of the Revolving Housing Loan Fund for Civil Servants in Tanzania."

Diamond, D. B and Lea, M. J. (1995)
"Sustainable Financing Strategies for Housing: A Conceptual Framework for HABITAT II."

Diamond D. B., (1997)
"Public/Private Partnership in Housing Finance," Regional Seminar on "Maintaining Sustainable Mortgage Finance Schemes in Africa: Lessons and Perspectives for Developing Countries", Accra, Ghana, December.

-- (1998)
"Next Steps Toward Housing Finance in Tanzania" A Report presented by PADCO for USAID and NHC

Diyammett, B. D., Mabala, R. S., and Mandara, R (1998)
"Poverty and Diffusion of Technological Innovations to Rural Women: The Role of Entrepreneurship." *REPOA Research Report* No.98.2.

Doutetien, H. A., (1999)
"Role of the Private Sector in Housing Delivery in Benin," Paper presented at the Shelter Afrique Symposium on Improving Housing Delivery in Africa in the Next Millennium, held in Cotonou, Benin, June, 1999.

Drakakis - Smith (1981)
Urbanization, Housing and the Development Process, Croom Helm, London.

Driss, Taoufik (1999)
"A review of the Impact of Institutions Involved in the Housing Sector in Tunisia", A paper presented at the Shelter Afrique Symposium on Improving Housing Delivery in Africa in the Next Millennium, held in Cotonou, Benin, June.

Edwards, Michael (1990)
"Rental Housing and the Urban Poor: Africa and Latin America Compared," in Amis, P. and Lloyds, P. (eds): *Housing Africa's Urban Poor.* International African Institute, Manchester University Press.

Ermisch, John (1990)
"Modelling the Income-Household Formation Relationship," *Discussion Paper* (No. 1) for Scottish Home.
Ferguson, Bruce (1999)
"Microfinance of Housing: A Key to Housing the Lower, Moderate-Income Majority?" *Environment & Urbanization: Healthy Cities, Neighbourhoods and Homes*, Vol II No. 1, April, 1999.
Gilbert, A et al (1997)
"Low-Income Rental Housing : Are South African Cities Different?" *Environment and Urbanization: The Struggle for Shelter,* Vol. 9, No. 1, April.
HABITAT (1992)
Improving the Living Environment for a Sustainable Future.
-- (1993)
Habitat in Sub-Saharan Africa.
-- (1996a)
"Sustainable Financing Strategies for Housing and Urban Development - A Contribution to the City Summit: Housing Finance", 1996, pp. 17-26.
-- (1996b)
Cities and the Environment - World Resources: A guide to Global Environment, 1996 - 97.
-- (1996c)
HABITAT Agenda and Instanbul Declaration, 2nd United Nations Conference on Human Settlements, Instanbul (June, 1996).
-- (1996d)
An Urbanizing World: Global Report on Households, Oxford University Press.
-- (1996e)
The Human Settlements Conditions of the World's Urban Poor.
Halfani, M (1994)
"Urban Research in East Africa: Tanzania, Kenya and Zambia - Towards an Agenda for the 1990s," in Stren, R. (ed.): *Urban Research in the Developing World: Africa*: Centre for Urban and Community Studies, University of Toronto.
Halla, F. F. and Majani, B. B. K (1997)
"Environmental Management Strategy for Dar es Salaam, Report Prepared for Dar es Salaam City Commission Through the Sustainable Dar es Salaam City Project (SDP).
Hardoy, J.E, (1995)
"Reflections on Latin American Urban Research" in Stren, R (ed): *Urban Research in the Developing World: Latin America.* Centre for Urban and Community Studies, University of Toronto.
Hasan, Arif (1994)
"Replicating the Low-Cost Sanitation Programmes Administered by the Orangi Pilot Project in Karachi, Pakistan," in Serageldin I. et al (eds.): *The Human Face of the Urban Environment* - Proceedings of the 2nd Annual World Bank Conference on Environmentally Sustainable Development, World Bank, Washington DC, September.
Hecht, Bennett, L. (1994)
Developing Affordable Housing - A Practical Guide for Non-profit Organizations, John Wiley & Sons, Inc.
Hoek-Smit, M. (1990)
"The Urban Housing Sector in Tanzania - Analysis of the Urban Housing Survey." Report Prepared for the World Bank and URT.

Hughes, Gordon (1991)
"Cost-Benefit Analysis: Housing and Squatter Upgrading in East Africa," in Tipple and Willis (eds): *Housing the Poor in Developing World - Methods of Analysis, Case Studies and Policy*. Routledge, Chapman and Hall Inc.

Hui, Eddie Chi Man (1999)
"Willingness to Pay for Better Housing in Hong Kong: Theory and Evidence (of Dwelling Space)." *Urban Studies Journal*, Volume 36, No. 2 February, University of Glasgow.

ILO (1999)
Key Indicators of the Labour Market, Geneva.

IUCN/UNEP/WWF. (1991)
Caring for the Earth. A Strategy for Sustainable Living. Gland, Switzerland.

Jakande, Lateef, (1994)
"**Secondary Mortgage Markets** in Africa" Welcoming Address to the Symposium on Secondary Mortgage Markets in Africa, Abuja, Nigeria, May,

Jambiya, G. Kulindwa, K., and Sosevele, H. (1997)
"Poverty and the Environment: The Case of Information Sand-Mining, Quarrying and Lime-making Activities in Dar es salaam."REPOA Research Report No. 97.1

Jazari, I; M. Alamgir and T. Panuccio (1992)
"The State of the World Rural Poverty: An Inquiry into its Causes and Consequences," International Fund for Agricultural Development (IFAD), London.

Kabwogi, C. M. (1997)
"The Implementation and Impact of Rent Control in Tanzania" Unpublished *PhD* Thesis, University of Sheffield.

-- (1999)
"Evaluation of the Sale of National Housing Corporation Low and Medium Cost Houses."

Kamuzora, C. L. and Gwalema, S. (1998)
"Labour Constraints, Population Dynamics and the AIDS Epidemic: The Case of Rural Bukoba District, Tanzania" - *REPOA Research Report* No. 98.4.

Kanyama, A. K. (1995)
"Can the Urban Housing Problem be Solved Through Physical Planning: An Analysis Based on Experience from Dodoma, Tanzania, 1995:1

Kaseva, M.E; Mbwete, T.S.A.; Katima, J.H.Y. and Mashauri, D.A. (1999)
"Constructed Wetland Systems for Domestic Wastewater Treatment - Promising Technology for Application in Developing Countries," Paper presented at the 1999 Annual Seminar for Engineers, "Engineering for Sustainable Development - Tanzania Urban Development: Strategic Issues", Arusha, Tanzania, December, 1999.

Kashuliza *et al*, (1998)
"The Role of Informal and Semi-formal Finance in Poverty Alleviation in Tanzania: Results of a Field Study in Two Regions." REPOA Research Report No.98.1.

Katima, J.H.Y. (1999)
"Sustainable Urban Environment: How Close Are We?" Paper presented at the 1999 Annual Seminar for Engineers, "Engineering for Sustainable Development - Tanzania Urban Development: Strategic Issues," Arusha, Tanzania, December, 1999.

Kearns, A and Malcolm, J (1992)
"Scottish Housing Associations and Their Tenants: A Base-line Study of Customers and Services: The Characteristics of Tenants and Tenancies." *Research Report* (No. 20) for Scottish Homes.

Keles, Rusen (1990)
"Housing Policy in Turkey", in Shidlo, G (ed): Housing Policy in Developing Countries, Routledge, Chapman and Hall Inc.
Khan, M. A (1995)
"Sustainable Development: Key Concepts, Issues and Implications" Key Note Paper given at the International Sustainable Development Research Conference held in Manchester, UK, March.
Kihunrwa, E.D. (1981)
"Physical Development Control in Dar es Salaam, Tanzania." *M.A.* Dissertation, Institute of Planning Studies, University of Nottingham, U.K.
Kilonzo, B. S. (1996)
"Rodents As a Potential Cause of Poverty in Tanzania: The Need for Appropriate and Sustainable Technology for their Control" Paper presented at a workshop on Poverty Alleviation in Tanzania, 25th - 27th March.
Kim, Joochul (1990)
"Housing Development and Reforms in China," in Shidlo, G. (ed): *Housing Policy in Developing Countries.* Routledge, Chapman and Hall Inc.
Kirobo, A.Y. (1977)
Filmed-House in Manzese, Dar es Salaam. Practical Experiences from the Construction of a Demonstration House for the Film "Jijengee Nyumba Bora" (Building a Better House), Building Research Unit, Ministry of Lands Housing and Urban Development.
Kironde, L. J. M., (1985)
"Three Decades of National Housing Corporation: The Evolution of the Land Use Structure of Dar es Salaam 1890 - 1990 - A Study in the Effects of Land Policy((excerpt from *PhD.* Thesis).
-- (1996)
"A Brief Review of Policies and Programmes Related to Human Settlements Development in Tanzania" - Consultative Workshop on the preparation of a National Report for the HABITAT II Conference, January.
-- (1998)
The Access to Land by the Urban Poor in Tanzania With Some Reference to Structural Adjustment Programmes. The Case of Dar es Salaam. *UCLAS Research Series* 99.1.
Kombe, W.J. (1999)
"Urban Poverty, Service Provision and Land Development in Tanzania - Predicaments and Prospects," Paper presented at the 1999 Annual Seminar for Engineers, "Engineering for Sustainable Development - Tanzania Urban Development: Strategic Issues", Arusha, Tanzania, December, 1999.
Kothari, C.R. (1990)
Research Methodology - Methods & Techniques. Wishan Prakashan, 2nd Edition
Kulaba, S. M. (1980)
"Housing, Socialism and National Development in Tanzania: A Policy Framework
Kusnetzoff, F. (1990)
"The State and Housing in Chile - Regime Types and Policy Choices," in Shidlo, G (ed.): *Housing Policy in Developing Countries*, Routledge, Chapman and Hall Inc.
Kweka, A. N. (1996)
"Strategies for Poverty Alleviation in Tanzania - Produce, Participate and Control." Paper presented at a workshop on Poverty Alleviation in Tanzania, 25th - 27th March, 1996.

Kwelegano, Thomas M., (1997)
"National Development and Urban Management in Botswana," International Conference on Planning, Legislation, Housing and Environment (ICPLA IV), Dar es Salaam, October, 1997.

Kyessi, Alphonce (1996)
"Shelter Situation in Tanzania: What prospects for National Housing Corporation" - High level Consultative Workshop on NHC's Policies and Activities, July, 1996.

-- (1997)
"City Expansion and Urban Agriculture in Dar es Salaam: Lessons for Planning."

Kyulule, V. L. and Kihiyo, V. B. S. (1996)
"Dynamics and Reproduction of Poverty: A Case of Kilombero District." Paper presented at a workshop on poverty alleviation in Tanzania, 25th - 27th March, 1996.

Lall, Vinay D. (1996)
"Housing and Urban Indicators: India Case Study - Comparative Urban Scenario." *Society for Development Studies*, p. 12.

Lee-Smith, Diana (1990)
"Squatter Landlords in Nairobi: A Case Study of Korogocho," in Amis, P. and Lloyd, P (eds): *Housing Africa's Urban Poor*, International African Institute, Manchester University Press.

Leitman, J., et al, (1992)
"Environmental Management and Urban Development: Issues and Options for Third World Cities," *Environment and Urbanization*, 2 (4).

Ligthelm, A. A, and Wilsenach, A (1995)
"Development, Poverty and the Environment, with particular reference to Eastern Transvaal Region." Paper presented at a Seminar for Journalists on Environment and Sustainable Development in Southern Africa, Cape Town, South Africa, December.

Likwelile, S. B. (1998)
"Poverty and Poverty Alleviation in Tanzania." Research on Poverty Alleviation (REPOA).

Liviga, A. J, and Mekacha, R.D.K (1998)
"Youth Migration and Poverty Alleviation: A Case Study of Petty Traders (Wamachinga) in Dar es Salaam." *REPOA Research Report* No. 98.5.

Lugano, W.; John, G.R. and Mkilaha, I.S.N. (1999)
"Aspects Affecting Urban Public Passenger Transportation in Dar es Salaam," Paper presented at the 1999 Annual Seminar for Engineers, "Engineering for Sustainable Development - Tanzania Urban Development: Strategic Issues," Arusha, Tanzania, December.

Lupton, M., and Wolfson, T., (1994)
"Low-income Housing, the Environment and Mining on the Witwatersrand, South Africa", in Williams and Main (eds.): *Environment and Housing in Third World Cities,* John Wiley & Sons.

Lyimo, F.F. (1999)
" The Quantitative and Qualitative Approaches in Social Science Research." Paper prepared for Research Methodology Training Workshop, Dar es Salaam, March.

Maddala, G.S (1989)
Introduction to Econometrics. MacMillan Publishing Company.

Magembe, E. J. A. et al., (1980)
"Housing Production in Selected Areas of Dar es Salaam", 1980.

Mahanga, M. S. (1998)
"Securitisation: The Essence for Creating Secondary Mortgage Markets for Housing Finance in Tanzania." *MSc.* Finance Dissertation, University of Strathclyde.

Main, Hamish, in Williams and Main (eds), (1994)
Environment and Housing in Third World Cities, John Wiley & Sons.

Main, H. and Williams, S. W. (1994)
"Marginal Urban Environments as Havens for Low-Income Housing: Third World Regional Comparisons," in Williams and Main (eds): *Environment and Housing in Third World Cities.* John Wiley & Sons.

Makombe, I. A. M. (1996)
"The Role of Women's Empowerment in Poverty Alleviation in Tanzania." Paper presented at a workshop on Poverty Alleviation in Tanzania, 25th-27th March, 1996.

Malpass, Peter and Means, Robin (eds.) (1993)
Implementing Housing Policy. Open University Press, Buckingham.

Malpezzi, Stephen (1991)
"Discounted Cash Flow Analysis: Present Value Models of Housing Programmes and Policies," in Tipple and Willis (eds.): *Housing the Poor in Developing World - Methods of Analysis, Case Studies and Policy.* Routledge, Chapman and Hall Inc.

Mascarenhas, A. (1994)
"Environmental Issues and Poverty Alleviation in Tanzania," in Bagachwa (ed): *Poverty Alleviation in Tanzania: Recent Research Issues,* Dar es Salaam University Press and REPOA.

Mashauri, D.A. (1999)
"The Water and Sewerage Sector in Perspective: Success and Failures in the Outgoing Millennium", A paper presented at the AWEC Conference on Water Supply and Sanitation Services in the Next Millennium, Arusha, Tanzania, November.

Massawe, A.A.F. (1996a)
"The Housing Problem: A Conceptual Portrait of an Aspect of Urban Management", in Massawe, A.A.F.(ed.), "Urban Management - Issues, Problems and Trends," *IDM Local Government Series,* No. 1, 1996, Institute of Development Management, Mzumbe, Tanzania.

-- (1996b)
"Evolution of A Housing Policy in Tanzania", in Massawe, A.A.F. (ed.), "Urban Management - Issues, Problems and Trends," *IDM Local Government Series* No. 1, 1996, Institute of Development Management, Mzumbe, Tanzania.

-- (1996c)
"Squatting and Urban Policies", in Massawe, A.A.F. (ed.), "Urban Management - Issues, Problems and Trends", *IDM Local Government Series* No.1, 1996, Institute of Development Management, Mzumbe, Tanzania.

-- (1996d)
"Housing Finance and Institutions in Tanzania", in Massawe, A.A.F.(ed.), " Urban Management - Issues, Problems and Trends", *IDM Local Government Series* No. 1, 1996, Institute of Development Management, Mzumbe, Tanzania.

Materu, J. S. (1994): "Housing for Low-income Groups: Beyond the Sites-and-Services Model in Tanzania", *Ekistics,* 1994.

-- (1996)
"Sites and Services in Tanzania, a Case Study of Implementation." *Third World Planning Review,* Vol. 8 No.2.

Mbuguni, P. (1994)
"Gender and Poverty Alleviation in Tanzania: Issues from and for Research", in Bagachwa (ed.): Poverty Alleviation in Tanzania: Recent Research Issues, Dar es Salaam University Press and REPOA.

Mbuligwe, Stephen, E. (1999)
"Alternative Post-Municipal Water Treatment Options for Safer Drinking Water", A paper presented at the AWEC Conference on Water Supply and Sanitation Services in the Next Millennium, Arusha, Tanzania, November, 1999.

McCarney, P. (1995)
"Four Approaches to the Environment of Cities", in Stren, R, and Bell, J. K (eds.): Urban Research in the Developing World: Perspective on the City, Centre for Urban and Community Studies, University of Toronto.

McGregor, Alan,et al (1992a)
"Community Participation in Areas of Urban Regeneration", Research Report (No.23) to Scottish Homes.

-- (1992b)
"A Review and Critical Evaluation of Strategic Approaches to Urban Regeneration." *Research Report* (No.22) to Scottish Homes.

-- (1998)
"Community Based Housing and Local Economic Regeneration: A guide to the Potential", Scottish Homes and Scottish Enterprise.

Mchenga, A. S. and Hassan, O. (1998)
"20/20 Initiative Study on Zanzibar Housing Development."

Mehta, Satish., (1997)
"Low Income Housing Finance Initiatives: The HDFC India Experience" - Regional Seminar on "Maintaining Sustainable Mortgage Finance Schemes in Africa: Lessons and Perspectives for Developing Countries", Accra, December.

Milanzi, M.C. (1996)
"Urban Housing: A Challenge to Urban Authorities in Tanzania." in Massawe,A.A.F. (ed.), "Urban Management - Issues, Problems and Trends," *IDM Local Government Series* No. 1, 1996, Institute of Development Management, Mzumbe, Tanzania.

Misra, H. N. (1994)
"Housing and Environment in an Indian City: a Case of Squatter Settlement in Allahabad, India", in William and Main (eds): Environment and Housing in Third World Cities, John Wiley & Sons.

Mkapa, B. W. (1994)
"Opening Address to the Workshop on Poverty Alleviation in Tanzania, in Bagachwa (ed). *Poverty Alleviation in Tanzania: Recent Research Issues*, Dar es Salaam University Press and REPOA.

Mpuya, M, *et al*, (1990)
Housing conditions in Tanzania - "Illustrations", BRU Working Report No. 68, Building Research Unit.

Mtaki, Nelly (1999)
A Paper on Transportation Problems in Dar es Salaam at the Annual Road Convention, November, 1999.

Mtatifikolo, F. (1994)
"Implications of Public Policies on Poverty and Poverty Alleviation: The Case of Tanzania", in Bagachwa (ed): *Poverty Alleviation in Tanzania: Recent Research Issues*, Dar es Salaam University Press and REPOA.

Mutagwaba, W., Mwaipopo-Ako, R; and Mlaki, A (1997)
"The Impact of Technology on Poverty Alleviation: The Case of Artisanal Mining in Tanzania." *REPOA Research Report* No. 97.2.

Mutter, Michael (1994)
"Traditional Housing and Future Urban Planning Strategy in Katsina, Nigeria", in Williams and Main (eds): *Environment and Housing in Third World Cities,* John Wiley & Sons.

Mwakyagi, Jackson M., (1993)
"Low Income Housing Strategies in African City: A Case Study of Dar es Salaam, Tanzania" - Unpublished Research Proposal.

Mwapilindi, P. R (1997)
"New Thinking About Housing and Urban Development Policy: Agenda for the 1990s," *Journal of Building and Land Development,* Volume 4 No. 1.

Naimani, Godwin, M. (1999)
"Development of Research Instruments." Paper presented for Research Methodology Training Workshop, Dar es Salaam, March.

-- (1999)
"Analysis of Survey Data." Paper presented for Research Methodology Training Workshop, Dar es Salaam, March.

Narso, Monty., (1997)
"South African Report" - International Conference on Planning Legislation, Housing and Environment (ICPLA IV), Dar es Salaam, October.

Ndatulu, T.S. and Makileo, H.B. (1989)
"Housing Cooperatives in Tanzania." *BRU Working Report* No. 65, Building Research Unit.

Ngalomba, Flaviana (1992)
"Law and Practice Relating to Securities for Housing Loans in Tanzania." Unpublished *LLM* Dissertation, University of Dar es Salaam.

Ngowi, D.Y.K. (1996)
"Urban Land Use Planning: Policy Issues for Consideration", in Massawe,A.A.F. (ed.), "Urban Management - Issues, Problems and Trends." *IDM Local Government Series* No.1, 1996, Institute of Development Management, Mzumbe, Tanzania.

Nguluma, Huba, (1993)
"Towards Better Management of Self-Help Housing Through Utilization of Appropriate Building Materials and Technology in Tanzania." Paper presented at the Fifth Habinet Seminar on Construction Management for Sustainable Self Help Housing, Dar es Salaam 22nd - 26th November.

-- (1997)
"Sustainable Human Settlements and Environment: In Search of a Strategy to Improve Urban Infrastructure in Tanzania." Unpublished *Msc.* Thesis, Royal Institute of Technology, Stockholm.

Nhachungue, E., and Dgedge, A; (1997)
"The Green Zones of Maputo: A post - Independence of Urban Agriculture" - International Conference on Planning, Legislation, Housing and Environment (ICPLA IV), Dar es Salaam, October.

Nnunduma, B. J. (1996)
"Mass Housing Production Through Prefabrication Technology: Cost Implications and the Housing Finance System in Tanzania." Proceedings of the Workshop on Prefabrication in Housing Construction, p. 127 -130.

Nyerere, Julius K., (1968)
Ujamaa: Essays on Socialism. Dar es Salaam, Oxford University Press.

Okoye, T. O (1990)
"Historical Development of Nigerian Housing Policies With Special Reference to Housing the Urban Poor." in Amis, P. and Lloyd, P (eds): *Housing Africa's Urban Poor,* International African Institute, Manchester university Press.

Omari, C. K. (1994)
"Social and Cultural Factors Influencing Poverty in Tanzania." in Bagachwa (ed.): *Poverty Alleviation in Tanzania: Recent Research Issues*, Dar es Salaam University Press and REPOA.

Ondiege, Peter O., (1992)
"Public Sector and Urban Housing Development in the City of Nairobi, Kenya: Affordability and Implicit Subsidy and Possible Alternatives", Africa Urban Quarterly, Vol. 7, No. 1 - 2 Feb - March, 1992.

O'Riordan, J; Swai, F., and Rugumyamheto, A. (1997)
Educational Background, Training and their Influence on Female-operated Informal Sector Enterprises, REPOA Research Report No. 97.3.

Ouayaro, Eustache (1994)
"Ouagadougou Low-Cost Sanitation and Public Information Programme in Burkina Faso, in Serageldin, I et al (eds.): The Human Face of the Urban Environment - Proceedings of the 2nd Annual World Bank Conference on Environmentally Sustainable Development, Washington D.C., September 1994.

Pallihakkara, V. N., (1997)
"Housing Finance in the Urban Sector in Sri Lanka with Special Reference to the Experience of Housing Bank and Building Society", 4th International Seminar on Urban Finance in Habinet Countries, Nov. 1997 pp. 3-7.

Parker, R. S. (1995)
"Disaster Vulnerability: Lessons from Four Turkish Urban Areas", in Parker, R et al (eds.): Informal Settlements, Environmental Design Degradation, and Disaster Vulnerability: The Turkey Case Study, World Bank and IDNDR.

Payne, Geoffrey (1999)
"Land Management and Shelter Delivery: Issues and Options." Paper presented at the Shelter Afrique Symposium on Improving Housing Delivery in Africa in the Next Millennium, held in Cotonou, Benin, June.

Peil, Margaret (1994)
"Urban Housing and Services in Anglophone West Africa: Coping With an Inadequate Environment." in Williams and Main (eds.): *Environment and Housing in Third World Cities*, John Wiley & Sons.

Ponte, Stefano (1996)
"Free" to Remain Poor: Liberalization and Rural Poverty in Tanzania." Paper presented at a Workshop on Poverty Alleviation in Tanzania, 25th - 27th March, 1996.

Pennant, Thomas (1990)
"The Growth of Small-Scale Renting in Low-Income Urban Housing in Malawi." in Amis, P. and Lloyd, P. (eds.): *Housing Africa's Urban Poor*, International African Institute, Manchester University Press.

Potts, Deborah (1994)
"Urban Environmental Controls and Low-Income Housing in Southern Africa." in Williams and Main (eds): *Environment and Housing in Third World Cities,* John Wiley & Sons.

Premadasa, R. (1981)
Address to the 4th Session of the United Nations Commission on Human Settlements held in Manila in April.

Ranson, Ray (1991)
Healthy Housing: A Practical Guide, E & FN Spon - World Health Organization.

REPOA (1995)
"Guideline for Preparing and Assessing REPOA Research Proposals." *Special REPOA Paper* No. 9.

Richey, Lisa (1996)
"The Reproduction of Poverty and Poverty Reproduction: Population Policy and Reproductive Health in Tanzania." Paper presented at a workshop on Poverty Alleviation in Tanzania, 25th - 27th March.

Rumulika, M.K. (1996)
"Some Contextual Issues in Urbanization and Urban Management", in Massawe,A.A.F. (ed.), "Urban Management - Issues, Problems and Trends." *IDM Local Government Series* No. 1, 1996, Institute of Development Management, Mzumbe, Tanzania.

Rweyemamu, A.H (1974)
"Some Reflections on Decentralization in Tanzania," in Rweyemamu, A. H and Mwansasu, B. U (eds): *Planning in Tanzania: Background to Decentralization*: 121-31, Dar es Salaam, East Africa Literature Bureau.

Sa-Aadu, Jay (1997)
"What Have African Housing Policies Wrought: A Historical Perspective of Housing and Housing Finance Issues in Africa" - Regional Seminar on "Maintaining Sustainable Mortgage Finance Schemes in Africa: Lessons and Perspectives for Developing Countries," Accra, December.

-- (1999)
"Housing Finance Systems in Africa: Perspectives, Policies and Strategies in the Next Millennium", A paper presented at Shelter Afrique Symposium on Improving Housing Delivery in Africa in the Next Millennium, held in Cotonou, Benin, June, 1999.

Salewi, K.W. (1999)
"Employment Intensive/Labour Based Technology in Public Works: An Engineering Science for Poverty Alleviation and Sustainable Development." Paper presented at the 1999 Annual Seminar for Engineers, "Engineering for Sustainable Development: Strategic Issues", Arusha, Tanzania, December.

Sanders, Donald, H. (1995)
Statistics: A first Course, McGraw - Hill, Inc. fifty edition.

Saris, A. H and R. Van Den Brink (1993)
Economic Policy and Household Welfare During Crisis and Adjustments in Tanzania, N.Y. New York Press.

Scottish Homes (1994)
Scotland's Housing into the 21st Century: Strategy.

Semboja, J, (1994)
"Poverty Assessment in Tanzania: Theoretical, Conceptual and Methodological Issues", in Bagachwa, (ed): Poverty Alleviation in Tanzania: Recent Research Issues, Dar es Salaam University Press and REPOA.

Shelter Afrique (1993)
"Corporate Profile."

-- (1995)
"Private Sector Housing Delivery in Africa: Problems and Opportunities." Background paper for the Private Sector Round Table Meeting, Johannesburg, October.

-- (1997)
Feasibility Study for the Development of a Market-Oriented Housing Finance System in Tanzania: A Report prepared for the Government of Tanzania.

Shidlo, G. (1990)
"Housing Policy in Brazil," in Shidlo, G. (ed.): *Housing Policy in Developing Countries*, Routledge, Chapman and hall Inc.

Shubert, Clarence (ed.) (1996)
"Building Partnership for Urban Poverty Alleviation: Community Based Programmes in Asia; HABITAT 1996.

Silayo, E. H. (1997)
Provision of Surveyed Plots in Urban Areas, The Journal of Building and Land Development, Vol. 4, No.2 April.

Simime, A.G.B. (1996)
"Urban Slums and Shanty Towns : A Challenge to Urban Health Administration", in Massawe, A.A.F. (ed.), "Urban Management - Issues, Problems and Trends", *IDM Local Government Series* No. 1, Institute of Development Management, Mzumbe, Tanzania.

Stephens, Carolyn (1994)
An Overview of Health, Poverty and Environment: The Nexus - Overview, in Serageldin, I. et al (eds.): *The Human Face of the Urban Environment*, Proceedings of the 2nd Annual World Bank Conference on Environmentally Sustainable Development, Washington D. C., September.

Stren, Richard, E (1990)
"Urban Housing in Africa: the Changing Role of Government Policy," in Amis, P. and Lloyds, P. (eds): *Housing Africa's Urban Poor*, International African Institute, Manchester University Press.

Struyk, R., and Turner, M. A. (1991)
"Econometric Analysis: Measuring the Impact of Rent Controls in Urban Housing Markets", in Tipple and Willis (eds.): *Housing the Poor in the Developing World - Methods of Analysis, Case Studies and Policy*, Routledge, Chapman and Hall, Inc.

Sweet, M. L. and George S. (1976)
A Study of Housing Finance: Mandatory Housing Programmes. Praeger Publishers, Walters, 1976 p.2.

Swere, R.M.A; Mneney, D. and Ishengoma, D.M. (1999)
"Urban Sector Rehabilitation Project - IDA Credit 2867 - TA" Paper presented at the 1999 Annual Seminar for Engineers, "Engineering for Sustainable Development - Tanzania Urban Development: Strategic Issues", Arusha, Tanzania, December.

Syagga, P. M. and Kiamba, J. M (1992): "Housing the Urban Poor: A case Study of Pumuani, Kibera and Dandora Estates in the city of Nairobi, Kenya", African Urban Quarterly, Vol.7, No. 1 - 2 Feb - Feb - March, pp. 79 -89.

Teedon, Paul (1990): Contradictions and Dilemmas in the Provision of Low-income Housing: The Case of Harare, in Amis, P. and Lloyds, P. (eds): Housing Africa's Urban Poor, International African Institute, Manchester University Press.

Temba, E. I (1996)
"Environmental Problems and Women's Poverty in Rural Tanzania", a paper in a workshop on Poverty Alleviation in Tanzania, 25th - 27th March.

Temu, A. E (1996)
"Rural Financial Markets in Low Income Countries: Key Features, Operational Problems and Opportunities for Supporting Poverty Alleviation" Paper presented at a workshop on Poverty Alleviation in Tanzania, 25th - 27th March.

Tibenda, Ivan K. B. (1997)
"Are we Moving Towards or Away from Sustainability in Uganda", International Conference on Planning, Legislation, Housing and Environment (ICPLA IV), Dar es Salaam, October, 1997.

Tinios, P., Sarris, A.H., Amani, H. K. R, and Maro, W (1993)
"Household Consumption and Poverty in Tanzania: Results from the 1991 National Cornell - ERB Survey" - Paper prepared under the auspices of the CFNPP, African Economic Policies Project Supported by USAID.

Tipple, A. G. and Willis K. G. (eds.), (1991)
Housing the Poor in the Developing World - Methods of Analysis, Case Studies and Policy, Routledge, Chapman and Hall. Inc.

UCLAS-Institute of Housing Studies and Building Research (1997)
Report on The National Housing Corporation as a Landlord.

UNEP (1992)
The State of the Environment (1972-1992): Saving Our Planet: Challenges and Hopes.

United Kingdom (1997)
"Eliminating World Poverty: A Challenge for the 21st Century", White Paper on International Development, presented to Parliament by the Secretary of State for International Development, November, 1997.

United Nations: (1978)
"Non-conventional Financing of Housing for Low-Income Householders" - UN Publication No. E. 78 IV. 12, 1978, pp. 9-15.

United Republic of Tanzania (1971)
The Building Acquisition Act. No. 13 of 1971.

-- (1972)
"Tanzania Housing Bank Act. No. 34 of 1972."

-- (1980)
"Towards a National Housing Policy." Report on a Conference organized by Building Research Unit and Centre for Housing Studies.

-- (1990)
"National Housing Corporation Act No. 2 of 1990."

-- (1994a)
"JICA Study on Water Resources Development in the Ruvu River Basin."

-- (1994b)
"Urban Sector Engineering Project: Short-Term Consulting Services for the Institutional Strengthening Programme." Draft Report on Dar es Salaam Stage 2 Study (TASKS), prepared by Devco Ireland, April, 1994.

-- (1995)
"Rehabilitation of Dar es Salaam Water Supply System - Feasibility Report"

-- (1996)
"Urban Sector Rehabilitation Project: IDA Credit No. 2867 - TA. Project Implementation Plan for Dar es Salaam Water Supply Component."

-- (1997a)
"National Environmental Policy."

-- (1997b)
"The Study of Applicability of Simplified Sewerage, Dar es Salaam."

-- (1997c)
"Study for the Augmentation of Dar es Salaam Water Supply - Serviceplan, 1997."

-- (1997d)
"Policy Implications of Adult Morbidity and Mortality - End of Phase 1 Report."

-- (1997e)
"National Employment Policy."
-- (1998)
"The National Poverty Eradication Strategy."
-- (1999a)
"National Human Settlements Development Policy (Draft)."
-- (1999b)
"Country Report Presented at the First Healthy Cities Workshop for the Anglophone Countries of the African Region," Nairobi, Kenya, November, 1999.

Uronu, William (1999)
"Provision of Water Supply and Sanitation Services in the Poor Urban." Paper presented at the AWEC Conference on Water Supply and Sanitation Services in the Next Millennium, Arusha, Tanzania, November, 1999.

URT/UNICEF (1994)
"Report of the Water and Environmental Sanitation Task Force; Mid-term Review of the Government of Tanzania/UNICEF: Country Programme, 1992-1996."

Vanderschueren, F., Wegelin, E. and Wekwete, K. (1996)
"Policy Programme Options for Urban Poverty Reduction: A Framework for Action at the Municipal Level, Urban Management and Poverty" UNDP/HABITAT/World Bank (Urban Management Programme), Washington D.C.

Wambura, R. M (1996)
"Reducing Rural Poverty in Tanzania: The Role of Appropriate Extension Approach,", Paper presented at a Workshop on Poverty Alleviation in Tanzania, 25th - 27th March.

Wangwe, S.M. and Tsikata, M.Y. (1999)
" Macroeconomic Development and Employment in Tanzania." Paper presented at the National Round Table Meeting on Employment Policy, Dar es Salaam, May.

Warioba, M.M.D. (1999)
"Management of Local Governments in Tanzania - Some Historical Insights and Trends", Institute of Development Management, Mzumbe, Tanzania.

Wegelin, E. A. and Borgman, K. M (1995)
"Options for Municipal Interventions in Urban Poverty Alleviation: Urban Poverty II: From Understanding to Action" *Environment and Urbanization*, Vol. 7, No. 2, Oct. 1995.

Whittington, Dale *et al* (1991)
"Contingent Valuation: Estimating the Willingness to Pay for Housing Services: a Case Study of Water Supply in Southern Haiti", in Tipple and Willis (eds): *Housing the Poor in Developing World - Methods of Analysis, Case Studies and Policy.* Routledge, Chapman and Hall Inc.

Wikan, Unni (1990)
"Changing Housing Strategies and Patterns Among the Cairo Poor, 1950-85," in Amis, P. and Lloyd, P. (eds): *Housing Africa's Urban Poor,* International African Institute, Manchester University Press.

Willis, K. G. and Tipple, A. G. (1991a)
"Discriminant Analysis: Tenure Choice and Demand for Housing Services in Kumasi, Ghana", in Tipple and Willis (eds.): *Housing the poor in the Developing World - Methods of Analysis, Case Studies and Policy,* Routledge, Chapman and Hall, Inc.
-- (1991b)
"Methods of Analysis and Policy", in Tipple and Willis (eds.): *Housing the Poor in Developing World - Methods of Analysis, Case Studies and Policy.* Routledge, Chapman and Hall Inc.

Willis, K. G. (1991)
"Regression Analysis: Determinants of Overcrowding and House Condition in Ghanaian Housing Markets", in Tipple and Willis, (eds): *Housing the Poor in the Developing World - Methods of Analysis, Case Studies and Policy*. Routledge, Chapman and Hall, Inc.

World Bank (1992)
The World Bank and the Environment - Fiscal Year 1992.

-- (1993)
" Tanzania: Poverty Profile." World Bank Population and Human Resource Division, East African Department, Africa Region.

-- (1995)
Tanzania - Country Report, The World Bank, Washington DC.

-- (1996a)
World Bank Research Programme, 1996 - Abstracts of Current Studies.

-- (1996b)
"Macro-economic Adjustment and Poverty in Africa: An Emerging Picture" (Demery, L and Squire, L, *World Bank Research Observer*, Vol. II No. 1, February.

-- (1998a)
Poverty Reduction and the World Bank: Progress in Fiscal Years 1996 and 1997.

-- (1998b)
Africa Recovery Journal.

World Health Organization (WHO, 1995)
Building a Healthy City: A Practitioners Guide. A Step-by-step Approach to Implementing Healthy City Projects in Low-Income Countries.

Yahya, Said S. (1990)
"Residential Urban Land Markets in Kenya," in Amis, P. and Lloyd, P (eds): *Housing Africa's Urban Poor*, International African Institute, Manchester University Press.

APPENDIX I: HOUSEHOLDS SURVEY QUESTIONNAIRE

1. STUDY AREA
   - City/Municipal...
   - District...
   - Settlement (Area/Block)..
   - Formal ☐ /Informal ☐ settlement
   - Road/Street...
   - House No. ....

2. PARTICULARS OF HOUSEHOLD
   - Name of Head of household ....
   - Male ☐ Female ☐ Age..
   - Married ☐ Unmarried ☐ Divorced/Widower...
   - Number of other dependants: male ...... female...
   - Number of Rooms..
   - Religion...
   - Tribe ....Home District...
   - Do you have own house back home (village)? YES ☐ NO ☐
   - If married is spouse: co-resident ☐ Not co-resident ☐

3. TENURE
   - Owner occupier ☐
   - Renting
     - NHC ☐
     - Private ☐
     - Employer ☐
     - Other public ☐
   - Rent per month T.shs...
   - Other payments: -Electricity T.shs...
     - -Water T.shs ....
     - -Others (specify) .... T.shs. ....
   - If owner occupier
   - Self constructed / purchased ☐
     - - through compensation money...
     - - own savings/loan...
   - Inheritance (family)...
   - Wholly owner occupied ☐ Partly rented ☐
   - Rent received per month T.shs. ....
   - How land/site acquired..
   - Length of stay in the house .... years

4. HOUSING CONDITION
   - Physical Condition and Environment of the House : Good................ Poor.................
   - Age of the House: .... ☐

¨ Type of roof: -Corrugated iron sheets ☐
- Asbestos ☐
- Tiles ☐
- Other (specify)................................
¨ Roof Ceiling: Yes.......... No..............
¨ Type of walls: - Bricks: Well plastered...... Not plastered.........
- Mud (swish) ☐
- Other (specify) ....

¨ Compound house? YES ☐ NO ☐
¨ Single - storey ☐
¨ Multi-storey House ☐
¨ Planned House ☐
¨ Unplanned House ☐
¨ Access Road:
- Available and good ☐
- Available but poor ☐
- Not available ☐

5. EMPLOYMENT AND INCOME

¨ Head of Household:
- Formal ☐ Informal / Self ☐
- Others(specify) ....

¨ Other workers / income earners in the household: Number.......................
- formal ☐ Informal / Self ☐
- Others (specify)...........................

- Monthly Average expenditure pattern of the Household.

- Food	T.shs. ....
- Clothing	T.shs. ....
- Rent	T.shs. ....
- Medical	T.shs. ....
- Charcoal / Kerosene	T.shs. ....
- Transport / Vehicle fuel	T.shs. ....
- Education	T.shs. ....
- Utilities (water, electricity etc.)	T.shs. ....
- Entertainment and Recreation	T.shs. ....
- Drinks and Tobacco	T.shs. ....
- Savings	T.shs. ....
- Others	T.shs. ....
TOTAL	T.SHS. ....

¨ Total monthly income of the household T.shs..............................

6. SERVICES

¨ Are the following services available?
- Piped water supply?

YES ☐ adequate ☐
NO ☐ not adequate ☐

If NO or inadequate what is the source of water
- Shallow wells ☐
- Private vendors ☐
- Own private well ☐
- Others (specify)..

- Sewage system
  YES ☐ Efficient ☐
  NO ☐ Inefficient ☐

- Garbage disposal system
  YES ☐ Efficient ☐
  NO ☐ Inefficient ☐

- Sanitation Conditions

  Sanitation facility available YES ☐ NO ☐
- Type of Sanitation System
  - Twin pit pour-flush latrine ☐
  - Ventilated Improved pit (VIP) ☐
  - Shallow Sewerage ☐
  - Small -bore sewerage ☐
  - Conventional septic tank ☐
  - Conventional Sewerage ☐

- Are services freely provided?

  - Water: YES ☐ NO ☐ - market rates
  - Subsidized ☐

  - Sewage: YES ☐ NO ☐ - market rates
  - Subsidized ☐

  - Garbage collection: YES ☐ NO ☐ - market rates
  - Subsidized ☐

How far are you satisfied with your housing conditions/structure and with services offered by Dar es Salaam Water Supply Authority, Dar es Salaam City Commission (local government) and the central government such as water supply, health care, access roads, drainage system, sanitation, sewerage and solid waste collection (tick appropriately):

- Very satisfied ☐
- Satisfied ☐
- Just adequate ☐
- Unsatisfied ☐
- Do not know ☐

Do you think (poor) condition/environment and inadequate space of your house is affecting (tick):

	YES	NO
1. Your income-generating capacity		
2. Your children's health		
3. Your children's school attendance/Performance		
4. Your Social and mental satisfaction and thus productivity		

- Do you think unsecure land tenure (unplanned and unserviced plots) affects the urge and incentive of households and other stakeholders to improve the housing structures and other housing conditions, environment and services around them ?

  Very Much......... Somehow.............. Not at all............

- Do you think the poor services are a consequence of lack of financial resources?
  YES ☐ NO ☐

- If yes, are you willing to pay more for such services? YES ☐NO☐

- If yes, what additional amount would you be able to pay if the levels of services were to be improved as follows:

  Level I: Provision of piped water, drainage system and better access roads
  Level II: Provision of the above (level I) plus sewage and sewerage systems and health care centres
  Level III: Provision of all the above (levels I and II) plus surveyed and serviced Plots (for unplanned settlements) and provision of housing loans.

Level	Additional Willingness To Pay (T.Shs)
I	
II	
III	

- If access to credit were available, can this induce you to improve your housing and its environment? Yes ☐ Somehow ☐No ☐

7. IN-HOUSE INCOME GENERATION

- Have extensions/modifications been done to the houses to cater for other income generating ventures? YES ☐NO ☐

- If yes, for what purpose?

  Additional renting out. ☐
  Residential ☐
  Commercial: Type of business...........................
  Additional own business venture. ☐
  Type of own business.......................................

- What other income generating activities are conducted within the housing compound?

Poultry ☐
Piggery ☐
Cattle rearing ☐
Gardening ☐
Others, specify...

- Total Additional income from extensions/other income generating activities in/around the house T.shs.......................... per month.

8. CBOs AND NGOs PARTICIPATION

- Are you a member of any community organizations in your Ward/area? YES ☐ NO ☐

- If yes,

	Is it Effective? (Tick)		
	Very Effect.	Effective	Ineffective
1.Name of CBO............................ Purpose................................... 2.Name of CBO............................ Purpose................................... 3.Name of CBO............................ Purpose...................................			

- If No, Why ?
  - No CBOs established in the area ☐
  - They are ineffective ☐
  - I don't know their usefulness ☐
  - Others (Specify) ☐

- Have you participated in any Self help activities for housing/service improvement in the last three years in your ward/area? YES ☐ No ☐

If yes, specify 1.......................................
2.......................................
3.......................................

If No, why?
No initiatives ☐
Not effective ☐

- Are there any NGOs supporting housing/services improvement projects in the Ward/area?
YES ☐ NO ☐
If yes, name 1..................................
2..................................
3..................................

9. ANY OTHER COMMENT?...
....

APPENDIX II: Housing Markets in Selected Asian Cities

Various (legal and illegal) housing sub-markets can usually be identified, ranging from squatter housing through to legal and illegal low-income housing sub-divisions to "regular" developer-provided middle class housing and higher income housing. Typologies vary from city to city, but typically about one-third of the urban population in major South and Southeast Asian cities live in slums and squatter settlements, and about 60-80% of housing supply is provided and financed through informal sector mechanisms.

In **Dhaka, Bangladesh**, housing is supplied overwhelmingly by the informal sector, mostly through efforts by individual households. Financing is largely from personal savings and informal credit. Public sector involvement is limited to allotment of plots to middle and lower income groups. Land developers and apartment builders are catering to the needs of the upper middle and higher income groups. The number of houses built is small, and mostly consists of multi-storey apartments.

In **Ahmedabad, India**, the most dominant sub-market is the formal private sector followed by the informal sector. The share of the public sector in terms of provision is only 10% of total supply, the formal private contributes almost 60% and even outpaced the informal sector. Formal housing efforts have catered only to the middle classes and above, hence the only recourse left for the lower income groups has been to live in "hutments" (slum housing). In the informal sector, slum landlordism and quasi-legal developments are increasingly becoming commonplace.

In **Bangkok, Thailand**, five major housing sub-markets catering for the needs of low-income groups can be identified. These consist of:

- National Housing Authority (NHA) land-and-house projects which take the form of subsidised walk-up apartments, the construction of houses on serviced plots and core houses in sites and services projects.
- Low-cost houses produced by the private sector, which has recently moved into mass production of housing, selling three times as fast as other land and houses packages on the market.
- Informal land subdivisions, which play an important role in low-income housing in Bangkok. They are effectively a form of sites and services provided by the private sector and offer plots, unpaved roads, water, and electricity. For many, they are the first step on the housing ladder.
- Slums and squatter settlements. Over 80% of all slum dwellers rent land legally and live in houses which they have owned for long periods.
- Low-cost rental housing. This type of accommodation is provided by the informal as well as the formal private sector.

In **Karachi, Pakistan**, the individual owner has been the main producer of housing (83.7%). Developers produce relatively small numbers of expensive units, hence the low and medium income group have to opt for shelter in the informal sector, which produces about 60% of total housing production. The poor are also effectively excluded from access to government plot development schemes, firstly by standards and prices which cannot be afforded by 40-50% of the population; secondly by the long waiting period before a plot can be occupied; thirdly by the allocation procedure. Consequently the poor are forced to resort on illegal subdivisions. Among the sources of financing, own savings take a very prominent place (74% of the households). Such savings are often mobilised through informal rotating saving and credit associations.

In **Indonesia**, in sample cities for a representative survey of urban households - Jakarta, Bandung, and Medan (large cities), Yogyakarta, Bandar Lampung, and Balikpapan (medium cities), and Serang, Jambi, and Pukang (small cities) - the survey showed that urban Indonesia has two systems for the delivery of housing, i.e., the popular or household based system and the formal system. The former system provides houses through incremental construction (80% of all housing) and is highly responsive to consumer demand. The purchase of property is made through savings from wages (cash or gold), sale of personal property or funds obtained from family. Informal subdivision of land is a major way in which land enters the residential housing market. Lower income rental units are developed by individual property owners. Main actors who provide these units are; family entrepreneurs, commercial entrepreneurs or employers.

Source: Vanderschueren, *et at*, 1996

Appendix iii: *Recommendations by Habitat on Urban Housing and Infrastructure Finance for Poverty Alleviation*

Problems	Possible Solutions
MICROFINANCE AND POVERTY ALLEVIATION The poor and women do not have access to credit.	Nurture development of microfinance and community-based credit institutions by providing adequate regulatory framework. Give support in the form of refinance or tax breaks ntil their operation reaches a sustainable level. Promote microfinance institutions' efforts to broaden their revenue base through savings mobilization.· Allow microfinance institutions to charge market interest rates.· Improve credit worthiness of the poor by enhancing financial discipline through microfinance. Encourage linkages between formal and informal sector financial institutions to address the multiple credit requirements of the poor.
The potential to use credit to finance housing and urban services for the poor is not fully utilized.	Approach housing and basic services as an integral part of poverty alleviation packages highlighting income generation activities. Provide small, short-term finance to support incremental approach to improve housing and urban services provision. Promote community development finance institutions and co-operatives engaged in housing and service delivery.
HOUSING FINANCE *Housing finance system is weak and narrow-based.*	Promote policies contributing to macroeconomic stability and financial deepening. Enforce property rights, individual titling and foreclosure laws.· Establish market-based housing finance system linked to the broad financial sector and capital markets.· Allow competition for funds at positive real interest rate and also for potential borrowers.

	Facilitate a smooth transition from directed-credit to market-based systems.· Establish adequate regulatory structure and supervisory mechanisms.
Housing finance institutions lack long-term sources of funding.	Strengthen mechanisms and incentives for savings mobilization. Tap domestic capital markets (pension and mutual funds, and insurance companies). Introduce a form of liquidity facility (secondary mortgage market or refinance mechanism). Explore cross-border finance
Housing finance does not support various housing options.	Encourage loans for home improvement and rental housing, not just home purchase. Use innovative loan products to make mortgages more affordable.· Offer flexibility in the use of loan proceeds.· Improve housing delivery systems to make housing more affordable.
Subsidies are inefficient and inequitable; They are not sustainable and fail to reach the poor. ·	Define the target groups clearly (the poor or the middle income groups). Move toward separating subsidies from finance (targeted lumpsum subsides combined with market based loans).· Provide capital subsidies or tax incentives to developers of private rental housing.
URBAN INFRASTRUCTURE FINANCE ***Revenue base of urban local authorities is weak and narrow.*** ·	Rationalize tax assignment and intergovernmental transfer systems in the context of simultaneous decentralization of responsibilities and financial resources. Increase local autonomy in setting taxes and charges· Rationalize and improve collection of land and property taxes. Explore non-conventional local revenue sources.
Pricing of services is inadequate	Raise the tariff level to accurately reflect value of services to users and cost of provision. Address the financial capacities of the poor with increasing block tariffs and transparent subsides.

	Use cross-subsidization as an interim measure.
Revenue collection is poor.	Improve information and administrative system for billing, payment and collection of taxes and charges. Combine billing for one service or a tax with that of another with greater enforceability (water service billed with property tax, for example). Use computerization of realistic standards. Make payment systems convenient to users (use banks and other financial institutions). Follow up on arrears with necessary sanctions.
Willingness to pay by some users is low.	Engage users and communities in the design of services, determining standards, and monitoring to more closely match costs and benefits for all classes of users.· Identify and address service quality or billing problems that may be responsible for poor payment by users. Improve communications with citizens, elected councillors and media on the linkage between payments and service delivery.
Municipalities have only inadequate access to capital	Allow market-based municipal borrowing within debt-carrying capacity.· Assist municipalities in establishing credit worthiness through technical assistance and incentives to improve their financial efficiency and transparency. Provide credit assessment and credit enhancement mechanisms (credit rating agencies and bond insurance). Use BOOT type of arrangements to finance commercially viable projects.· Establish, if necessary, municipal credit institutions and use them to enhance financial discipline and project preparation by municipalities.· Promote cross-border finance by securing adequate legal and regulatory environment.
Service delivery and resource management are *inefficient and not transparent.*	Reduce cost of services by streamlining staffing, reducing leakages, utilizing joint-service arrangements among municipalities, and by engaging the

	communities in service delivery. Promote private sector participation by providing an enabling legal, regulatory, supervisory framework, and ensuring fair competition. Improve systems of financial information, control and budget management. Introduce performance-oriented evaluation system.

Source: HABITAT(1996)

Appendix IV: *Recommendations for Action to Improve the Land Tenure Situation for the Poor*

The major recommendations of the Inter-regional UMP/UNCHS Seminar on Urban Land Management, Regularization Policies and Local Development in Africa and the Arab States were as follows:

1. Central government should recognise the multiplicity of land delivery mechanisms in urban areas and accept the roles played by the various actors and rationalise them as appropriate.
2. Public land delivery will need to be carried out in a transparent and market-oriented manner. It is recommended that, in the interest of efficiency and equity this is devolved to the local government level. For this to work effectively, it will be necessary to strengthen local governments' institutional, fiscal and human capacities.
3. Expeditious land tenure regularisation of irregular settlements should be pursued as a central element of (local) government land delivery. Additionally, but not necessary in conjunction, high priority should be given to the provision of basic services in these settlements.
4. These efforts should be supported by simple, unified systems of land information assembly, management, and documentation, accessible and comprehensible to the public to ensure that land title registration will be cheap, quick, and simple.
5. The use of fiscal instruments (property tax, capital gains tax, incentive subsidies) in the management of land delivery should be promoted by central and local government.
6. The state should actively promote the economic empowerment of the disadvantaged members of society, particularly women, and especially remove structural impediments to their access to land.
7. The customary land tenure system should be made more market oriented through enhancing the transparency of its availability, utilisation, and pricing, supported by the development, integration, and adoption of a land information system as well as dialogue with the customary controllers of land.
8. The role of NGOs and CBOs in mobilising resources for land and housing delivery, dissemination of information on land related issues (management and delivery), and mobilisation and organisation of the community must be utilised as a positive force in enhancing transparency in the land market.

Source: Vanderschueren, et al, 1996.